Memoir Of Thomas Archer

John MacFarlane

MEMOIR

OF

THOMAS ARCHER, D.D.,

MINISTER OF OXENDON CHAPEL, LONDON.

BY THE

REV. JOHN MACFARLANE, LL.D.,

LONDON,

AUTHOR OF "THE NIGHT LAMP," "THE MOUNTAINS OF THE BIBLE," ETC. ETC.

LONDON:

JAMES NISBET & CO., 21 BERNERS STREET.

MDCCCLXVII.

TO

The Widow

WHO WAS WORTHY TO BE HIS WIFE,

THIS MEMOIR OF DR ARCHER

IS AFFECTIONATELY INSCRIBED

BY

The Editor.

PREFATORY NOTE.

THIS Memoir has been drawn up at the urgent request of Dr Archer's nearest and dearest friends. It makes no pretensions beyond a humble effort to meet their affectionate and reverential wishes.

While the life of Dr Archer included only what is, in so far, common to the diligent men of his profession, there are some fresh settings and varied illustrations, which impart to it peculiar interest. He was a member and minister of the United Presbyterian Church of Scotland, and never acted inconsistently with such a position. But he was more. From his London centre, he was necessarily drawn forth into scenes and conditions not met with in the pastoral life of the North. These new points and juxtapositions will impart some variety to the biography, and make it more interesting to the reader.

The "memoir" is becoming one of the demands of the age. It is good that it is so, especially within the pale of the Christian Church, where such books can only stimulate to what is better, by truthfully representing what is good. The excellence of Christianity as a Divine faith is certainly made more conspicuous by such grateful embalming of useful memories. Not designed for society at large, but simply conceded to the cravings of select friendships, the *religious memoir*, at all events, should be tenderly judged of and respectfully handled. With such a hope, the Editor has consented to the publication of the present volume.

Since the "Memoir" was printed, four of Dr Archer's discourses have been added, in compliance with the earnest wishes of friends.

LONDON, CLAPHAM,
September 1867.

CONTENTS.

CHAPTER VIII.

CHAPTER IX.

CHAPTER X.

DISCOURSES BY DR ARCHER.

CHAPTER I.

THE BEGINNING.

IN Perthshire—pronounced by Sir Walter Scott to be the most varied and beautiful of all the provinces in Scotland, to have the most picturesque if not the highest mountains, and to justify the application to it of the line,

" Beauty lying in the lap of Terror,"—

THOMAS ARCHER was born. Perth, the " fair city," founded by the Romans, and " beautiful for situation," was his native place; and his birth-day was the 19th of September 1806. His remarkable appreciation of the grand and sublime in nature, which, in after-life, took him oft to the mountains and lakes of Switzerland and Italy, may be from this accounted for. His eyes from childhood had feasted upon a prospect which, as seen from the " Wicks of Baiglie," is perhaps unrivalled in the world. Stretched out before him lay the valley of the Tay, which drew from the Romans, when it burst upon their view, the exclamation, " Ecce Tiber!" In its centre rose the town itself, with its two Inches and the two hills of Moncrieff and Kinnoul, while the huge Grampians in the distance marked out

A

nature's ramparts alike against Highland or Saxon raids. But
he was still more indebted for the formation of character to his
parentage, and the home and church associations of early life.
He was connected with some of the oldest and most respectable
families of the city, whose descendants are now almost extinct.
Both on the father's and mother's side, his ancestors had been
for generations members of the famous Incorporation of Glovers.
His grandfather, the late Bailie Joseph Forrester, was one of the
leading men who, in 1733, followed the Rev. William Wilson,
then one of the ministers in the Established Church in Perth,
when he seceded from the Church of Scotland along with
Erskine, Fisher, and Moncrieff. Bailie Forrester accompanied
Mr Wilson to the " Glover's Yard," on his being refused admission into his pulpit, after his sentence of deposition had been
passed by the General Assembly, and there stood by his venerable and self-denying minister while he addressed the multitude that had convened to join their testimony with his against
such tyrannical proceedings. He continued, while he lived, one
of the most zealous and influential promoters of the Secession
cause. This branch of the family was originally from Stirling-
shire, where they possessed considerable property, which was
taken from them in the reign of Charles II., because of their
decided sympathies with the Covenanters. Thomas Archer in-
herited from such an ancestry what proved better to him than
" houses or lands"—even the blessing of the Lord of the Cove-
nant. He was not proud of such descent, but he was ever
thankful that the blood of martyrs and confessors flowed in
his veins; and he was through life mindful of the obligations
under which he was in consequence laid, to walk worthy of

such distinction, and to carry forward the cause for which they so nobly suffered.

James Archer and Christian Forrester were the parents of a numerous family, of whom the subject of this memoir was the youngest son and the last survivor. It has ever been a laudable wish, in Scotch families, to have one at least of the children devoted to the Christian ministry. Whether the parents in this instance acted under such a motive in respect of their son Thomas, is not known. It seems rather that, having marked in him, from a very early period, a decided predilection for the sacred profession, they gave to it all the encouragement in their power. In this they were kindly aided by their ministers, the late Rev. Jedidiah Aikman and Dr Newlands, who took notice of the boy's dispositions and tastes, and warmly superintended his upbringing. Serious impressions were also deepened in his heart by the precious and friendly intercourse he was permitted to have with such venerable men as Drs Pringle and Young of Perth, Dr Jamieson of Scone, and Mr Jamieson of Methven. He received his elementary education at the public seminaries of the city, some of which, at that time, were in considerable repute. He often spoke of his obligations to Mr Riach of the English classes, Mr Dick of the Grammar School, and Dr Anderson of the Academy. From all accounts he was a diligent student and an apt scholar, giving early promise of the excellence to which in future he attained. His natural temperament was at once joyous and generous. Remembering him in those days, a writer in a Scotch journal thus refers to him: " How vividly and distinctly do we recollect him as a frolicsome, light-hearted, laughter-loving youth, who, as if by acclamation, took commandingly the lead in all the romps, sports, and pastimes of boys of his own age and standing! All looked up to him; and though he mingled in these sports, and enjoyed to the very utmost these hours of recreation, he was, when quite young, extremely fond of reading, and eagerly devoured what books he could get." Roaming, as he often did, amid the picturesque beauties of his native district, he could not fail to imbibe a passionate fondness for such scenes; and he accordingly indulged himself, frequently climbing to the summits of " Moncrieff" or " Kinnoul," where, with book in hand, he would sit for hours, storing his mind with useful knowledge, and refining his heart in the exercises of love and adoration, as he gazed upon the wondrous works of the Creator.

It does not seem to be indigenous to the Scotch mind to be demonstrative as to periods or means of conversion. Hence, while some can note the very day, and describe the very means, that were blessed for their new or second birth, most of Dr Archer's countrymen are shy about referring either to the one or the other,—not that they are not genuinely pious, but, from peculiarities of religious education, or from national temperament, they are neither prone to certify to themselves their actual conversion, nor to reveal to others what may be their spiritual condition. It is difficult to determine which of the two characteristics is the preferable one. On the one hand, there is a danger of taking for granted a change which has not been undergone, and on the other, there may be a reticence which defrauds the Author of our faith of the praise which is due to Him, and at the same time beclouds the evidence for the existence and power of Divine grace in the heart. Be this as it may, we have no clue to the period of the spiritual quickening of this boy. From the circumstance of his early choice of the ministerial profession, we may infer that at the same time he must have felt the power of religion. From his tenderest years, indeed, he had given proof of piety. He was much indebted in this respect to constant intercourse with an aged grandmother who was an eminent saint. For hours every day he used to sit beside her,—question her, and be questioned by her; while he eagerly drank in the precious instructions which she gave him upon the most important of all subjects. This, and his occasional remarks on the books which he read to her, suggested to the old lady's mind the idea of his future calling; and so, with something almost approaching to prophecy, she once remarked, "Well, well; we cannot tell what may be *His* plans, but perhaps the bairn may be appointed, some of these days, to preach the Word even in yonder great Babylon !" (referring to London). It is of more consequence to ascertain the fact than to discover the date of our new birth. Some are sanctified from the womb; some are called in the spring-time of their days, but only evidence it by their lives; some are so suddenly and strikingly arrested in a career of unbelief, and brought into saving acquaintance with Jesus Christ, that no doubt can exist as to the time or manner of their union to Him ;—but a great many others—perhaps the majority of real Christians—have long passed from death to life without being aware of it. Gradually, under the use of the means of grace, and the influences of holy examples and awakening providences, they have been growing in spiritual stature, and are just as safe for eternity, as perhaps their more favoured brethren who can exultingly affirm their

effectual calling. Dr Archer was never heard to refer to this
deeply interesting portion of his religious history; but of his
actual personal piety, from a very early period, there can be no
justifiable doubt. In other and after years that piety was known
by its fruits; nor let this reference be undervalued: its importance in a biography is elemental. Learning and labour
have been expended in simply ascertaining the dates and locali-
ties of the nativities of illustrious men. Of how much deeper
interest to us should be the spiritual quickening of immortal
souls! By certifying their conversion, we are placed in more
favourable circumstances to enjoy the glimpses of their future,
and even for forecasting their " eternities." It is especially
pleasant and encouraging, when the compiler of such a memoir
as the present, has such a foundation to build upon.

Having finished his elementary education in Perth, Thomas
Archer, in his fifteenth year, was entered an alumnus of the
University of St Andrews. His name stands in the books of
the United Colleges of St Salvador and St Leonard's as having
studied there during the sessions of 1824-5, 1825-6, 1826-7.
His professors were—for Greek, Dr Alexander; for Latin, Dr
John Hunter; for Logic, Dr James Hunter; for Mathematics,
Dr James Duncan; for Natural Philosophy, Dr Thomas Jack-
son; and for Moral Philosophy, Dr Chalmers. He was,
therefore, singularly fortunate in the men who superintended
his university studies. Dr John Hunter was a Latin scholar of
high distinction, and edited several editions of the classics. He
possessed a most retentive memory, one instance of which may
here be quoted. He was one day reading " Virgil " with his
class, when he suddenly announced his discovery of a difficulty

in the passage, the construction of which he could not explain. " I will give it my attention," he said, " in the evening, at home, and let you know to-morrow." This he did in the following terms : " Gentlemen, I solved the difficulty, and I had no sooner done so than I remembered that the very same difficulty occurred to me when reading the same passage forty years ago, and that I solved it in precisely the same way. Though I have often read the passage in my class since then, I have never noticed that difficulty till now." The mathematical professor was quite noted for his odd manners and quaint expressions, though an accomplished and successful teacher. Dr Alexander was equally distinguished for his Greek and his wit, and happily influenced his pupils to an enthusiastic study of that beautiful language. But it was of Dr Chalmers that our student retained the strongest and most loving memories. The celebrity of this truly great and good man had attracted many to St Andrews from all parts of the country. Edinburgh and Glasgow had been hitherto the popular colleges; but the name of "Chalmers" in some degree turned the tide in favour of the Fife school of learning. It certainly decided Thomas Archer to pursue and finish his studies there. His admiration of, and veneration for, his eloquent instructor, scarcely knew bounds. He delighted to tell of the special marks of friendship he had received from him ; how he had given him much of his society, by not only inviting him to his house, but by asking him frequently to accompany him in his rambles by the shores of the "far-resounding ocean." These were not only seasons of intense pleasure, but of immense advantage to the student. To the end of life they influenced both his ministerial character and usefulness. It was indeed evident that he chose Dr Chalmers' for his model, and had imbibed not a little of the spirit of his masterly and fervid eloquence. In his future lot, Dr Chalmers took a kindly interest, and was even desirous to secure his talents for the Established Church. Had he succeeded, no doubt Thomas Archer would have entered that Church under the highest auspices, and might probably have gained some of the richest ecclesiastical prizes. But he could not be persuaded, even under such temptation, to renounce his connection with the Church of his fathers. His naturally independent and self-relying spirit stood him in good case at this juncture : he unhesitatingly and positively refused to apostatise from his principles as a Seceder. This disappointed the professor, but only increased his esteem for the pupil. On one occasion, " The Great Advantages of Church Establishments" had been given out as a subject for an essay by the class. On the evening before the essays were to be read, Dr Chalmers and Mr Archer met each other strolling on the beach. "Well, Thomas," said the Doctor, placing his hand familiarly on his shoulder, " have you written your essay?" " I have," replied the student. " And, pray, which view do you take?" " The one opposed to yours, Doctor," was the instant reply. " Oh, you do !" said the somewhat surprised philosopher ; " well, come up and breakfast with me to-morrow morning, and bring your essay with you, and let me hear it." This request was, of course, complied with, and when the reading of the essay was finished, Dr Chalmers said, " Powerful—very powerful—and startling reasoning ; but it may be as well that you do not read it in the class !" And it was, consequently, not read there. It is well known that the eloquent and learned divine was, at that time especially, a keen and staunch defender of the Church and State principle, and he might think it inexpedient, and perhaps inconsistent, to allow this young Voluntary such an advantage. Anyhow, it speaks well for the manliness and discernment of the student, whose honest opinions could thus influence the professorial judgment. It may only be added, that from the numerous certificates and prizes which he obtained from all his professors, it is clear that he must have, in a high degree, dis-tinguished himself as a student in the university.

At the close of the session of 1827, Mr Archer bade farewell to his "Alma Mater;" but he never forgot the happy and busy days he had passed within her walls. There he laid the foun-dations of that busy and useful life during which he so success-fully and completely justified early promise; there his literary tastes had been formed and richly nourished; and there, too, his personal piety and firm purpose to devote himself to the sacred profession had been not only unshaken but fully con-firmed. It is especially due to Dr Chalmers to record, that he never omitted, in the midst of his intensest enthusiasm, to set before his students the primary necessity for pure and undefiled religion, and to inculcate the consecration of all talents and endowments to the service and glory of our Redeeming God. Inspired with zeal from the lip and life of such a preceptor, and now fully qualified to enter upon the second division of his educational curriculum, he made the usual application to the Presbytery of Perth to be received and admitted into the "Theological Hall." He passed his examinations easily and creditably, and forthwith proceeded to Glasgow, where at that

time the Hall was kept. There were then only two professors
of divinity—the late Dr Dick and Dr Mitchell—of whom it
may safely be affirmed, that they were eminently qualified to
discharge the important duties of their respective chairs. They
were not only accomplished Christian gentlemen, but scholars
of erudition and ability rarely to be met with. Under their
joint training some of the most distinguished ministers of the
United Presbyterian Church were educated ; and it is not difficult even still to trace to their influence, much of that elegance
of mind and dignified deportment which, in addition to solid
acquirements, impart to the pastoral character both ornament
and strength. Dr Archer, in after-years, did nothing more
than agree with his fellow-students, when he rehearsed the
privileges and benefits of their memorable professoriate. Then,
as now, it was required that candidates for the ministry should
study for five consecutive sessions in the divinity classes.
Thomas Archer did so, for the first two years under Dr Mitchell,
and for the remaining three under Dr Dick. During the inter-
vals of session he continued under the inspection of his native
Presbytery; and whether in the Hall of Theology, or at the bar
of Presbytery, he uniformly made most respectable appearances. He continued to make progress in his study of the
original languages of Scripture; and his sermons, lectures, and
critical exegeses, which were from time to time required from
him as "trials," obtained for him not only the good opinions of
his fellow-students, but the warm applause of professors and
presbyters. Great expectations were formed of his powers and
popularity as a preacher, which were ere long verified.

The Rev. Mr Redpath, in his able "funeral sermon" for Dr

Archer, in adverting to the length of the literary and theological curriculum through which the Presbyterian students of all denominations must pass, makes the following judicious observations :—

"Views of divine truth, to be of any worth, need to be gradually formed in the mind. They are not like pieces of furniture, which are made to order, and which, when once transferred to a room, retain the same place and dimensions ; but rather resemble plants, the growth of which is most healthy when least forced, and when they are allowed to pass through the vicissitudes of the season, and to draw from rain, sunshine, and air, as well as from the culture of man, every aid to a natural and steady progress. The student needs to examine every important truth on all sides, and, in many relations, to seek all the light which books and instructors, as well as his own reflections, can furnish, before it can strike its roots very deeply in his mind, or yield fruit for the refreshment and sustenance of others. It is good to have ample opportunity afforded to professors, ministers, Christian friends, and, most of all, to the student himself, to ascertain his aptness for the work of the ministry. And while I am quite willing to concede that there are exceptional cases, such as that of the missionary to the heathen, I am inclined to think that the general adherence to the rule has been productive of advantages which can scarcely be overrated. In this, as in every department of education, the remarks made by Lord Stanley the other day hold good, that it is not by trying to do too much at once, but by doing a little at a time, and doing it well, that the most satisfactory progress is made. 'Time is thus given, the wall is not run up in haste, the bricks are set on carefully, and the mortar is allowed time to dry; and so the structure, whether high or low, is likely to stand.' Another advantage which the United Presbyterian Church has pre-eminently enjoyed is, that there has been always only one Theological Hall for all her students. These, numbering from 150 to 180, come from all parts of the kingdom to study under the same professors, at a time of life when warm and lasting friendships are most likely to be formed. The opportunities of intercourse thus furnished enable them to appreciate one another's excellences, and, by full and free discussion, tend to produce a harmony of sentiment, and a mutual confidence and good understanding, which have contributed not a little to the efficiency of the Church."

Immediately after leaving the Hall, at the close of his fifth session, Mr Archer went upon his "trials for license" before the Presbytery of Perth. These trials were all sustained; after which, in November 1831, he obtained his license to act and preach as one of the "probationers" of the Church. Thus at length was reached that "mark" to which he believed himself to be called from on High, and towards which he had been pressing and praying for the previous ten years,—a long period of training for the Church, it may by some be thought, but not considered extreme by the Churches in Scotland, whose people, without exception, demand and obtain a fully educated ministry. If ever such a ministry was required, it is certainly in the present day a necessity. Talents and genius and learning are all enlisted on the side of latitudinarianism, if not of infidelity; the public, the religious mind of all classes, is now unusually whetted; and unless we be prepared to leave Christianity in the hands of " sciences falsely so called," the pastors of every denomination must be equipped for serious encounters with the speculative and sceptical. It is a sorrowful narrowing of the great object of the Christian ministry to confine it merely to the plain and simple preaching of the Gospel to lost men. Into what dismal and destructive regions should the world soon pass, if, through neglect or misapprehension, the Christianity of the atonement were to be submerged in the lethal stream of rationalism !

As it was not then permitted to " students of divinity" to preach in public, so the *first* sermon, which was not preached till the Sabbath after license, was considered an epoch in young life. The student himself looked forward to it with fear and trembling, and all his kinsmen and acquaintances took note thereof as a day of days. No " reading" of sermons was then tolerated. The discourse, therefore, had not only to be carefully written out, but committed to memory, word by word. To Mr Archer this was not such a herculean task as to others. He had a retentive memory, and could easily mandate what he had thoughtfully composed. Notwithstanding, he anticipated with anxiety his first public appearance in the " fair city." It came at length, and, as is usual, it was made in the pulpit of the church in which he had been brought up, and of which the late amiable Dr Newlands was then the occupant. An immense congregation crowded to hear their young townsman, and some who had thought that the bounding, lively, frolicsome boy should never be fit for the pulpit, were there to be convinced that, as in the case of Chalmers himself, and of many others besides, the boy is not always "father of the man," and that solid manliness and imposing seriousness may grow up out of a rollicking and roving disposition in "childhood's years." On the occasion referred to, every available corner in the building was packed, and some had even climbed up to, and sat upon, the rafters of the ceiling. The preacher was listened to with rapt silence. He got through without "sticking," which in itself is considered, in the circumstances, to be a decided feat. But there was more than this—he captivated the hearts of all. The sermon was quite "*sui generis*" with his later productions, full of fervid and eloquent disquisition, and delivered with the earnestness and force of his best days. His popularity in his native city was from that day established, and it continued undiminished to the latest visit he paid to Perth.

The practice of sending out young men, at the commencement of their student-career, to preach to the public, is, to say the least of it, questionable. They are not then qualified, and, if not qualified, ought not to be so employed. Besides, the duty of publicly instructing others is by far too sacred and responsible to be intrusted to such tyros, who are in great danger of either not propounding truth, or of doing it in such a way as to make the Cross an offence alike to the educated and ignorant. Loose habits of study are also liable to be formed—desultory thinking must necessitate desultory preaching—and such often continues to be their degenerate style through life. On the other hand, a fixed law, forbidding to preach till license has been obtained, is not to be commended. Preaching is an art, and the finest of all arts. It cannot be gained at one leap. There is no royal road to it, any more than to learning. The only way, then, by which it can be secured, if we desire the youthful candidate to be in some degree proficient, is to allow him some gentle and prudent practice in anticipation. This can be easily done by and under Presbyterial arrangement, at once to regulate the proper times, and ensure the amount of such an exercise. It is good that the law, in this respect, is being prudently relaxed. The consequences to the student must be, at the beginning of his probationary stage, much more easiness and comfort and success as a preacher; and to the Church herself, an accession of labourers of much more self-possession and matured experience. There have been cases where students have broken down just on the eve of license, and where they either abandoned the profession or unduly delayed their entrance upon it; and all this traceable to the terror that fell upon them in the prospect of their first and earliest essays. This may suggest the question as to whether committing sermons *verbatim* to memory is the most judicious or effective mode of preaching. Some of the most acceptable ministers of the Gospel have been known to regard " mandation " as a process of slow murder. If it was not such to men of Dr Archer's class, it was owing to the possession of an extraordinary memory. Though at the very outset he wrote his sermons fully out, and mandated them carefully—often for this end sitting up whole nights to meet the Sabbath requirements—he was ere long driven to the easier and better plan of making an ample sketch of his subject, and preaching therefrom.

If we are cast upon times when effective preaching has become a great necessity, it is to be desired that the practice of *reading* sermons shall be confined to the narrowest possible limits. By all means let such as absolutely cannot commit to memory enjoy the boon. " The man," says Dr Vaughan, " who can address an auditory from the pulpit as the senator has to address the Speaker in the chair, or as the barrister has to address the twelve men in the jury-box, possesses a great advantage. But there are men who must be allowed to read, or they always fall below their own idea of how they should acquit themselves, and, being dissatisfied for the most part with their best efforts, are liable to become disheartened in their work." The case of Dr Vaughan's own son, the accomplished author of " Hours with the Mystics," is very much in point. The father writes : " My son's memory was not of a sort easily to recall words. When he had been at the pains of writing his sermons, he could scarcely deliver a sentence as he had written it. He was thus shut up, so far as language was concerned, to the alternative of either reading entirely, or extemporising entirely. If the speaker who must always repeat his language from memory can hardly be expected to rise to great eminence as an orator, the same may be said of the man who can never avail himself of premeditated words, but must always depend for them on the moment. Had my son entered on his career as a preacher only a dozen years later, he would probably have been allowed to read in the pulpit; and as he would have been able by that means to ensure the exact enunciation of what he wished to say, he might have been led to concentrate his strength on his pulpit discourses, and have left us many finished compositions of that order, in place of much we now have from his pen."*

* Memoir of Robert Alfred Vaughan, by Robert Vaughan, D.D.

Dr Archer used to say that, when he had gained some practice in the *memoriter* plan, one reading of anything he had composed with care, placed it in his recollection. He traced this to a circumstance in his boyhood, which he used to tell his class of young men, when impressing on their minds the great benefit to be derived from cultivating memory, not so much as a natural gift, but as a faculty to be earnestly sought after and improved by practice. For some misdemeanour at school he had been punished. The punishment was to commit to memory five hundred lines of "Virgil." He felt the task to be a severe one, but he mastered it, and ever afterwards found mandating comparatively easy.

Mr Archer soon became one of the most popular probationers on the field. The "vacancies" sought after him. Ere long he received a unanimous call to the church at Lasswade, near Edinburgh, which he might have accepted but for the claims of Oxendon Chapel, London, which were submitted to his preference. The Rev. Mr Broadfoot, long the minister of that chapel, had retired in consequence of infirm health. To the fathers and brethren, whom he consulted, he deferred. To supply " Oxendon " with a popular and efficient minister was a great desideratum. He was consequently sent to the Metropolis, in the hope that he might prove the object of that church's choice. He accordingly preached his first sermon there on the last Sabbath of December 1831. His text was from Romans v. 1: " Therefore, being justified by faith, we have peace with God, through our Lord Jesus Christ." Few are now alive who heard that sermon. They who remain speak of it as an able and eloquent production; and he became at

B

once the general favourite. They saw in him a mind cast in no
common mould, and did him the high compliment of compar-
ing him, as a preacher, to their first pastor, Dr Jerment, even
when in his palmiest days. He had but a small audience—the
congregation having from various causes dwindled down to a
select few. He was not, however, discouraged. It was with
him then, as it was ever afterwards, a purpose to look upon
difficulties as things to be overcome. He continued in Oxendon Chapel for three months, preaching three times every
Sabbath, and once on a week-night. This must have proved
no easy task to a young beginner, who not only had no stock
to fall back upon, but who had to resist the powerful temptation of a first visit to roam over London and see its "lions,"
that he might be secluded in the study to prepare for the
pulpit. On leaving London, a unanimous call was sent after
him. Fears were entertained that the depressed state of the
congregation would indispose him to accept. But he at
once set aside the call from Lasswade, and accepted London,
in the self-denying purpose of his mind, to attempt the resuscitation of the "Oxendon" cause. Of this choice none
of the parties ever repented. Accordingly, having delivered
all his trials for ordination to the satisfaction of the London Presbytery, he was publicly and solemnly set apart to the
pastorate on the 3d of May 1832. His former pastor, the
Rev. John Newlands, D.D., of Perth, came up to the ordination. The Rev. John (now Dr) Young, of Albion Chapel,
gave the charge, and he was introduced to his congregation on
the forenoon of the following Sabbath by Dr Newlands. In
the evening he himself occupied the pulpit, preaching to a

large and interested audience from Proverbs xi. 30: "He that winneth souls is wise." The sermon was delivered with solemn animation, and characterised by that fervour and power which distinguished him to the end of his life. A few still remember it, and delight to speak of the burning zeal for souls which it so impressively displayed.

In a letter addressed to Mrs Archer after his death, there is a touching reference to his earliest efforts in Oxendon :— "These sermons," says the writer, "must have made a deep impression on those who heard them—certainly *one* heard who never forgot them. When my dear father was on his death-bed, eighteen years afterwards, his mind being anxious about his state, I said to him, 'Father, you know in whom you have believed : through Jesus Christ you have peace with God.' 'O yes,' he replied; 'justified by faith, we have peace with God, through our Lord Jesus Christ—that was our minister's first text, and what a grand discourse it was! I have often thought about it, and the comfort it has given me ought not to be less now.'"

But Oxendon Chapel, Haymarket, London, has a history previous to all this, which is not generally known, and which deserves a chapter to itself.

CHAPTER II.

OXENDON CHAPEL.

XENDON CHAPEL was built for the famous Richard Baxter. Mrs Baxter had a high appreciation of her husband's preaching powers. He allowed her to manage all his temporal concerns; and when it became dangerous for him to preach in the neighbourhood of St James' Market-house, from the annulling of the " King's Dispensing Declaration " and the passing of the " Test Act," she determined to build him a chapel elsewhere. She accordingly purchased on lease a piece of land in Oxendon Street, with a ground-rent of £30 a-year, and erected upon it the chapel, which was opened for public worship in 1676. It has been said that she did this at her sole expense. It might have been at her sole risk, but it appears that, without any appeal to the friends of her husband, many of them sent in handsome contributions. We have seen a list of these, and among others there are the names of Alderman Ashurts and Mr Booth, £100; Lady Acmine, £60; Sir James Maynard, £50; Countess of Warwick, £20; Sir James Langholm, £20; Countess of Clare, £10; Sir Edis

Harley, £10; Countess Tyrconnel, £6; Lady Fitzjames, £6; Lady Chuton, £5; Lady Richards, £5; etc., etc. In the death of Mrs Baxter, in 1681, the great Puritan sustained a heavy loss. Howe preached her funeral sermon, and her husband, in sketching her character, says, " She was the meetest helper I could have had in the world." Baxter only preached once in the new chapel. It so happened, that one of His Majesty's principal secretaries, Mr Henry Coventry, lived only next door. To him it was a nuisance, and he determined, if possible, to have it shut up. He brought the matter twice before the House of Commons, but got no seconder. A warrant was then taken out upon what was called the " Oxford Act," in order to have Baxter imprisoned for at least six months, who, knowing nothing of this, had gone down into the country, leaving the Rev. Mr Sheddon, from Derbyshire, to preach for him on the following Sabbath. Mr Sheddon was accordingly arrested while in the pulpit; and suffered imprisonment, until released by " Habeas Corpus," procured through Lord Chief Justice Hale. Mr Sheddon was of very infirm health, and suffered much in prison. Mrs Baxter paid him many seasonable and soothing visits. Even after this Coventry was not satisfied. He was determined to get quit of his neighbours, the proscribed schismatics. He employed men to beat drums under the chapel windows during public worship; and when this did not succeed, he actually marched soldiers to the doors, and forcibly prevented the congregation from assembling. Mr Baxter now lost hope of being suffered to preach any longer in that place; and in the following year he offered it to Dr Lloyd, rector of St Martin's-in-the-Fields, who agreed to take it, and to pay the ground-rent only—£30 a-year—but nothing whatever for the chapel itself. For above a century after this, it was used as a chapel-of-ease to St Martin's. On examining the title-deeds, it appears that in 1768 it was sold to Samuel Joynes, Esq., and leased by the Rev. Whitely Heald. In 1788, Dr Charles Peter Layard leased it for twenty-one years, agreeing to repair the building at an expense of not less than £400, and to pay an annual pepper-corn rent for the first five years, and £65 per annum thereafter. After sixteen years' possession Dr Layard died, and his executors gave the remainder of the lease to Dr Hamilton, who does not seem to have completed it, as in 1807 the freehold was bought by a Presbyterian congregation in the city for £1400, inclusive of all the fixtures, organ, etc., etc. Up to 1821 it is invariably described as "that wooden building;" but in documents drawn up at that date it is referred to as "that wooden building, lately of wood, now of brick," which seems to indicate that its Presbyterian purchasers had pulled down the wooden, and erected a brick building in its stead. This may account for the lapse of a year and a half before it was re-opened for worship in connection with the Presbyterian Church.

This event took place on the 10th of July 1808. The opening sermon was preached by the Rev. George Jerment, D.D. His text was taken from Acts vii. 48, compared with 1 Kings viii. 27; and the collection amounted to £104, 6s. 6d. As the first Secession minister of Oxendon Chapel, it is proper to give some account of this much-esteemed servant of Christ. He was a native of Peebles, and his father was the Antiburgher minister there. His early piety decided him to prepare for the

Christian ministry. After studying at the grammar school of his native town, and at the University of Edinburgh, he entered the Divinity Hall, at that time under the able tutorship of the Rev. William Moncrieff of Alloa. He had just received license as a probationer, when he was sent to London to assist for a time the Rev. David Wilson, pastor of the church in "Great St Thomas Apostle," Cheapside. Mr Wilson is well known for his admirable vindication of Hervey's "Theron and Aspasio" from Mr Sandeman's scandalous attack upon that interesting and popular work. His congregation determined to give him a colleague, and applied to the Antiburgher Synod in Scotland to supply them with a suitable person. Young Jerment was at once fixed upon, and having obtained a unanimous call, he was ordained there in September 1782. Upon the death of Mr Wilson, two years afterwards, Mr Jerment became sole pastor. His chapel has sometimes been said to have been situated in "Bow Lane." This is not correct. There is no chapel of any kind there ; but lower down on the east side, "Great St Thomas Apostle" turns out of it at right angles, and two doors from the south-east end of that street it still stands. Their lease having expired in 1807, Dr Jerment and his people removed to Oxendon Chapel immediately on the completion of repairs, which cost about £3300, of which £1000 was raised by Dr Jerment himself among his friends. It will interest some, in these days of innovation, to be informed that the "organ" was sold for £30, to help in the cost of these repairs. Some may live to see and hear another in its place. The times are changed, and we are changing in them. In 1789, Dr Jerment married the daughter of Mr Moncrieff, his theological professor. She was, by all accounts, one of those daughters who excel. To her husband she proved an helpmate indeed. "Do what I will," he said concerning her, "it is all right in her eyes. When I go from home, return when I may, early or late, I am always welcomed with a pleasant smile ; never a frowning look, never a murmuring lip or chiding tongue seen or heard." One night, in 1795, this worthy woman went to bed in sound health. Before morning she was in heaven. All who know the widow of Dr Archer will at once perceive a remarkable resemblance in some points between her and Mrs Jerment. To them both the comfort and usefulness of their husbands were paramount to selfish considerations. Dr Jerment married a second time in 1797, the lady being a daughter of the Rev. A. Moncrieff of Abernethy. On the 21st October 1812, he lost his only son, a youth of much promise, and only twenty-six years of age. He never recovered from this shock. He died upon the 22d of May 1819, and one of his latest death-bed confessions was, " This truly is the happiest day in all my life ! I speak this not as words of course, but as the sincere words of a dying man." It has been justly recorded of him that, "in the zenith of his days, his style, both in his preaching and in his writing, was nervous, classical, and generally elegant." The celebrity of the latter procured for him the degree of D.D. His chief pieces are—" Early Piety," " The Religious Monitor," " The Trump and Harp," " Bishop Leighton's Life," " Mr Wilson's Life." He also finished Dr Gibbon's " Lives of Eminently Pious Women." Dr Jerment was one of the fathers and founders of the London Missionary Society. His spirit was greatly ahead of that of his people, who opposed his taking such a step. In fact, a turmoil arose. Notwithstanding, he stood to his point, and thus spake to his people from the pulpit: "Were it to come to this issue,—support *that* cause and leave us, or give it up and abide with us,—I have no hesitation in saying, I would do the former, were it this very day." Dr Morrison, in his "Memoir of Dr Jerment,"* pays him the following just tribute: "In the missionary direction his services were most highly appreciated, and his attendance was very assiduous, and devoted. His examinations of missionary candidates, both as to their theological sentiments and piety, were characterised by the meekness of wisdom; and when missionaries of superior attainments offered themselves to the Society, his sound knowledge and correct scholarship became peculiarly manifest." The venerable Dr Waugh also thus alludes to him in a sketch of his character: "Dr Jerment possessed strong powers of mind, which he had much improved by reading and reflection. He had a vigorous judgment, a well-stored memory, and a rich but chastened imagination. He was, moreover, the faithful minister of the cross of Christ; in his own family kind and indulgent, and in his friendships warm and steady. During his last illness he appeared to enjoy much of the countenance of his Lord; and notwithstanding his severe bodily distress, his mind was quite collected and composed. He spoke familiarly of his dying situation, and not only expressed his entire satisfaction in the Lord's calling him hence at His own proper time, and his being happily delivered from all fears about his eternal state, but the highest assurance of his being with the Lord God and the Lamb for ever and ever. His faith, indeed, seemed to be most triumphant, and his hope

* Fathers and Founders of the London Missionary Society.

without a cloud. A little before his departure he sang, with his family standing around his bed, the closing part of the seventy-third Psalm, beginning with the 26th verse." The liberal and catholic spirit of this good man was useful in the counsels of the Church, when the union of the two great branches of the Secession in Scotland was on the *tapis.* He was a decided advocate in its favour, and though far away from the seat of its chief interest, he did what he could to promote it. The following letter, written the year before the union was consummated, will be read with pleasure. It was addressed to the late John Finlay, Esq., then of Newcastle; and the much respected "Union Secretary" there :—

"No. 32 RICHARD STREET, ISLINGTON,
LONDON, *April* 6, 1819.

"DEAR SIR,—It rejoiced Mr Broadfoot and me to hear that there was a meeting of Seceders in Newcastle relative to the proposed union between the two branches of the Secession Church, and that they are to meet again on the 12th current. (I hope and pray, harmoniously and more fully and decidedly), about the same important and pleasant business.

"The information which you desire concerning our movements in London shall be readily given in a few words. The four ministers met twice to consider the subject; first, on the 21st of January, and again in my house, on the 11th of February. At the former meeting I had the honour to fill the chair. The utmost harmony prevailed. We agreed that no sacrifice of truth was to be made, and that the peace of the congregations was not to be disturbed; that the union was practicable, and

the object to be pursued regularly and with caution ; that the
original testimony was the principal basis of a proper union ;
that in our several congregations the evening of Sabbath the
31st of January be devoted to public prayer for the Divine
guidance and blessing; that the people should be informed of
our proceedings ; and that our sessions should, with the con-
currence of the people, send a petition to their respective
Synods.   It was also agreed that the four sessions should meet
conjunctly for prayer and conference.   At the meeting of our
session, early in February, I submitted to them several resolutions, which were approved ; and at their request I engaged to
draw up a petition to the Synod against the next Lord's-day.
On the *Thursday* of that week, the second meeting of ministers
was held.   I read to them the resolutions of our session, which
they adopted, and requested that copies of the resolutions and
the petition might be sent them before next Lord's-day.   This
was done.   I read the petition to our session after sermon in
the morning.   The resolutions were read to the people in the
afternoon, and their approbation of our views and plan was
given by the usual sign.   After sermon the ministers and elders
subscribed the petition, which was drawn in the name of the
people as well as in their own.   The petition was sent off
next day to the Presbytery-clerk, for the purpose of its being
transmitted by the Presbytery of Edinburgh to the Synod.   The
four sessions have met twice conjunctly, and most agreeably.
They are to meet again this month.   The people of all the
congregations here are keen for the union.   •

    " I hope that something will be done by the Synod wisely
and peaceably to promote the good work.   May they be led

in the *midst* of the paths of judgment!—I am, dear Sir, yours truly, GEORGE JERMENT.

"Mr Finlay.

"*P.S.*—Kind regards to Mr Pringle and Mr Syme.—I had almost forgotten to say, that you will oblige me much by communicating, as soon as convenient, the result of the meeting in Newcastle next Monday. The friends here are anxious to obtain all information. The elders are to hold their third general meeting a few days after the 12th, and it will rejoice their hearts to learn that you have had a happy meeting. I shall send this letter to the care of Mr Pringle, as you have not given your address. G. J."

Dr Jerment died in the sixtieth year of his age, and in the thirty-seventh of his ministry.

Two years before Dr Jerment's death, the Rev. William Broadfoot was called and admitted to be his co-pastor. Their collegiateship was brief, but happy. Previous to his removal to London, Mr Broadfoot had been settled at Kirkwall, in Orkney, and was the first Secession minister in those islands. After nineteen years of successful labour, he accepted of a call to Oxendon Chapel, where he laboured for twelve years, and then, on the 4th December 1830, he resigned his charge, having, from an affection of the throat, been prevented from discharging his regular duties for some time previously. "This union," says Dr Morrison, "proved for many years a happy one; though latterly it was somewhat clouded by discontents which arose among the people, mainly, perhaps, originating in the declension of the congregation. The result was his retirement, and

the appointment of his present successor, the Rev. Thomas
Archer, whose talents and graces have contributed largely, by
the Divine blessing, to restore the cause to all the prosperity of
bygone years, and who promises to become one of the most
useful and successful preachers in the Metropolis." Mr Broadfoot, however, did not altogether leave public life. Very soon
after his resignation, he was appointed theological tutor at
Cheshunt College. Having discharged the duties of this important chair to the satisfaction of the trustees and the students,
he passed away to his eternal rest upon Tuesday the 6th of
June 1837, in the sixty-second year of his age. While the
Secession minister at Kirkwall, he not only gathered together a
large and influential congregation there, but was instrumental
in planting several others in Orkney. He was the founder and
patron of nearly all the benevolent societies in these interesting
islands, and was particularly fortunate in advancing the cause
of sound religious and useful education—a cause to which,
throughout his life, he was warmly attached. His settlement at
Kirkwall is connected with a very interesting anecdote. For
twelve years previous, four individuals had been constantly
engaged in praying for the establishment of a gospel ministry
in Orkney. Their prayers were heard. Mr Broadfoot was sent
to them, and he became, under God, one of the most successful
revivalists of religion in his day. He was equally effective as
the tutor at Cheshunt. One of his students, afterwards a minister in the Countess of Huntingdon's connection, thus writes
of him: "When we assembled in the lecture-room, he himself
commenced our engagements with prayer, and often with a
simplicity and elevation, a fervour and affection, which could

not fail to impress, not only with a feeling of his own devotion
of spirit, but also of his great concern in our welfare. . . . No
course of study connected with divinity could be more zeal-
ously or devotionally conducted, or with a more constant
and decided bearing upon the great object, than they were by
him. . . . . . His taste, though correct, was not so much distinguished by attention to the minuter elegances of language as
to the subjects of thought. He relished what was accurate,
beautiful, and useful, and felt it intensely ; but he delighted in
extended views and manly statements of things, and as truly
despised what was turgid and bombastic. . . . . As an individual, if God shall spare and graciously succeed me in the
ministry, I shall connect it instrumentally with the advantages
which I enjoyed under my beloved tutor, as a student. My
recollections of the college, as associated with him and his
esteemed colleague, will be sweet, fresh, and lasting, and
cherished, I hope, as among the most favoured of my life."
This affectionate testimony is more than corroborated by
one of the resident tutors who succeeded him at Cheshunt :
"I need not tell you," he writes, "that sound sense, learning,
and love for the truth as it is in Jesus, order, punctuality, kindness, were evident ingredients in his character. His great
anxiety was to raise the intellectual and religious tone of his
students, and to teach them to grasp the great truths of the
Gospel, in all their Scriptural statement, unqualified with metaphysical refinements. He seemed desirous that 'their faith
should not stand in the wisdom of men, but in the power of
God.' I consider his mind to have been well-balanced, too
warm and devout for neology, too humble and sensible of

responsibility for Antinomianism, too substantial and massive for visionary notions, and too active and zealous for mere formal morality. He took a lively interest in the extension of the Church, and lost all sectarian considerations in the paramount importance of saving souls; and it was almost impossible to be with him and not be rendered a more public man. Being of a denomination not in any respect agreeing with the principles of the Countess of Huntingdon's College, he had the good sense and catholicity to put out of sight those minor differences, and, in fact, never to think of them, while his whole soul was absorbed in his endeavours, under God, to render the ministry efficient. The grief the students manifested at his death, showed how much hold he had upon their affections, and that this hold must have been taken by the kindness of his behaviour towards them."

During his last illness he was uniformly cheerful. The disorder in his throat prevented conversation. He could only whisper, and even that much with pain. "We cannot speak much," he said, two days before he died, "but we can pray much." He did not, however, anticipate his death to be so near at hand. On noticing the alarm of his friends, he said, " I do not think that death is in the cup, but I may be mistaken: the Lord's will be done." On the morning of the day on which he departed, he had a fainting fit, and it was feared that his soul had fled upward. On opening his eyes and seeing his beloved wife and children around him, he said, "A little while longer among you;" then, taking farewell of his family in order, and smiling sweetly on each, he peacefully passed away.

Mr Broadfoot had three sons who highly distinguished themselves in the army, and fell gloriously on the battle-fields of Asia :—

1. James Sutherland Broadfoot, lieutenant in the Bengal Engineers, fell in the battle of Purwan Durrah on the 2d November, 1840.

2. William Broadfoot, captain in the 1st Bengal European Regiment, and military secretary to the President at Cabool, fell in the insurrection at Cabool on the 2d November, 1841.

3. Major George Broadfoot, C.B., of the 34th Madras Light Infantry, political agent for the North-West Frontier of India, and for the affairs of the Punjaub, acting as A.D.C. to the Governor-General, fell at the battle of Ferozashar, on the 21st December, 1845. Sir Henry (afterwards Viscount) Hardinge thus noticed him in his despatches—" He was as brave as he was able, and second to none in all the great qualities of an accomplished officer." His loss was recorded as a public calamity in both Houses of the Imperial Parliament. A beautiful marble monument, called the " Broadfoot (Madras) Testimonial," was afterwards raised to his memory by a public subscription throughout the Presidency of Madras.

A writer in the *United Presbyterian Magazine* for 1862 gives the following graphic description of the locality of the chapel in which Dr Archer commenced his long and laborious life as a preacher of the Gospel :—

" The locality of Oxendon Chapel is anything but agreeable. In fact, its *entourage* is worse than Dr Cumming's, if that be possible. It is surrounded in all directions by night-houses, supper-saloons, oyster-shops, casinos, cafés, chantants, and

C

various other social evils, whose glittering attractions thrust themselves into most unpleasant prominence before the frequenters of the chapel, even on Sunday evening. It is, in truth, a neighbourhood consecrated to dissipation; and in its week-night aspects, may be said to represent London on the spree. The Continental proletarianism which always hovers about Leicester Square—seedy, out-at-elbows, and altogether dubious-looking—is another marked feature of the locality; while among the secular influences which affect it there is in one direction the Alhambra Palace, with its attractions, equestrian and acrobatic, and in another, Dr Kahn's Museum, with its delicate arcana. Any one, in fact, who wants to see the great metropolis in its most debased, black-leg, and altogether graceless moods, has only to take a five minutes' walk in any direction from Oxendon Street. And in the midst of this rabble-rout, this Vanity Fair, stands the unpretending little chapel, a very tolerable emblem of modest virtue shrinking abashed from the contact of brazen and triumphant vice."

Here, also, is a curious notice of the chapel, taken from one of the papers of the *Spectator* in 1711 :—" This is to give notice to all promoters of the holy worship, and to all lovers of the Italian language, that on Sunday next, being the 2d of Dec., at 5 in the afternoon, in 'Oxendon Chapel,' Oxendon Street, near the Haymarket, there will be Divine Service in the Italian tongue, and will continue every Sunday at the above said hour, with an Italian sermon preached by Mr Cassotti, Italian minister, author of a new method of teaching the Italian language to ladies."

Such is a brief sketch of the church-history of Oxendon

Chapel, from 1676, when it was built for Richard Baxter, down to the 3d of May, 1832, when Dr Archer was ordained as Mr Broadfoot's successor, covering a period of no less than one hundred and fifty-six years. Its rise is coeval with one of the most persecuting periods in the annals of our national religion. Living, as we now do, in happier, freer, and holier times, such scenes as Coventry the Secretary caused to be enacted before and against the humble chapel in Oxendon Street, can scarce be realised as possible.   The flight of Baxter from his " wooden chapel," after having preached in it only for one Sabbath, cannot now be re-illustrated.   Places of worship are rising up on every side in London, and are built of wood, or iron, or brick, or stone, to be filled with worshippers of all religious persuasions, no man daring to say to any of them, " What doest thou ?"   The " drums" of state secretaries dared not be beaten at the doors of the humblest conventicle, any more than at those of the Chapels Royal.   But the question presses itself— Are we still secure ?   Under God we may ; under the present innovations of Anglican and Popish infidelities, we may not. Unless the inhabitants of these British Isles awake immediately to a perception of, and arise to avert, the danger threatened against our homes and altars, another " Five Mile Act" may be passed, the fires of Smithfield may be re-kindled, and the dragoons may again be let loose to do the discipline-work of the State-church militant.

CHAPTER III.

THE PULPIT.

M R ARCHER, immediately after ordination, set to work with head and heart. Not ignoring the antecedents of Oxendon Chapel, he at once saw that success depended, not on what it had been, but, under Divine blessing, upon the zeal and fidelity of its new minister. His was a brave attempt. It is hazardous, in any circumstances, to take in hand with a declining interest. It is peculiarly so in London, where, on every side, there is abundant supply of pious and powerful preaching, and where the winning cause is irresistibly attractive. A young and inexperienced man there, is in danger of overvaluing his capabilities, and of discovering, in failure, the mistake of his choice. Of course, it must ever be the same Gospel that is to be preached; but it does not follow that all are qualified to preach it with equal variety of style and power of attractiveness. There are exceptions to all rules; but it has been generally found, that striking success in the Metropolis, belongs not so much to rare genius as to maturity and experience. Church-goers there, are for the most part under some degree of religious conviction. There is little temptation to frequent ordinances from a regard to public opinion. The merchant in the city owes little of his success to a mere character for piety. It is enough if he be known as a man of honour, integrity, and good business habits; and there is no account whatever taken on Monday morning of his Sabbath-keeping. It may hence be inferred, from his attendance at the sanctuary, that he is there upon principle, and is sincerely seeking the " finest of the wheat " for his soul. A successful young preacher in London is therefore the more to be marked, as indicating an unusual kind and amount of excellence. Thus it was with Mr Archer; for, though he did not all at once reach it, he gradually and surely commanded popular regard. Finding the congregation in a declining condition, and as yet distrustful of what might be his own adaptation to the duties and responsibilities of such a charge, he determined with himself that he should not fail; or, if he did, that it should not be chargeable to any shortcoming on his part. The compiler has it in his power to report of the progress made, within little more than twelve months after his ordination. He and Mr Archer exchanged pulpits in the summer of 1833, for six weeks, and, even at that early period, the chapel was well attended; and the impression was, that the new ministry was to be blessed with a steady and happy revival. The sequel will prove that the impression was a right one. Though not numerous, there were in the congregation some substantial people—honest, thorough-going Presbyterians, who were resolved to countenance the pastor in all his plans and proposals for a resuscitation of good old Oxendon;

not that they were bigots in their preference of denominational
peculiarities, but that they felt that there was a place, and an
important one, too, for Presbytery in London,—a place which
had hitherto been but sparsely occupied, and which now gave
promise of additional Gospel ministration to a populous neighbourhood. The esteemed secretary of the congregation at
that period, thus writes:—"When Dr Archer entered on his
ministry at Oxendon Chapel, the church was in anything but
a prosperous condition; the seat-holders were few and by no
means wealthy; the building was not in good repair, had not
been painted for many years, and was as dingy and unattractive
a place of worship as could well be imagined; there was also
a heavy debt upon it,—drawbacks these sufficient to have discouraged the most stout-hearted. He was not, however, to
be discouraged. Confiding in *Him* whose help was all-sufficient, he went on working hard, determined never to flinch
from the task he had undertaken. For some time the prospect
was dark, and showed few signs of brightening. Nevertheless,
his great anxiety to promote the spiritual wellbeing of his
flock, and more especially the young,—his gentle, affectionate,
and genial bearing with whom, brought many young men
around him, and endeared him to all with whom he came into
contact,—soon made his talents and attainments more widely
known. Before, however, anything like prosperity had been
reached, and while seat-rents and collections were inadequate
to meet the ordinary expenditure, the congregation was suddenly called upon to pay off the debt, thus creating almost
unsurmountable difficulties. In the midst of these, with a noble
devotedness to the cause, he intimated to the managers that in

lieu of the stipend that had been guaranteed to him, he was willing to accept whatever sum was over after paying the ordinary expense. This generous and disinterested conduct, on the part of the pastor, led to increased energy on the part of the people. The result was the adoption of means which, with his valuable influence and assistance, immediately relieved the church from embarrassment, preventing the necessity of curtailing his income, raising funds to put the chapel in thorough repair, and ultimately getting rid of the debt. Had this noble sacrifice not been offered, the probability is, that little zeal or energy would have been manifested to get out of the difficulty; but his generous example stimulated all to redoubled exertion, and from that time may be dated the commencement of the prosperity of Oxendon."

Mr Archer had taken the proper measure of his position. He saw that upon the *pulpit* must lie his main dependence. Other things might be accessories—this was a necessity ; not that he undervalued what is usually understood to be *pastoral work* among the members, but that to preaching-power, in the first instance, must success be looked for. He had himself seen and known cases where comparatively humble enough talents had kept and even gathered together a goodly flock, the lack of real pith and compass being made up out of great painstaking in private intercourse and social blandishments. But his quick eye soon perceived that London was not Perth, and that its peoples must be touched from other and more telling heights at once of mind and manner. He therefore set himself to hard study, and produced and delivered, from Sabbath to Sabbath, discourses of unusual elaboration. Of course, he was not at all times equal—who is?—still we question if more earnestly-composed or more thoroughly-mandated compositions were ever thrust into the very foreground of pulpit-life by one so young in years and so inexperienced. The Chalmerian fervour did not always descend upon him, but there were few of his sermons that did not faintly echo that wonderful orator. It was thought, indeed, by some of his compeers, that he slavishly copied Chalmers. No doubt he had caught some of the fire of the "old man eloquent," when under his tuition at St Andrews, but there was in his own natural temperament not a little of that *ingenium perfervidum* for which his countrymen are famous. The best thing, however, that can be said of his earlier performances is, that he baptised them with the loves and lights of the Cross. He himself once said that, "as blood was the best nourishment for the vine, so must the roots of the one he had undertaken to cultivate, be saturated with the blood of Christ." This he did, and did it very assiduously. Hence the growth of that Oxendon plant, whose fresh shoots and numerous branches have since been found, not only throughout the United Kingdom, but in the Colonies also, and other parts of the world. In a comparatively short time he got quit of the terror of the pulpit, composition became easier, slavish preaching from mandated notes he discontinued, and then he fell, as a general rule, into the habit of first sketching, and then mentally filling up his subject, so that both less time and less labour were consumed upon pulpit preparations, while his preaching became more free and easy, and, of course, more effective. His most intimate friends at once detected the difference between his ordinary prelections and his occasional public sermons and speeches. The latter, unquestionably, did more justice to his parts as a scholar, a thinker, and an orator; they were more condensed, more logical, more constructively and powerfully eloquent. They were not, however, more interesting or instructive than his ordinary ministrations. To those his *foreign* reputation might be traced,—to these, his regular and growing usefulness. This indeed is, in general, the test of a well-filled pulpit. It is comparatively easy to get up an occasional discourse which fills for " nine days" the mouths of the public. It is quite a different thing to provide food sufficient for hungry souls, Sabbath after Sabbath, and to send them away fed and satisfied. Mr Archer could do both ; but he did the last best. It is thought by some, that, in his ordinary work, he often far excelled even his finest and most popular pieces.

This is easily accounted for. For *special* occasions some men set themselves earnestly to work, and produce what is striking. They have studied for it. They have read and thought and prayed for it, and they may or may not have succeeded. Mr Archer was as conscientiously a student for his ordinary as for his extraordinary pulpit displays. Not that the same amount of mental effort was required, but that he invariably made himself master of whatever he brought before his people or the public. He had habits of study. He might not be always in his library, reading or writing at his desk, but he had acquired the power of abstraction to such an extent, as to return to his theme at any time, and anywhere, and work it out clearly and earnestly. Often when walking through the crowded streets of London he was inwardly digesting his discourse for Sabbath. Of a sudden he became silent and seemed unconscious of the presence of his companion. "What are you thinking about, you look so grave?" asked his wife one day as they threaded their way through the gay and giddy throng. "I am studying," he replied, "for Sabbath, and have just got a magnificent idea for my subject, which, I hope, I shall be able to work out." His rule was, immediately on returning home after the Sabbath work was over, to select his text and subject for the following Lord's-day. He thus had it in his mind throughout the week. He aimed at having his discourses all finished by the Friday evening, and in general succeeded. His idea was, that ministers should have Saturday for relaxation and recreation. He thought that working late, as many do, almost into the Sabbath morning, was sure to jade and wear out the mind, to the loss of that elasticity so useful to make the services of the pulpit profitable as well as comfortable to the worshippers. The exceptions to this rule were so few, that one such may be referred to here. It happened on a week previous to the dispensation of the Lord's Supper. The solemnity of such an occasion he always deeply felt, and prepared accordingly for what was called the "action sermon." Much to his discomfort, he could not decide upon a text. Even after he had selected one, and sketched out his subject, he threw the sketch aside, and tried a second, and a third, and a fourth, with like results. He could not decide; he could not be satisfied; and Saturday evening found him, as it rarely if ever did, quite out at sea,—no text, no subject, no sermon ready for the morrow. He was advised to drop all thought, and, if possible, all anxiety, and go to rest. Reluctantly he complied. He slept soundly till about three o'clock in the morning, when his watchful and anxious wife heard him ask, "Are you awake?" On replying that she was, he said, "Then, please, get up, strike a light, and write to my dictation. I have dreamt not only a text, but the very divisions of the subject." His wish was at once complied with. The text was taken from the first and second verses of the forty-second Psalm: "As the hart panteth after the water-brooks, so panteth my soul after thee, O God. My soul thirsteth for God, for the living God: when shall I come and appear before God?" Only a small portion of the introduction, that he dictated at this midnight hour, can now be found. It is here given *verbatim*, and by such of his own people as heard it when amplified, it will be easily recognised.

"These words have all the freshness and warmth of sincerity; they flow with all the simplicity of intense desire, from an awakened soul, and indicate the existence of a holy agony only to be subdued by the felt presence of its object. However dull and insensible the spirit may have been to the charms of piety,—however engrossed by the cares, or dissipated by the blandishments of life,—there have been waked up desires of burning force, of irrepressible vehemence, which carry it onward till lost in the full delights of Jehovah's immediate society, and in the splendours of heaven. The causes of this new passion of the soul may vary at once in the character or mode of operations, but the end and results are the same—the consecration of every power to the one grand object, the final unrestrained converse of the soul with God. Uttered, therefore, with truth and fervour, the text intimates one of the most interesting states, and forms one of the most hopeful symptoms of the Christian's experience. The sleep of spiritual death has been

broken, and the throes of a new life are felt. The first bursting buds of the spiritual spring are seen, beauteous in themselves, and still more so because ominous of the rich and everlasting harvest. The spirit of the living God has breathed
upon the slain and slumbering, and that spirit, met by the
desires of the incipient Christian, will issue in the activity and
vigour and joy of the matured saint. The language we are
about to examine, while thus expressive of one of the most
interesting eras in the history of man,—of the noblest hopes
which can impell, and the most glorious destinies which await
him,—is not less the expression of conscious destitution and
essential helplessness. It comes from one deeply, painfully
alive to his necessities—from him who wanders in a dry and
thirsty land. We are not, therefore, to imagine that the consciousness of this destitution is followed by the *instant* utterance of this cry. Human pride does not at once submit to the
Gospel—does not at once receive God. There are processes
sometimes painful and tedious; there are transition-states more
or less rapid. How interesting and instructive to trace the
progress of a soul in this work, to witness the agonised heavings of a new creation, only to rest in the beauty and order
and joy of the new creature ! "

He then dictated the following heads of thought and discussion :—

" I. Let us consider the object of the Christian's desire—

" (1.) *God.* This is the grand distinction—the worldling
seeks *earth* as his portion—if he ever thinks of God, it is not
as the end at which he aims—the Christian, on the contrary,
looks upon earth, all its attractions and acquirements, as vain

—exclaiming, as in Psalm xxxix. 7,—'And now, O Lord, what wait I for? My hope is in thee.'

"(2.) *God in salvation*—not a vague, impalpable conception —not as seen in creation and providence, but as in Micah vii. 7,—'Therefore I will look unto the Lord; I will wait for the God of my salvation: my God will hear me '—the full meaning of salvation—the ultimate of life—John xvii. 3—devout old Simeon holding the babe in his withered arms, Luke ii. 28.

"II. The nature and characteristics of the Christian as typified by '*thirst.*'

"(1.) Thirst indicates vehement desire—gold—revenge— blood—the Christian from the cross, shown by a marked rest-lessness, a holy impatience, etc.

"(2.) Such thirst wholly absorbs the mind—every faculty and feeling of gratification yield to it—'one thing I do '—Satan's devices are many to allure, but he knows the attempt to be vain—God is the great object—Oh! a new aspect! heavenly steadiness, zealous superiority—God ever present, renders the being invisible to all surrounding objects—the pilgrim sees not the beauties of the scenes through which he is passing when parched and fevered with thirst—so with the Christian—joys and cares he shuns alike—sees only Christ—say not, this is Utopian—David did not reach this, but he aspired after it— hear his prayer, 'Unite my heart '—seek then God's presence, and ye shall find God's presence—'Ye shall find me when ye shall seek me with all your heart.'

"(3.) We are not to expect this passion to develop itself in wishes or words, not in actual or visible excitement—but in private meditation—special ordinances—the Lord's supper.

" (4.) Such is its importance and intensity, it will lead to many sacrifices.

" (5.) Thirst is only eradicated by a change in constitutional action and laws—like manner—the spirit retains its features—soul craves. after God—seeming contradiction, John xiv. 14—shades of uneasiness—pain from His absence—admiration of the Saviour—nearness to Him—never destitute of joy—the saints' thirst brings them to Him—this was David's experience —saints all feel that none deserve—this is the process—come to the Fountain — portals of God's temple—overwhelming splendour of its inmost shrine—such desire! shall it be vain? Scripture forbids—prayer with faith secures a good right to heaven, etc.

" III. The realisation of this desire.

" (1.) The soul that thirsts appropriates God when it finds him—Simeon clasps the Redeemer—so he is presented to us —' The Lord is our portion.'

" (2.) The soul is filled with joy.

" (3.) The soul is inspired with new strength.

" (4.) The soul catches new purity—law of nature—affinities —final promise, ' We shall be like him!' wondrous thought!

" IV. Let me now mention one or two encouragements.

" (1.) The largeness and suitableness of the object.

" (2.) Not less encouraging the freedom and universality with which that object is presented.

" (3.) And, as if to hush every murmur, the invitation is couched in the most affectionate terms."

With this sketch thoroughly mastered, he ascended the pulpit, and preached from it a truly noble sermon, with fine freedom of utterance and marvellous fervour. It happened to be the season of the year in which many strangers visit London, who seek for " Lions" on the Sabbath, as well as on the other days of the week. Oxendon Chapel was crowded. One who heard him on this occasion says: " It proved a most remarkable sermon, not only for its richness of thought in illustration, its deep and fervent piety, its heartfelt stirring appeals, but for its burning and impassioned eloquence. It made an impression that could not be soon effaced, and God commanded upon it a rich blessing. Sometime after, he received no fewer than twenty-three letters from different individuals, in various parts of the country, and some even from Australia, in which the writers informed him that that discourse had been the means, under God, of their conversion, and thanked him cordially for it. How many more were thus seemingly edified cannot be told: *that* day will reveal it."

In the earlier period of his ministry, Mr Archer's discourses were more doctrinal than practical. As he advanced, however, he reached the happy medium wherein truth and duty, faith and works, were faithfully combined. The spirituality of his teaching gradually increased, up to the last year of his life. He was ever decidedly evangelical. Modern innovations had not then been so unblushingly intruded. They became somewhat rampant by the mid-time of his ministry, and, as will be seen in the sequel, he was not behind the bravest of his compeers in analysing, exposing, and condemning them. These, however, were the "detours" of his pulpit-work, and were never permitted to interfere with, or cast into the shade, the grand and elemental doctrines that save guilty sinners. He was never

ashamed anywhere, or at any time, of "Christ and him crucified." He traced all the good he had been honoured to do to
the preaching of such Christianity as has from the "fulness of
the times" added to the Church such as are saved. It was the
good old Gospel of his own and of the Church of his fathers,
that brought back the people to Oxendon, and raised himself
to a high position as one of the most effective preachers in the
Métropolis. It was not the massiveness of his thoughts, the
clearness of his views, the depth of his research, the brilliance
of his eloquence, nor the simplicity and memorableness of his
prelections, that brought such success. Such adjuncts have
by themselves been often tried, and as often failed. In Mr
Archer's hands they proved powerful helps, only because they
were all baptised by the spirit of Christ, and then consecrated
to the service of the pulpit.

It was long a prevailing opinion, that what has been called
the "Scotch lecture," could not be made popular or acceptable
in England. And there was some reason for this. Reading
and expounding a passage of Scripture was considered by many
to belong to a lower order of mind; and when the service
was made up of it, the complaint was, that the occasion had
been trifled with,—in fact, that the congregation had been de-
frauded of their dues of sermonizing. This mistake may have
had its rise in the superficial and perfunctory mode of discharging the duty. Merely to read and cursorily to paraphrase
the passage is not critically to expound it: such is not the
nature of the "Scotch lecture." In that peculiar method of
discourse, the one or the other of these two plans is adopted:
The general scope or drift of the passage selected is seized,

and, obedient to this, the several verses or clauses are explained; or the lecturer goes over the entire paragraph verse by verse, keeping always carefully in view the context, and giving what appears to be the mind of the Spirit in each succeeding verse or sentence. The latter is the most prevalent plan. The Scotch pulpit has almost universally acted thereon; and to this, it has been thought, may be traced the very general acquaintance with Scripture which obtains in the North. Mr Archer did not fail to give his people the benefit of such a lecture. For many years after his ordination, it was his regular practice to do so on the Sabbath forenoons. His thinking powers fitted easily into such an exercise, and he became proficient in it. His expositions of Scripture, especially of the Psalms and Epistles, were much appreciated for their clear and vigorous style. In preparing them he read much and prayed often. Having a most retentive memory, he was able to pour out stores of knowledge, accumulated from his varied reading. He was particularly happy and beautiful in his occasional readings of and remarks upon the Psalms. He commented on one if short, and only on a portion of one if long. His hearers used to say that this division of the service alone afforded food for contemplation during the entire week. And here it is but just to tell of him, that he was peculiarly sensitive as to the use of other men's thoughts and words. He invariably noticed quotations from his authors, and gave their names. The revival of Oxendon was mainly due to these expositions. If well done, the "lecture" cannot fail to be as popular as it is instructive, and it is a good sign of the times that it is now more resorted to by ministers of all denominations in England, and deservedly sought after by the people. Many desired the Oxendon lectures to be published; but, like most of his pulpit discourses, they were all delivered from notes, and not in a form that could be sent to the press.

The frequenters of Mr Archer's ministry might in general calculate on his being in his own pulpit every Sabbath. In the beginning of his way, he was almost a fixture there. He used to say to newly-ordained young men, " *You* would not have been called if your preaching had not been acceptable to your people, and it is not fair to deprive them of your services. Then, if strangers come to the church and find him absent whom they came to hear, they may not return. You will, no doubt, find the labour arduous at the commencement; but take courage, pray, and persevere, and you will be sure to prosper. Remember that a wandering shepherd is very apt to make a straying flock." His own practice in this respect was much thought of by his people. Still they saw one disadvantage which it had. His keeping himself so exclusively to his own pulpit, prevented the public at large from becoming acquainted with his talents, and thus his more extensive usefulness was for a while delayed. Taking advantage of one of the anniversaries of his induction, the proposal was made to him, that the sermons should be preached by ministers of different denominations, instead of always selecting those of his own. He saw the propriety of this, and consented. Consequently, on the 17th of December 1837, the three diets were served successively by Dr Morrison of Brompton, Mr Sherman of Surrey Chapel, and Dr Leifchild of Craven Chapel. In the forenoon and evening Mr Archer occupied the pulpits of Drs Morrison and Leifchild.

He thus became known to these large and influential congregations, and his own chapel stood out into more importance among her sisters in the neighbourhood. From this day he himself ceased to live and work amid the unknown. His sermons were, from this time, eagerly sought after. The applications indeed were almost innumerable. It was only a few of these that could be entertained. He was robust in health, and in spirits buoyant. Then, his marvellous facility in preaching or speaking, almost on the spur of the moment, not only brought him many requisitions, but tempted him often to exceed limits. Indeed it was not an unusual occurrence, that when he had gone only to *hear*, application, on the unexpected failure of another to appear, was both made and responded to by him. On a few minutes' notice he would mount the pulpit or the platform, and continue the subject in a style so fluent and telling, as to suggest the thought of his having been prepared to do so. His brethren in the city often, very often, applied to him at the eleventh hour, and seldom if ever unsuccessfully. Very late one evening, Dr Leifchild called at "Hans Place." On being announced, he said, "Well, brother, I am come as usual in an extremity. You must preach to us to-morrow morning. We expected ———, a great gun, you know, and he has just sent word that he cannot come. A pretty affair, indeed! So I put on my hat, and said to my wife, 'I shall go and seek out brother Archer, and get him if I can;' and so here am I, and you will consent." "Very likely, indeed," replied he, smiling; "and at such short notice, too! As you expected such a powerful piece of artillery to be fired off, what execution do you expect my pop-gun to do? No, no; I am

not going to occupy *his* place, and see the looks of disappointment, and perhaps of disgust, when I mount the rostrum."
" Disappointment and disgust, indeed !" rejoined he. of Craven
Chapel, " I can assure you that no man enters my pulpit who
is more welcome to my péople than you are ; and I can vouch
for the fact, that gleesome gladness will be depicted on every
countenance as soon as your well-known face appears."   " But
what a short notice to prepare a suitable discourse," continued
Mr Archer.   " What nonsense," said Dr Leifchild ; " what nonsense you talk ; *prepare*, indeed ! why, you are always ready.
Give us any of the following : ' Power from on high ;' ' Mighty
to save ;' ' Mighty rushing wind ;' ' Curse ye Meroz ;' ' Plant
of renown ;' ' Mercy of God,'—all of which I have heard, and
many more equally magnificent ; but any one of these will do
famously."   " I suppose I must comply," said the obliging
Oxendonian ; " and you shall find me there, God willing, in
good time."   Dr Leifchild seized his hand, and in bidding him
" Good-night," added, " You are really a noble fellow, a real
boon to London, and a friend indeed to me, because a friend
in need."   So eagerly indeed were his services sought for, and
so yielding was he when at all in his power, that it was no
unusual thing for him to start early in the morning, travel fifty
or sixty miles, preach a special sermon, and then return to town
to deliver a lecture on some religious or scientific subject in the
evening.   Three sermons a-day he sometimes attempted ; and
into them all he so earnestly threw his whole soul, that they
who heard only one out of the three, thought the effort enough
to task his strength.   Home he came, however, late at night,
cheerful and fresh.   Such labours were constant for years, and

were continually augmented as he became better known. There
are not many cities or towns in England where his name is not
mentioned as a household word, and even yet held in grateful
love. No doubt his genial, happy disposition in private contributed to this. He soon endeared himself to all of every per-
suasion. His was no sectarian soul. He was so thoroughly
catholic, and so obliging to all and sundry, that many could
not tell to what denomination he belonged. To any curious
inquirer, however, upon the point, he would smile, and say,
" I am a Presbyterian to the back-bone." And so he was, but
he was more,—he was a Christian in every bone of his body,
and in every corner of his heart.

When he had laboured for three or four years, his people
determined to give him a token of their appreciation of his
valued and successful labours. A snuff-box was at first proposed, but objected to on the ground that he did not take
snuff, and that such a present might induce him to begin a
habit very prejudicial to a public speaker. A silver tea and
coffee service was then agreed to. When purchased, it was
found that a *surplus* remained. With that a silver salver was
bought,—Mr Gray (Mrs Archer's uncle) adding, " If there be
any difficulty in raising the funds, come to me, and I will
pay the difference." The testimonial was then placed in a
handsome oak chest (also a present from one of the congregation), when the whole was presented to him along with the
following address :—

" Reverend and Dear Sir,—We, in the name of the congregation among whom you labour in Oxendon Chapel, sensible
of the great importance of a Gospel ministry in general, and

especially of that ministry under which Providence has placed us, feeling, we hope, its salutary influence upon our spirits, and wishing to see the Lord's work prospering in the midst of us, desiring to give you all encouragement by our prayers and any other means competent to us in our station in the Church, —we, as a testimony of our Christian esteem and love for your person and ministry, do now present this small token from the congregation, hoping you will receive it with the same feelings in which it is presented to you, trusting that mutual love may ever exist between you and the congregation, and that by this Christian union the Lord's work may prosper among us, so that both he that soweth and they who reap may rejoice together, and that, when the Chief Shepherd shall appear, we may receive a crown of glory that fadeth not away.   This is the sincere and heartfelt prayer of your affectionate congregation.   ' Now unto Him that is able to keep you from falling, and to present you faultless before the presence of his glory with exceeding joy, to the only wise God our Saviour, be glory and majesty, dominion and power, both now and ever. Amen.'"

It may be proper here to refer to other similar tokens of esteem which, during the course of his ministry, he received from his attached hearers and friends.   These things prove the fidelity of a pastor.   In 1840, the non-commissioned officers and privates of the 1st Battalion of the Scots Fusilier Guards attended his ministry.   On leaving, they raised among them the sum of £8, which was presented to him by a serjeant, corporal, and private, in token of their appreciation of his faithful ministry, and of the anxiety he had manifested for their spiritual welfare. This was most gratifying to him : he used to speak of it in after-days. He valued gifts, not for their intrinsic worth, but for the feelings which they represented.

In 1855, Dr Archer and his lady were invited to a soiree to be held in the chapel. W. S. Lindsay, Esq., was in the chair. After a feeling and effective address, in which he did ample justice to the talent and worth of his friend and pastor, he presented him, in name of the congregation, with a massive silver tea-tray, valued at eighty guineas, twenty-three volumes of standard works, handsomely bound, and a purse of seventy sovereigns.

In 1860, six gentleman joined and purchased for him a large folio pulpit Bible, which he continued to use to the close of pulpit-work. In a letter to Mrs Archer, similar tokens are feelingly referred to :—" Only think, my dear Martha, how surprised I was when I went into the vestry yesterday morning, to see a magnificent new pulpit-gown and cassock; and how astonished I was, when I went into the pulpit, to find a beautiful crimson-velvet cushion for my Bible ! I had no notion of these things, and they rather overcame me. I told my people once more that I could not thank them in words ; but you know my heart feels to the very utmost these marks of kindness. . . . I got such warm greetings after the service—so many good wishes for us both, and lots of love for you. It really does my heart good to witness how you are beloved by the dear Oxendon friends—and so you ought to be, for you have laboured among them to the utmost of your power, and you are rewarded here by their love. A richer reward awaits you on high."

Several valuable gifts were made to him, at different times, by grateful members of the church. We only record two others, because of their coming from a different quarter. He frequently visited the "Gore Lane Schools" on the Sabbath afternoons, and preached to the poor. He was presented with two handsomely-bound quarto volumes,—the one upon "Constantinople and the Scenery of the Seven Churches of Asia," and the other upon "Syria, the Holy Land, Asia Minor," both beautifully illustrated. Upon "Constantinople" was inscribed:

"To the Rev. THOMAS ARCHER, as a small token of esteem and regard for his kind and continued exertions in preaching the Gospel to the poor inhabitants of Gore Lane, Kensington."

Upon "Syria" was inscribed:

"To the Rev. THOMAS ARCHER, in grateful remembrance of the pleasure and information received from attending his interesting and talented lectures on the 'Fulfilment of Prophecy,' from his sincere friend,   MARY RAY."

In 1844, he received from the Senatus of the College of Princeton, New Jersey, the degree of D.D. He would not, however, use the honour till the diploma conferring it had arrived. He highly appreciated this distinction; and all the more that it came to him from the other side of the Atlantic, and especially from that old and British-founded College, which had become famous as the seat of learning where Wetherspoon, Edwards, and Alexander had presided. Dissenting ministers in this country are laid under great obligations for such just and generous notices of their personal and literary worth. Their non-conformity excludes them from the diplomas of Oxford and Cambridge; and the Scotch Universities are, though growingly liberal, still somewhat chary of conferring degrees beyond the pale of the State-church. It were to be regretted if our American brethren were to receive the impression that their diplomas were not highly prized among us. They may be assured of the contrary. The only drawback is, that we have no similar means by which their preferences can be reciprocated.

The pulpit of Oxendon Chapel was ever kept sacred for the promulgation and defence of "the faith once delivered to the saints." Dr Archer's discourses were, in the main, simple though powerful elucidations of evangelical truth. He taught men the way to be saved. He knew that way well, and never faltered or doubted upon the subject. He was not one of that new school where it is said men are "feeling their way," or as yet only "searching for truth." He had found the way and the truth and the life, and preached the Gospel therefrom with no "uncertain sound." At the same time, he was quite alive to the grievous aberrations of the school referred to. It was in the mid-time of his ministry that the "new views" made bold to come forth to the light. He set himself at once to analyse and expose them. He saw that hatred to the doctrine of vicarious expiation lay at the bottom of it all, and gave his attention for a time to a more thorough and rigorous examination of that vital point in dogmatic theology. His published lectures on "The Atonement," "Puseyism," "Popery," etc., which may afterwards be referred to, are sufficient evidence that he had detected, and had courage and ability to confront, the danger. He was chiefly concerned about the progress and power of what has been called "the Broad-church School," and thoroughly sifted its pretensions. His conclusions were, that "Rationalism" was only a wolf in sheep's clothing,—a Trojan horse with its belly full of deadly weapons,—a masked battery where the sentinel, with peace on his lip, had the poignard under his gabardine. He was at no time deceived by its specious compliments to Christianity, while everything supernatural was eliminated from its system. In a masterly style he set himself to expose the narrowness of this boasted "breadth;" and he succeeded at least in confirming the faith of his own flock in the "good old way." Such fearless and telling preaching as his was, is loudly called for still. Dim and flickering lamps must not be substituted for God's "true lights," and the playthings of a ritualistic toy-shop must not displace the spiritualities of our Divine faith. It is said, "The schoolmaster is abroad;" if so, he has hitherto sought rather to drive us from than to bring us to Christ. He tells us we have been befooled, that we have as yet to learn what true Gospel is, and that we must now unlearn what our fathers taught us, and unsay what the prophets have affirmed. Assuredly, men like Dr Archer are the best friends of Christ and of the world, who so unravel the tortuosities of pretension, and simplify Divine truth, as to conquer for the Gospel the convictions alike of the thoughtful and the unlettered. Some amiable and even accomplished minds have of late allowed themselves to be spiritually seduced. They who have the key by which propitiatory Christianity can be opened and reached, must endeavour to lead them back to that Cross which has ever signalised its triumphs, by first of all humbling the pride of human intellect. The religion of *mercy* must be laid bare to the very core, and apostolic fervour and simplicity must characterise and emphasise the work of the evangelical pulpit. It was when the Gospel was distilled from the lips of its Divine Author, in plain and transparent propositions, that the "common people heard him gladly." In its outset, Christianity had no help from letters, or metaphysics, or dialectics ; none from synods, councils, or assemblies. Placed in the hands of the unlettered Galileans, with a world for its antagonist, it surely won its way from the fisherman's hut to the city on the seven hills. And so it must ever be. Despite of all the braggings of our age, the bit and bridle must be put into the mouth of its pseudo-liberalism, that reason may be reminded of her proper place, and be thrown back upon the knees of a humble and teachable faith. Such was Christ's, and such ought to be his servants' way. He pandered to no pretty conceit; he dallied with no natural prejudices; he elaborated no argument; he condescended to no demonstrations of fundamental doctrine. His mysterious system of mercy took for granted the very points our modern rationalists demand to be proved. All is strikingly axiomatic. Where, in all the Bible, is any proof led for the existence of a God, or indeed for any of the cardinal principles of the remedial religion? All is simply asserted or affirmed. Herein lay Christ's power as a preacher : "Verily, verily, I say unto you," was the authoritative preface to his lessons. Higher than imperial, he applied Divine force to his offer of a free salvation, and then tinted it all round with the heavenly hue of his Father's mercy. As if there was no other song to be sung, the key-note of his music was mercy; as if there were no other tale to be told, his only readings were those of mercy; as if God had but one attribute, he constantly unveiled mercy. There were ten thousand other themes upon which he might have easily discoursed, but he waived them all off. Had he willed it, he could have given all the explanations haughty minds demand, and assigned satisfactory reasons for every doing and saying within the compass of revelation. He could have drawn aside the curtain, and shown us how he proceeded in the creation of worlds, and in the begetting of intelligences; he could have given us, in a sentence, the age and history of our little planet; he could have swept away all the mist that hangs over the entrance of moral evil; he could have shown us clearly what now we but dimly see—the nature and necessity of atonement, the adaptation of his life and death to the demands of law and justice, the process of the Holy Spirit's work in regeneration and sanctification; and the entire links of every chain in his general and special providences. He could thus have captivated the convictions of all reasonable beings, and made infidelity of every shade an utter impossibility. But he never did so condescend. He came but with one view before his own mind—the salvation of the soul; and with but one truth to tell, and one way of telling it; he told it as one having authority. Never was he betrayed into the region of the exact, and he never paid homage to prying curiosity. Such was his plan, solemnly and wisely taken, and, up to this hour, strictly adhered to. He still simply teaches *mercy*, he still exemplifies *mercy*, and pays as little heed to the proposals of an aspiring, as to the pettishness of an offended reason.

Such were the convictions of the preacher and pastor of Oxendon, and he acted them fully and fearlessly out. In language equally clear and bold, he denounced the present demand for what is called a re-adjustment of Christianity on a basis compatible with the spirit of the age. He characterised that basis as simply one of scepticism. He had no fears of the doctrine of vicarious propitiation becoming " stale, flat, and unprofitable." He denounced the new pulpit of modern thought as, after all, not new, but an old one reconstructed and re-varnished. He admitted that from it came some fascinating thoughts, that it wreathed some beautiful garlands, and produced some tempting fruit. All such things he regarded at best as academic icicles suspended from a frozen zone. His Swiss tours had taught him that, among the glaciers of the Alps, summer productions and winter formations might be seen in immediate contact,—where the full ears of corn touched the icy lake, and the ripe cherries could be gathered with one foot standing on the ice. With the eye of an eagle, he saw those extremes meeting in the rationalistic theory. He saw them in the bosom of the Anglican Church, veering around State-Presbyterianism in the North, and swooping, as evil birds of prey, above the ark of modern non-conformity; and he traced it all to the old offence of the Cross—to the spiritual whore-mongery which prefers human merit to Divine mercy. It was when carried by burning zeal into this region of apologetics, that his acute and comprehensive intellect was seen to fine advantage. His mind was never muddled. His tactics were

never dastardly or compromising. He demanded that the
"old landmarks" should remain,—that neither standard nor
standpoint should be deserted. He was more afraid, however,
of secular infidelity than even of Popery,—regarding the former
as more dangerous, from its air of intellectual *abandon*, and
even from its benevolent pretensions. He feared that such
infidelity might, after all, turn out to be "the great apostacy;"
and hence he laboured in his sphere to protect especially
young minds from its ensnaring influence. He was more particularly anxious to guard them against the idea that the
Gospel either had or could become effete. His sarcasm was
sometimes very withering when he referred to the bugbear that
the age had run ahead of the Gospel; and it would be well
for the Church and for the world if such drivelling were met
on all sides by equal manliness and demonstration.

It must ever be the consolation of the Church, that no age
whatever shall outrun the religion of the Cross. God provided
that religion for mankind-sinners as such, and down to the
end of time, the need shall be the same and the supply the
same. Man has no right to expect either that new wells shall
be dug, or that the old ones shall be emptied. The Scavatori
from Naples dug up the other day, from among the ruins of
Pompeii, an urn of bronze filled with pure water, sweet to the
taste, and unaltered in quality. Thus they who lived eighteen
centuries ago, and they who live now, quaff the very same
water. The bronze urn has survived the vicissitudes of ages,
and its contents are found to be still good for all uses. So it
is with "the things that are not seen,"—they are immutable
and eternal. More than eighteen hundred years ago, out of

the "Great Fountain of Life" was the Gospel urn filled; and,
let modern thought dig away as it pleases, that water shall
never be found either deteriorated or diminished. It sprang up
then, in the experience of thousands, even unto everlasting life.
It is still springing; and it shall so spring till time shall be no
more. "Jesus is the same yesterday, to-day, and for ever."

Dr Archer's popularity as a preacher continued unabated to
the end. There certainly were modifications, as he drew
towards the evening of life, but these were not of such a kind
as to render him less effective and useful. There was the
mellowing of autumn,—there was the golden hue of a fine sunset,—there was the subdued tone of a spirit that, after long
communion with God and truth, is about to go where it shall
see Him "face to face." For two years before he died, he
was a severe sufferer from bodily ailments, but these were
scarcely discernible when he was fairly set a-going in the
pulpit. The compiler had an opportunity of judging of this,
somewhat unexpectedly. On a cold and dismal Sabbath evening
in December 1862, he had been called to visit a sick friend in
the immediate locality of Oxendon Street. His own pulpit
was to be occupied by another, and, as it was now the hour
of "evening sacrifice," he determined to step into Oxendon
Chapel, and worship with the brethren there. He was fortunate in finding Dr Archer in the pulpit. He preached from
the words, "The powers of the world to come,"—a sermon of
great grasp of mind, in some portions of severe and keen
logic, and brilliant throughout with flashes of fine eloquence.
It was in every respect equal to anything the compiler had ever
heard from him in his freshest days. He remembers still the

look of kind surprise which met him as he stepped into the vestry, and thanked the preacher. "I do not believe that a better sermon has been preached to-night in London," was the tribute paid, and which got for an answer, "I had no idea that you were to be a hearer." This was the last time the compiler ever heard him preach, and the impression left is as deep and quick as ever.

At a time when the occasion called for it, Dr Archer used the pulpit to call attention to events that excited the public mind. This was not his habit, but he did not decline it, when he could improve what was passing for the benefit of his people. Two instances may be quoted. When the Duke of Wellington died, he preached from these words in Jeremiah xlviii. 17, "How is his strong staff broken!" In the first part of the "sketch," as he called it, he discoursed on the Duke's "influence for good amongst ourselves," and then on his "influence in regard to his own order." The second part was devoted to an analysis of his character, where he specified the Duke's "conviction of the obligation of duty," "his great concentration of action," "his perfect reality and transparency," "his perfect truthfulness," "his great disinterestedness;" and he wound up the whole by an eloquent illustration, furnished in the history of the Duke, of the "temporary fickleness, and the ultimate stability, of popular opinion." The whole piece is unique and piquant, being at once a just and bold estimate of one of the most remarkable men of his age. Again, during the Crimean war, he delivered a characteristic discourse from Psalm xlvii. 9, "The shields of the earth belong unto God: he is greatly exalted." His divisions were :—"I. In the war, let us marshal

E

the forces. II. Let us now ascertain the causes and the circumstances of the war. III. We might now advert to the
prospects of the war." The national mind was at the time
greatly excited, and in this discourse he dexterously met
an earnest and deep craving for suitable and serious thought.
Both these discourses were afterwards published, and received
that amount of approbation which they richly merited. Such,
however, were but the exceptions to his rule. " Christ and
him crucified" ever formed the staple of his preaching, and
secured for him through life, the cordial love and confidence of
his attached people.

We conclude this chapter by giving an extract from a somewhat facetious, but, upon the whole, truthful and friendly,
sketch of Dr Archer as a preacher, both throughout and at
the end of life, which appeared in the denominational
magazine* of 1862 :—

" Let us describe, if we can, Dr Archer—*Sagittarius*, as we
have heard some of his people who were disposed to air their
classics term him, with loving banter, after a more than usual
telling shaft had sped from his bow. Dr Archer's preaching
appears to us to have greatly changed in style within the last
dozen years. It·has passed from the declamatory stage to the
hortatory, from the combative to the persuasive. Formerly it
always struck us as highly pugilistic in tone. Of course, as a
true minister of the Church militant, he was bound to exhibit
an aspect of general pugnacity to the world, the flesh, and the
devil ; but, besides being assailant in the abstract or general
sense, he descended to the concrete and particular. He

* *United Presbyterian Magazine*, p. 308.

always seemed to us to be on the look-out for an opponent
worthy of his steel, either a somebody or a something—the
something being frequently a particular failing or sin embodied
by a bold style of personification in a somebody, towards whom
the Doctor indulged himself in a highly vigorous and animating
display of intellectual fisticuffs.   Many a sounding rap we
have heard him administer to the carcase of an opponent.
Nor were these opponents impersonal or untangible ; on the
contrary, they were generally flesh-and-blood celebrities of the
day, whom he, in the interests of the good cause, 'pitched
into' with manifest relish.   But his attacks were not in bad
taste, nor were they undeserved.   It was always some conspicuous offender against Christianity, humanity, or common
sense, that he took in hand.   We well recollect a choice
instance of this many years ago, when the Doctor, physically
speaking, was a much younger and stronger man than he is at
present.   It was at the time the news reached this country of
the harum-scarum pranks the then Governor-General of India,
Lord Ellenborough, played in connection with the gates of
Somnauth.   His silly and unstatesmanlike action was loudly
condemned by public opinion at the time,—notably so by pulpit
opinion.   If pulpit denunciation could have done it, then
assuredly would the tame elephant have been utterly squashed,
extinguished, and annihilated there.   To this concerto on the
'drum ecclesiastic,' Dr Archer contributed his share.   We
felt it to be a treat to witness the gusto with which he put the
unfortunate culprit on his legs, and then pounded away at him,
to the intense delight of an audience exhilarated by this
specimen of his prowess.   We must say that, on this occasion,

he took the measure of his man very neatly. This was one instance of what we used to consider his favourite style. . . . . Dr Archer is at this day (1862) as animated as he was twenty years ago, and though we have heard of his health suffering lately, there is nothing of this visible in his preaching or his personal appearance. Beyond a doubt, he is a capital preacher. He deserves to be better appreciated than he is, for his singularly lucid, free, and telling way of discoursing from a practical text, is not only very interesting, but eminently fitted to instruct. He has a habit of saying to his hearers, 'Now, take this thought with you,'—a mode of address that in some men would savour of vanity; but his audience might do worse things than carry Dr Archer's thoughts with them. Testing them by our own recollections, we should say that they will not become stale by lapse of time, nor pall by repetition, but, like generous wine, will improve with age. We heard him preach a sermon not long ago, which we take to be an excellent specimen of his style, from the text, 'When thou art converted, strengthen thy brethren.' We must say we have rarely listened to a sermon more telling and effective. Its division was particularly clear, and the four heads were grouped in a rather neat alliteration, not at all forced, but well fitted to aid the memory:—' Peter's danger; Peter's defence; Peter's deliverance; Peter's duty.' Very sound and clear exposition, forcible appeals, illustrations that, if not very striking, were at least quite to the purpose; and one or two bursts that, if uttered by certain popular idols, would have been pronounced eloquent, set off by a free, fluent, and animated delivery, distinguished this sermon. . . . . Twenty years ago, Dr Archer was one of

the popular preachers in the Metropolis, and was much sought
after in Dissenting pulpits generally. In those days his readi-
ness, his animation, his pluck, made him a great catch for
public sermons. We have heard him somewhat vaguely blamed
by Scotchmen as being 'too English,'—whatever that may
mean. The general arrangements of his services were certainly very like those prevalent among English Dissenters, and
we have known Scotchmen grunt dissatisfaction, and say, they
might 'as well be in an Independent chapel.' But we are
quite sure the Doctor always had a warm side to his native
country, and a patriotic sympathy with all that concerned it.
We shall not soon forget with how thrilling an effect he once
introduced in a sermon the tragic story of the martyred John
Brown of Priesthill. To hear him quote the dialogue between
Claverhouse and the heart-broken widow was a new sensation
to a used-up man. . . . Dr Archer's personal appearance, and
even his gait, indicate the sort of man that one would expect to
succeed in London. Unlike some of his brethren, whom we
have seen stealing through the busy metropolitan thoroughfares,
absent, reserved, distract, and with eyes downbent, as if they
were practising the monastic 'custodia oculorum,' he walks brisk
and self-possessed, with a quick, glancing eye, which takes note
of everything about him. He always looks alert and confident,
and in full possession of his wits,—not the kind of man to
come into harsh collision with his fellows, in the busy walks of
life, and yet not the man who would take a buffet very patiently.
His general outline and bearing are in no sense professional,
but may be termed cosmopolitan in their independence of local
and class characteristics. From his frank and cordial manner

he is decidedly a favourite. We have heard men call him 'a good fellow,' and women 'a good creature'—two definitions that reflect the idiosyncrasies of the sexes as well as their partialities. His qualifications are well suited for our Metropolis, where an active, ready man will be both more popular and more useful than a studious dreamer."

CHAPTER IV.

THE PASTORATE.

THE young minister of Oxendon, in the midst of his onerous duties, began to feel the truth of the Scripture, "It is not good that the man should be alone." His choice of a wife was made in the fear of God. Confident that much, not only of the comfort but of the usefulness of a pastor, depended upon a prudent and pious helpmate, he sought one such from the Lord, and got her. There was in his congregation a gentleman, Mr John Gray, whose counsels and liberalities caused the Church to prosper. He was long and well known for large-hearted benevolence. He was a native of Dunse, in Scotland, and made it his special business to patronise his young countrymen when they came up to the Metropolis. One instance of his success in this way is worthy of being recorded: it refers to no less a personage than the late Dr Abram Robertson, Savilian Professor of Astronomy in the University of Oxford. When Robertson came to London he was penniless and patronless. He applied to the generous bookseller in Piccadilly, Mr John Gray, with whom he had been acquainted as a member of the same congregation in Dunse. Mr Gray at once took him into his own employment as porter. He had not been long in this situation when his master discovered his extraordinary liking to mathematics. He was at once sent to Oxford, Mr Gray accompanying him. There, at the first, he became servant to a gentleman who resided in the city, and whose two sons were prosecuting their studies at the University. It was soon noticed that the young men made rapid progress in mathematics, and the teacher inquired at their father whether they had the assistance of a private tutor. It was discovered that the lads had been assisted by Abram, the servant. This led to his being employed as private tutor in the University, and ultimately to his appointment to the chair of Astronomy, which he so long and so ably filled.*

Mr Gray had a granddaughter who, on losing her mother at a very early age, was received into his family, and brought up under her grandmother's care. This old lady was also an eminent Christian. While meek and lowly, like her Divine Lord, she was in principle firm and unflinching. Her great wish for her grandchild was, that she should become a fearer of God and a follower of Christ. She regulated her upbringing accordingly. Everything was done that money could procure to make her an accomplished woman; and such she became. Mrs Gray used to say, "A good education is better than a fortune; the former can never be lost, the latter may take wings and fly away." The granddaughter would reply that "both would be best," and in after-life she found it to be so. On the death of this venerable lady, in 1828, her granddaughter

* See *United Presbyterian Magazine* for April 1867, p. 154.

went to reside permanently with her uncle, Mr John Gray, in
Piccadilly, a gentleman who not only equalled but surpassed
her father in acts of kindness and charity. God had blessed
him with an ample fortune, and he scattered it with a lavish
hand. He had infirm health, which made travelling about
necessary.. Every year he went from home seeking recreation
and recruiting, and sometimes visited the Continent. His niece
invariably accompanied him. In October 1835 they had set
off for Italy. At Paris he was attacked with serious illness,
and died there. The companion of his travels returned to her
former happy home with his remains, which were deposited in
the family grave at Bunhill-fields. She received the sincere
sympathy of many, but especially of her esteemed pastor, to
whom she was married on the 10th of November 1836. No
one who was privileged with the friendship of Dr and Mrs
Archer will refuse to bear their loving testimony to the suitableness of such a union. As the widow survives, all the truth
cannot be told. Simple justice, however, demands the record
on these pages of that estimable lady's devotedness to her
husband. It was almost perfect. Incessantly and unweariedly
did she labour along with him in the vineyard. Unencum-
bered with the anxieties of a family, she resigned herself entirely
to his help and comfort. In fact, she appeared fully as much
to be his colleague in the pastorate as she was his partner in
the household. The success of Oxendon was owing in part to
her unostentatious benevolence and sympathetic activities. Of
many a care she relieved him; to many a holy service she
guided him; from many a cause of grief she preserved him; in
many a season of trial she strengthened him; and whether at

home or abroad, in sickness or in health, in solitudes or in multitudes, she was ever at his right hand, to cheer with her smiles, mitigate with her fellow feelings, or relieve with her substitutions. So lovingly and admiringly did she proffer her heart and hand to aid him in all duties, that, on looking back upon the twenty-eight years of their companionship, we never see them apart. As they lived and loved together, so they worked and prayed together, even with one heart and soul, until death did them part. In short, we never knew a minister who was in every respect more indebted to his wife. At the head of his table she shone, not only as the hospitable mistress, but as witty in her herself and the cause of wit in others. From her early education, and especially from her frequent tours to and on the Continent, she had acquired alike ease and elegance of manners; so that it mattered not how many or how distinguished were the *savans* around her table, she coped with the best of them, and made them all feel, that while she appreciated their positions, she did not depreciate her own.

Thus happily settled, Dr Archer set afresh to his pastoral work. He preached better than ever. He laboured more abundantly than ever. He succeeded better than ever. In the former chapter, we saw him in the pulpit. We shall now look at him in other departments of professional life. We begin with his " Bible classes" for young women and young men. At an early period of his ministry he had formed such classes. He gave himself enthusiastically to their superintendence. To the religious improvement of young men he more especially devoted himself. He saw the many and powerful temptations to which, on coming from the country into Lon-

don, they were exposed, and he set himself to counteract evil
influences by pastoral zeal. At first he did not succeed: comparatively few young men attended. Good, however, was done,
and even some infidel minds were convinced and saved. He
determined to leave no means untried to gain their affections
and confidence. He invited them frequently to " Hans Place."
The smile that greeted them, as well as the judicious counsels
he gave to them, proved *their* place in his heart, and won for
him a place in theirs. He was wont to say, " My delight is to
entertain those who cannot return it, for they must feel that
my motive springs from pure love and an earnest desire for
their temporal and eternal welfare."

His class for young men was held at first in the vestry of the
chapel. When the attendance increased, it was transferred to
the school-room in Ship Yard, and ultimately to the chapel
itself. At the close of one of his courses of lectures, or "lec-
turettes " as he called them, in 1838, the young men presented
him with a handsome writing-desk, " in grateful acknowledgment of the talent and laborious research bestowed on the
course of lectures concluded March 1838." He was very
much pressed to re-deliver this course in public, but declined,
as he had resolved upon another course upon Popery, intended
for the general public, during 1839. In 1840, however, he
favoured the class with a course of lectures upon the following
interesting subjects :—

- " The Relations of Science and Scripture."

" Mosaic Account of the Creation compared with Geological
Discovery."

" Descent of the Human Family from one Pair."

"Mosaic Account of the Deluge, and Geological Discoveries."

" Geographical Divisions of the Globe after the Deluge."

" Confusion of Tongues, and Proof of one Original Language."

In 1841 he delivered an admirable set of twelve lectures to this class on " The Evidences of Christianity." He announced them as,—

" I. Statement of the subject—Responsibility for its discussion—Spirit of inquiry.

" II. Principles upon which the question is to be determined —Necessities of a revelation.

" III. Probabilities of a revelation—of its gift—of its evidence —and its contents.

" IV. Miracles: definition and tests of—Application of criteria to Scripture miracles—Amount of their testimony.

" V. and VI. Prophecy—elements and illustrations of.

" VII. Harmony between Scripture and science.

" VIII. Scripture theory of human nature.

" IX. Adaptation of the Scriptural remedy.

" X. Propagation of Christianity—Examination of Gibbon's secondary causes.

" XI. Social influence of Christianity.

" XII. Incidental testimony."

These lectures were attended very numerously, and were greatly blessed. Many were led to examine into the subjects, and not a few had their doubts dispelled and their faith established. Some, under powerful convictions, made a pro-

fession, and became zealous members of the Church. To
testify their gratitude and admiration, " the strangers," as they
were called, meaning those who had been privileged to attend,
though not belonging to Oxendon, invited him to a soiree in
Exeter Hall, which was presided over by William Leifchild, Esq.,
and who, after an impressive address, presented him, in their
name, with a massive silver salver and a beautiful copy of the
Bible. The inscription alludes " to their high appreciation of
his able course of lectures on ' The Evidences of Christianity,'
lately delivered at Oxendon Chapel, and their high regard for
his noble and disinterested efforts in the cause of truth.—
April 14, 1841."

In 1842 he again set to work, and delivered a course " On
Man and his Constitution :"—

" I. Man in his origin—theories discussed—Epicurean or
Atomic: Monboddo—French physiologists—German—Mosaic.

" II. Man in the date of his origin—Examination of the
Hindoo, Chinese, and Egyptian chronology—Verification of
the Biblical.

" III. Man in the identity of his race— History and present
state of opinion—Varieties admitted and defined—Illustrated
by analogies in the animal and vegetable kingdoms—Argument
from history and languages—Influence of climate and civilisation.

" IV. Man in his physical constitution—Its internal relations
and adaptations to the external world, illustrative of the loving
skill and benevolence of God.

" V. Man in his moral and mental constitution—Moral feelings: their nature, laws, and culture—Importance and means

of moral self-discipline—The intellectual powers—Their classification, phenomena, and laws—The immaterialism, responsibility, and immortality of the mind."

He continued year after year thus to labour.   His subjects
ever varied, and his enthusiasm never waned.   There were
lectures upon Palestine, Babylon, and Nineveh; and some of
them were illustrated from sketches by his distinguished friend
and countryman, David Roberts, R.A., who was laid in the
grave only a few days before him.   There were lectures also
upon the " Fulfilment of Prophecy," as illustrated in the history
of the Jews,—a subject in which, from boyhood, he had taken
the deepest interest.   The ground, indeed, over which he
travelled, was extensive and diversified.   There was scarcely a
department of useful knowledge that escaped him.   Still all
had but one aim—the establishment of the divinity of the Bible.
He issued, at the commencement of each session, cards of the
subjects to be discussed, but some of these cannot be found.

At the close of the course, in March 1851, his young men
presented him with Layard's " Nineveh," 2 vols., and Kitto's
" Cyclopædia of Biblical Literature," magnificently bound,
with the following inscription:—

" Presented to the Rev. THOMAS ARCHER, D.D., by the
young men attending his class (session 1850-51), as a small
token of their gratitude for his unwearied efforts to promote
their mental and spiritual advancement; and in acknowledgment of the benefit they have received from the able course
of lectures delivered by him during that period.

" London, March 1851."

In 1853 and 1854 the following synopsis was issued :—

"Subject.

"*The Bible.*—Its incidental testimony—Introductory remarks
—The object of the course—Incidental evidence—Its nature
defined—Its field described—Its importance defended.

"*Mosaic Records of Physical History.*—Creation—Interpretation of the text—Amount of its teaching—Biblical sketches
compared with geological conclusions.

"*The Deluge.*—Analysis of Biblical language—Results—Tes-
timonies to their truth from physical appearances.

"*Astronomical Phenomena as described in Scripture and verified
by Science.*—Ethnology—Objects and principles of the science
—Its relation to Scripture history—Its present condition—Its
growing harmony with Scriptural statements.

"*Archæological Testimony.*—General interest of the study of
antiquities—Higher importance of, in their Biblical relation—
Egypt—At once a region of productive and incidental evidence
—Its connection with Jewish history and Scriptural writings—
Progress of modern discoveries—Illustrations of its ancient
state—Verification and elucidation of Scripture from—Nineveh
—Frequency and style of Biblical allusions to its size, character,
and manners—Sketch of French and English researches—
Recent discoveries, and their bearing on the authenticity
and meaning of the Old Testament—Numismatic and pictorial
evidence—Monumental evidence—Traditional and legendary
evidence."

In 1856 and 1857, his subject in the class was announced
as—

"The Formation of Intellectual and
Moral Character.

" I. *Introduction.*—Practical importance of the subject—
Theory of mental and moral perfection—Means of attaining
it—Varieties of mind in degree, in direction—Classification of
powers—and, Arrangement of the course.

" II. *Memory.*—What is it?—Dr Brown's philosophy of—Its
relative place in the intellectual being—Its usefulness—Specimens of its varieties—Methods of strengthening it.

" III. *Judgment.*—Difference from reason—Its province generally—Laws of exercise—Mode of culture—Special application
in religion.

" IV. *Attention.*—Abstraction—Metaphysical questions on
—Concentration the highest practical result of—How to be
reached.

" V. *Imagination.*—Genius—Fancy—Distinction of—Their
relation to judgment, and comparative value—Refined and
controlled by reading and study—How to read.

" VI. *Taste.*—Is there such a thing?—Analogous moral question as to conscience—History of controversy on—Admitted
varieties of—Suggestions as to its formation and improvement.

" VII. *The Moral Faculties.*—Their variety—Relations—
Magnitude of their influence—Responsibility for their culture—
Helps to their advance, harmony, and benefit.

" VIII. *Conclusion.*—The religious sentiment and principle
—Their standard—Motives of action—Final results."

In 1858 and 1859 his subject was again—

"THE BIBLE.

"I. *Introductory Lecture.*—Importance of the subject, and mode of treating it.

"II. *The Bible.*—Its literary history—The antiquity and preservation of its manuscripts.

"III. *The Bible.*—Its claims—Inspiration of the.writers— What that is—How it can be proved—How it is vindicated— Brief review of the evidence.

"IV. *The Bible.*—Its purposes.

"V. *The Bible.*—Its science—Not minute teaching, but general suggesting.

"VI. *The Bible.*—Its ethics—The question of the foundation of morals—Their extent—Their motive principle.

"VII. *The Bible.*—Its politics—Liberty—Order defined— How to be harmonized—Biblical salutation.

"VIII. *The Bible.*—Its poetry—Examination of the poetic element generally—Application of its texts to Scripture—Illustrations of.

"IX. *The Bible.*—Its eloquence—Nature of, illustrated— Boundless variety of, in the sacred volume.

"X. *The Bible.*—Its style of teaching—Simplicity—Variety —Adaptation.

"XI. *The Bible.*—Its results—Personal—Domestic—National.

"XII. *The Bible.*—Its interpretation —Modern hermeneutics —Principle of analogy—Illuminating influence of the Spirit of God."

At the close of this session, his young disciples, anxious to

F

testify their gratitude for his untiring exertions on their behalf, presented him with a handsome mahogany davenport—made so high that he could stand while reading or writing. They were ever anxious to administer to his comfort, and noticing that of late he had begun to stoop slightly, they hoped he would find it more useful.

The following letter accompanied the gift :—

"London, *6th September* 1859.

" Dear Sir,—The young men who have attended your course of lectures upon the Bible have felt desirous of making some recognition of the affectionate regard and esteem they entertain for you,—also that it should come in some useful shape. A writing-desk for your study has been thought to be not altogether an inappropriate or an inconvenient article; and if it should prove not to be a superfluity, when we follow you in imagination, deeply immersed in thought, searching out the hidden mysteries of Christ our Saviour, whose faithful minister you are, we shall be glad in having made a suitable selection. We feel that this trifle is but a very imperfect recognition of the deep obligations we have incurred for the many years you have spent amongst us in anxious solicitude for our spiritual welfare. This debt we never can repay you, but our earnest prayers are that you may receive an acquittance at the great day of reckoning; and furthermore, we pray, that as our hearts have been brought into subjection to yourself, through your faithful teaching of the Gospel of Christ, so you may still more completely bring them into humble submission to our common Lord and Redeemer. The sentiments of esteem which we have so faintly and so inadequately expressed towards yourself, we are desirous also to communicate to Mrs Archer, whose piety, devotion, and many virtues, public and private, must be productive to you of considerable domestic comfort and happiness.

"Accept, then, this little gift, as the sincere offering of our affection, and as the expression of the hope that the pleasant relations which have so long existed between us may, for a considerable time, be yet prolonged."

At the close of the same session, the young women attending his class presented him with a pair of beautiful Bohemian vases, modestly expressing the wish that, in the gift selected, Mrs Archer might also have some enjoyment. This delicate attention to, and thoughtfulness of *her*, rendered the token much more acceptable. When looking at them in the drawing-room at Hans Place, he would express his feelings in reference to the surprise he got when they were presented to him. The numerous expressions of gratitude and respect which he from time to time received, were always by him most unexpected, and therefore the more highly appreciated.

In 1859 and 1860 he delivered what proved to be his last course to the young men's class; and for learning, eloquence, and power, it was in every respect equal to its predecessors. The subject was, — " Philosophy and Christianity — Their alleged antagonism—Policy of the allegation—Their real harmony—Philosophy the disciple of the Cross."

" I. *Philosophy.*—Its various meanings, various systems: the Platonic, the Baconian or Inductive.

" *Christianity.*—What is it? and how to be determined?

"II. *Philosophy and the Divine Existence.*

"III. *Philosophy of Hume.*— Theory of causation — Pantheistic theory—Biblical logic.

"IV. *Philosophy of the Human Being.*—The mental and moral powers of man, and their condition—Sceptical description contrasted with the Scriptural.

"V. *Philosophy.*—God's self-discovery to man—The authenticity of the Bible—How it is to be vindicated—What has it done?

"VI. *Philosophy and Christian Ethics.*—The foundation—The extent—The motive principle of Scriptural morality.

"VII. *Philosophy and the Christian Sabbath.*—Present aspect of the subject—Questions: On what does it rest?—How is it to be observed—What has been its practical influence?

"VIII. *Philosophy and the Christian Home.*—What did it accomplish in Greece? in Rome?—Christian homes? etc.

"IX. *Philosophy and Christian Rest.*—The heaven of the Philosopher and the Christian."

"That much and lasting good," writes one of his pupils, who had attended these classes from the commencement, "has been done by these means, there has been abundant proof. Socialists and infidels have become sincere professors; sceptics have had their doubts removed; and the careless, who would not have allowed themselves to be classed with either, have been led to see the importance of being decided.

"These yearly re-unions were to himself a source of great enjoyment, and he spared no pains, not only to make them attractive, but in the highest degree instructive and useful.

The average attendance was from 150 to 200 at the commencement.   When business became brisk, and the young men
could not so easily get out to attend them regularly, there were
seldom fewer at the class than from 100 to 150.   This sufficiently proved how highly the lectures were appreciated."

Dr Archer continued his class for young women, which was
always well attended.   In 1860 and 1861 he lectured to them
on the following subjects:—

" WOMAN.

" I.   *Woman.*—Her creation.

" II.   *Woman.*—Her constitution.

" III.   *Woman.*—Her employment for her livelihood.

" IV.   *Woman.*—Her occupations for her amusement.

" V.   *Woman.*—Her books.

" VI.   *Woman.*—In the sick-room."

In 1862 he continued this subject : —

"WOMAN.

I.

" *Introductory Statement.*—Woman's social state and development—Woman's relative position and mission—Woman's
individual responsibility—Outline of the topics.

" *Woman.*—What she is—General question of the comparative place of woman and man in the scale of humanity.

" (*a.*) *Woman.*—What she is physically—Her physical
organisation—Her physical education—Her physical occupations.

" (*b.*) *Woman.*—What she is mentally—Alleged inferiority of female intellect in art, science, etc.—Explanation of.

" (*c.*) *Woman.*—What she is morally—Consideration of the range, force, duration of her emotional nature—Prodigious sensibility—Danger of its excess—Advantages of its well-regulated action.

II.

" *Woman.*—What she should be—Her intellectual elevation—Her social ascendency—Great and proper sphere of woman's duties—Great results in filling it—The ideal of a woman educated for the circle in which she is to move.

III.

" *Woman.*—How she may become what she should be—The means within the range of all—Qualifications—Duty of forming clear conceptions of a model woman—Deep conviction of personal imperfection — Desire to reach a higher standard—Means to be employed.

IV.

" *Woman.*—Why should she aim at this standard ?

" (*a.*) To elevate herself in social rank.

" (*b.*) To possess the largest amount of social power.

" (*c.*) To employ her social power for the noblest social ends."

On the 28th of October 1863 he commenced the following course on—

"TASTE.

" *Taste.*—Its province—Its originality—Its extremes and their dangers—Its importance and means of culture.

" Principles applied—Sphere—Range and order of application.

I.

" *Taste in Dress.*—Sketch of its changes—History of, in caricature—Present time and modes—Rules of choice—Cautions.

II.

" *Taste in Reading and Study.*—Why read?—What read?—Novels and novel-reading—How read?

III.

" *Taste in Æsthetics.*—Importance of this department of mental culture—Woman's employments—Scope of—Music—Drawing—Modelling—Subordination of all to the useful.

IV.

" *Taste in Conversation and Companionship.*—Great end of both—What it should be—What it too often is—*Aim* loftiest and promote it—Themes of the one—Character of the other to be avoided.

V.

" *Taste in Morals.*—Personal, relative influence—Adoption of a high standard—Temptations to lower it—Firm courage to maintain, to elevate it.

VI.

" *Taste in Religion.*—Proneness to abandon the pure, the

simple in worship—Attractions of the showy and histrionic—
Neglect of the purer life—Historic illustration.

" Concluding address."

There was something unusually solemn in his leave-taking of
this young woman's class, after the course had been finished.
He thanked them for attending in such numbers (from seventy
to ninety was the average), and expressed his belief that he
himself, as well as they, had been greatly benefited. He also
gave them a promise that, if spared, he would, in the next
session, meet them again, and again administer to their moral
and spiritual necessities. But, alas ! he was not spared so long.
By that time he was reaping the gracious reward of his labours
of love.

It is worthy of record that, in addition to these Bible classes
for young men and young women, he for many years met the
girls and boys who had returned home from school during the
holidays, at Midsummer and Christmas, twice a-week, at eleven
o'clock in the forenoon in winter, and at six P.M. 'in the
summer. During successive years, he carried them through
the biography, botany, geography, and natural history of the
Bible. He had a happy mode of conveying instruction to the
young. He used to say to all teachers: "Make your sentences short and pithy. Never use a long word when a short
one will express the same meaning—the greater the simplicity
the better, and the more memorable." Hence, he was always
interesting and impressive. His winning way, his tender look,
his kind words, won the hearts of the little ones. A competent
judge of these meetings says: "It was a real treat to witness

the happiness depicted on their countenances, when seated in
the pews, before the 'lecturette' began. In his pleasant style, he
told them how glad he was to see them, and hoped they were
thoroughly enjoying their vacations. These little courtesies
over, he prayed shortly, and then commenced his subject. His
every word was listened to, and their gleaming faces told how
enjoyable they found it to be. At times he would put a few
questions, and their ready and correct replies proved how
thoroughly they had understood him. A short prayer closed
the service, which seldom exceeded an hour. About forty
children usually attended."

His attraction, indeed, to childhood was a marked feature. His
face gleamed at the approach of the little ones ; the sun seemed
to rise upon him when he caught them in his arms. Nor were
they overlooked even when his mind must have been weighty
with solemn thought. He had preached one Sabbath morning
to a crowded congregation, all the pews and aisles being occupied. The sermon had been one of his most powerful. As
he descended from the pulpit, his eye rested on the little
daughter of a celebrated physician, one of his hearers. He
patted her on the head, and kindly said to her, " Come away,
my little pet, with me into the vestry, and you shall have some
cake." Dr ——— remarked to Mrs Archer, " Well, well, I
have sat and listened with absorbing delight and edification
to his brilliant and eloquent discourse, and when he finished,
I said to myself, ' What a grand subject, and what a great mind
has unfolded it !' but his condescension in taking my little
child into the vestry with him, after such a display of genius,
reminds me of the great Luther when he went to Worms, with

his head and heart full of such important matters, stopping at
the Fair of Frankfort to buy toys for his children."

There were also connected with Oxendon Chapel, large day
and Sabbath schools. In them Dr Archer took a hearty
interest, frequently visiting them, and exciting to diligence by
giving them rewards. The day-school was a superior one;
the education given was of a higher kind than is generally
given in such establishments. It was held in Ship-yard,
Wardour Street. The lease expired in 1862, and the school
was then given up. Before its dissolution, however, the master
invited several of his old pupils to tea, to meet Dr and Mrs
Archer; and a very pleasant evening was spent. Some of the
young men were in important and responsible situations in the
city, and others were in comparatively high positions. All were
doing well, and attributed their success to the education they
had there received. They presented their teacher with a mark
of their esteem. Some of them told Mrs Archer that the books
they most highly prized were those she had presented to them.
A proof of the high repute of this school is the flattering
manner in which it is reported by the Government Inspectors,
who did not claim a right, but who were permitted to visit and
examine. The school received no Government support. Dr
Archer was a decided and consistent Voluntary. He held that
the financial law of the Church of Christ bound it upon her to
be self-supporting and self-extending. He therefore taught and
encouraged his congregation to maintain, out of their own free
gifts, whatever useful objects they might patronise. It must be
stated to their credit, that, according to their ability, they were
never, in this respect, behind. On the breaking up of these

schools, the pupils found admission into others in the vicinity. There, was, therefore, for some time, none such in connection with Oxendon. Ere long, however, he succeeded in interesting some of his young men in the revival of a Sabbath-school, which still exists and prospers. His people, indeed, never refused their countenance and support to their pastor, when he commended praiseworthy objects to their liberality. Many pleasing instances might be adduced, such as their collections of £100, in 1847, for the destitute Highlanders, and of £118, in 1862, for the Lancashire operatives, besides their regular and generous contributions to the Home and Foreign Missions of the United Presbyterian Synod, and to the London and other Missionary Societies. And why should it not be told here, that among the liberal donors, on all such occasions, were ever to be found the pastor and his wife?

The following is an illustrative and interesting incident :—

When the Rev. Hope Waddell was in this country, after hopefully planting the Christian Mission in Old Calabar, he begat among us a deep interest in the son and heir of King Eyo Honesty. Young Eyo had embraced Christianity, and great expectations were raised as to his influence upon the Mission in future years. On Mr Waddell's return to Africa, he took with him, from Mrs Archer, a handsome present for the heir-apparent. She received the following reply, which is copied exactly as it was written, in English :—

"CREEK TOWN, OLD CALABAR,
17th August 1849.

" MY DEAR MRS ARCHER,—I have received your kind, good, loveful letter by my dear minister, and I was very happy and kinds thank to receive it, and you good word in the letter, and thy kind presents, and it show me how kind our heavenly Father and our blessed Saviour is to his children who called upon him with pure and right heart, and my dear Mrs, I am quite glad to receive your kind and good and love-wishing letter, and I thank God for all this, for it is in his greater loveness that he gave unto me the kind friend as you be, and am very much full of your love in your letter, which I have received from you, also, my dear Mrs, I have sending you one of our country fans by my good friend Mr Goldie, and I hope to receive another letter from you again, and hope this letter will meet you and family and all Christian friends in good health, by the comfort and bliss of our greater Father, to lead you unto everlasting salvation and his mercy to guide you all unto eternal life, and all with my good belove compliment to you all.—I am, your truly particular friend,

" Young Eyo Honesty,

" *Creek Town.*"

To interest his people in the Calabar Mission, Dr Archer read this letter from the pulpit. After the blessing had been pronounced, one of the members said to him, " That young man ought to be encouraged." The idea was at once taken up by several of the congregation, and the result was, that in a few weeks, a box of highly valuable and useful articles was despatched to the mission, including some very precious presents to Young Eyo himself. When he received them he was laid up in bad health. On his recovery, he thus replied :—

"MRS M. ARCHER,

"DEAR MADAM,—I am extremely fearful that you consider me neglectful of your very kind letter, and the handsome present which I received last year from my dear Mr Waddell, and the same time I was very sick with pain in all my joints, and I was at plantation, and he bring it there unto me; and the same day Messas Horsfall com to see me, and I put on that fine dressing-gown, and I was very glad though the painful was so strong on me, but the kindness of a friend makes me feel a leetle better; and by the time I return to town I show all your present to my dear father, and he was surprising with grateful regard, and I give half of that snuff to him, and a little to dear Mr Waddell; and I am very glad to say, my dear madam, that the Lord, our heavenly Father, with his great mercy, has restore me again to health, and often dear Mr Waddell com and speak many good word of God to me, that afflictions are often accompanied with many valuable benefits; as David said, 'It is good for me that I have been afflicted, for before that I went astray.' Also the Lord was with me all the time that the pain trouble me, and I was quite glad, for I know that all things is from his merciful hands, and I have read the life of our Lord and Saviour which was presented to me by Mrs Grange, of Aberdeen, Scotland, and consider the character of our Redeemer, who suffered so much for us; He bare our griefs and carried our sorrows; He was a man of sorrow, and I pray to Him day and night to help and keep me; and often dear Mr Waddell pray with me many times when he come down to see me at bed of sickness, and I am glad that our prayers was granted, and I use to read the Hymn 274, which is, ' O thou from whom,' etc. And on the Sabbath-day I use in same Hymn-book, 212, verse 4th, ' Grant that all may seek and find thee, a God supremely kind, heal the sick, the captive free, let us all rejoice in Thee.' So, my dear madam, when I read this, and many other word in the Holy Bible, I feel happy by the word of our heavenly Father. And, my dear madam, this sickness is what hinder me from writing you by that time. So I am now have most sincerely to send you a thousand thanks for your kind present, and the good letter, and regard to the friend which sent the table-cover, with my best compliments. Also, dear madam, I hope the prayer which you say in your letter may be soon granted, and about the meeting in my house which you like to know. I do keep meeting in my house every Friday with Mr Waddell and some of my young friends, and I do keep prayer-meeting morning and evening with my boys ; and after meeting at my father's yard on Sabbath, Mr Waddell come to my house and have meeting with me and my people ; and after meeting at my house, we keep meeting in school-house ; and after school meeting, we have prayer-meeting at Mr Waddell's house, so I have all this meeting to tell you. And, dear madam, am now have to write a few lines to thank Mr Lindsay for the kindness of the gold watch, so I cannot say much more this time ; but I am sorry that you do not get the fan I have sent you, so I send you two other fan and two mats,—to hear how you will like them ; and I hope this letter will meet you with good health, as I hope that God our heavenly Father will be with you to keep you in his own care ; and my best compliments and kind regard to your dear husband, and all your family and friends. Also, please read Philippians, chap. i. verse 3. And I beg you to remember me in your prayer-meeting.—I remain, dear madam, your sincere and much obliged friend,

"YOUNG EYO HONESTY."

One of Dr Archer's sayings was,—" I do not care to have one or two rich people in my church who give very handsomely, because·when they are removed their loss is severely felt. What I like is, that *all* should do something, according to their ability, and then one or more should not be missed if removed." Regulated by such a principle, Oxendon made and maintained a character for being ever ready and willing to support good and holy objects. " I never ask my people, " said their pastor, " in vain for anything: they have always both purse and heart open to answer all demands."

CHAPTER V.

PUBLIC LIFE.

R ARCHER was not permitted to give to Oxendon a monopoly of his talents and labours. His popularity became now so great, that London and the churches round about sought their share. They did not seek in vain. Of course, he was necessitated to make selections, which were not always of the more ostentatious class. He loved to serve the meek and lowly, and many an unknown pastor and poor congregation can testify to his obliging disposition. Still, he had to *select*, as he invariably made it a point never to neglect any of his Oxendon claims for those of the outside world. In 1839 his attention was drawn to the insidious and plausible views of the Socialists. Their leader and apostle, Robert Owen, was busy propagating his principles. Dr Archer, ever ready to denounce error, as well as to advance truth, at once threw down the gauntlet, and challenged him to mortal combat. He delivered several lectures upon the subject in various parts of the Metropolis. One of these created a great sensation. He gave it at the Mechanics' Institute, Chancery Lane. It

G

happened to be on the night of the Queen's marriage. The room was crowded. Robert Owen himself was upon the platform. In a very effective style, yet most gently and courteously, he exposed the rottenness of Socialism, and unsparingly condemned the mis-leaders of the young and weak-minded.

Since commencing to write this Memoir, the compiler has received an account of the *acta* of this interesting night, from one who was on the same platform. Owen was evidently impressed—certainly not converted,—and became especially attentive when Dr Archer attacked the famous, or rather infamous, Social doctrine of "the power of circumstances." Owen had taught that no man is at all responsible for his "character," whatever that might be,—that "*character* was made not *by* men, but *for* men,—that they were entirely the creatures of circumstances." The lecturer, in clear and cogent reasoning, demolished this old piece of ungodliness, winding up his argument by a direct and irresistible appeal to the Socialists present, whether they did not, from their own present *consciousness*, feel, not only that they had faculties of judgment and reflection, but that they had full moral power to use them in the formation of opinion, and in the actions of life. The audience seemed to be electrified, and some of them, as it was afterwards ascertained, from that evening renounced the errors of Owen, and returned to the truths of Christ.

It happened, also, that the peculiar views of "Tractarians" were commanding much public attention. He at once set upon "The Tracts for the Times." He advertised a course of six lectures on "Popery, Puseyism, and Protestantism," and delivered them with great effect, in the following order :—

I. "The present aspects of Popery, and the history of Puseyism."

II. "The Protestant rule of faith."

III. "The Atonement—Its reality—Its importance and position in Christianity."

IV. "Justification by faith."

V. "Apostolical succession."

VI. "An intermediate state—Prayers for and to the dead."

His modesty took it for granted that he might have but a scanty audience. He had, therefore, given instructions to have only the lower part of the Chapel opened and lighted. He miscalculated both his own fame as an eloquent defender of the truth, and also the profound interest which the subject had awakened in the public mind. Oxendon was besieged by an eager crowd; not only the area, but the unlighted galleries, the aisles, and the very entrance-lobbies, were packed. Among the hearers were High and Low Churchmen, and Dissenters of every sect. The course was a decided success, and added to his reputation and influence. These orations were taken down, as delivered, in short-hand, and published without Dr Archer's knowledge. He had, therefore, no opportunity of correcting them. This only broadened and deepened the sensation, so that their sterling merits have been acknowledged both at home and abroad. They did much to fix public attention upon the innovations of Romanism, and to stir up the spirit of inquiry into the grand cardinal truths of that "Cross" in which he gloried.

During the same year, he also delivered two lectures on behalf of the Christian Institute Society—one at Hoxton

Academy Chapel, upon " The condition of the world at the
advent of Christ, and the expectation then prevalent of His
appearance ;" and the other at Orange Street Chapel, on " The
apostacy of man from his Maker."

The cause of Missions lay near to his heart. He looked at
none of the societies from their own denominational standpoints.
Hence he was frequently employed by them all, both in pulpit
and platform advocacy. Nor did he grudge time, money, or
labour. He arranged, however, that this " outside " work
should come on at the end of his winter duties in the classes of
Oxendon. Upon such deputation labours he was often out for
four days in the week. The " Moravian Mission " was one in
which he felt a deep interest, and often went out on its behalf.
He used to say that that Society " did the largest amount of
good, with the smallest amount of money, of any with whose
working he was acquainted." Of the London Missionary
Society he was ever an enthusiastic advocate, and was for
many years one of its directors. There was scarcely one influential auxiliary which he had not visited, and where his presence and services were not hailed with joy. This " deputation
work " was onerous, but he greatly relished it. It enabled him
to form many valuable friendships with brethren whose praises
are in all the Churches, and which were the sweeteners of his
life. Out of many may be noticed his illustrious friend, the
late Dr Harris, the Principal of New College, and the author
of " Mammon." They were men of like tastes ; both had well-
cultivated and otherwise most congenial minds; both were
popular speakers, and they rejoiced in each other's popularity.
They knew nothing of that small-mindedness which is jealous

of a brother's gifts. We shall have occasion to refer to their pleasant intercourse in a subsequent chapter.

At various times he did signal service for "the Sunday-school Union." Perhaps one of his most remarkable efforts was the sermon which he preached on the occasion of that Society's Jubilee, in Surrey Chapel, on the 12th of July 1853. His text was from Nehemiah vi. 3 :—"I am doing a great work, so that I cannot come down: why should the work cease, whilst I leave it, and come down to you?" With a vividness and force, which they who heard it can never forget, he eloquently discoursed upon "the *grandeur* of the Sabbath-school work, as evidenced by the greatness of the end proposed; of the *means* employed in its accomplishment; of the *motives* which inspire the prosecution of the work; and of the splendour of its results." Then followed a marvellous picture of the great work which had been already achieved, of that still being done, and of what yet remained to be accomplished. He concluded with a fervent and powerful appeal to teachers to devote themselves more unreservedly than ever to so glorious an enterprise. The effect was such, that the crowded congregation seemed with difficulty to restrain themselves from giving audible expression to their pent-up feelings.

He preached, also, one of the anniversary sermons of the "London Missionary Society," in May 1845. His text was from Zechariah iv. 6 :—"Not by might, nor by power, but by my spirit, saith the Lord of hosts." This is perhaps one of the most interesting of all his public sermons. His subject was, "The spirit of God in the concerns of the world," which he illustrated under the following observations :—

" I. We are not to conclude from the language and form of the text, which appear a contrast between power on the one hand and the Spirit on the other, that weakness is at all necessarily connected with this influence.

" II. Nor are we to interpret the text as if teaching that the Spirit is to act independently of, and unconnected with, human agency."

There is logical acumen, pictorial beauties, and brilliant analysis, in this piece, sufficient to account for the just celebrity to which, as a preacher, he had now attained.

On Thursday, the 20th of April, he delivered the Anniversary Sermon on behalf of the " Baptist Missionary Society," from Psalm lxvii. 1, 2 :—" God be merciful to us, and cause his face to shine upon us.   That thy way may be known upon earth, thy saving health among all nations."   He announced his theme to be, " Divine blessing essential to human salvation ;" and the following were his heads of method :—

" I. Let us first attempt to form an estimate of the scene of action.

" II. Let us examine the purpose to be gained, and the work to be done in this scene of action.

" III. Let us contemplate the agent by whose instrumentality the plan is to be carried out.

" IV. Let us review the fitness of the agent for the work.

" V. Let us examine the blessing here implored."

He concluded with the following burst of eloquent peroration :

" And now, brethren, amid the prospective glory and strength of the Church, let each of us exclaim, ' Eternal God, make bare thine arm and revive thy work in the midst of the years ! God be merciful to us, and bless us, and cause his face to shine upon us: that thy way may be known upon earth, thy saving health among all nations.' We require the *change for ourselves.* Our prostrate condition, our intellectual degradation, our worldly conformity, our carnal divisions, form alike the sport of hell and the grief of heaven ; draw forth the tears of the good, and furnish fuel to feed the fire of undying misery. We require it *for the world.* Revive the Church, and what new impulses do you give to its energies, and with what scrupulous solemnity will it redeem its fragmentary influence, its atoms of time and thought to Christ? All around us, the signs of the age, the movements of empires, demand it. The world is stirred, and we must move with it, move in its van, throwing in our course the light of liberty and life ; else it will move, and in its steady procession leave us behind as laggards, and despised or crushed amid the ruins of the systems over which it advances. All is moving ! Mind is universally restless. Revolutions are achieved in a day. The thrones of the earth, in their fawning submission to the popular will, or in their rough-shod, iron-hoofed tramp on popular rights, alike show that the prestige of sceptres is gone, and that kings must rule by another law than that of birth and succession—the law of truth and justice. Might is no more right ; but if knowledge proceeds, the axiom will stand—right is might ; principle is power ! In a moment the stern democracy tears the mask from hypocritical despotism, and consigns it to unmitigated, withering contempt. Amid the toppling of thrones and changes of nations, national religion is found to be the true conservative principle ; *national religion—* not the religion of the State, religion incorporated in the statute-book, endorsed by the Legislature that compounds for its personal neglect by professional homage—not the religion whose index is in the spire rising with picturesque beauty from the trees, whose shadows fall on the graves of the dead and mellow into beauty the humble temple of the living God—not the religion whose only monument is in the rich tracery, and noble creations, or fantastic symbolism of the cathedral,—but *religion living in the hearts of the people,* characterising their homes, fashioning their habits,—the religion that dignifies the palace and sheds lustre on the cottage,—the true glory of a land, and, amid the rottenness of its statesmen and the creeping craft and haughty daring of its churchmen, its highest chivalry, its cheapest defence. *All is moving!* Driven from the Western world, spurned even by Popery as intolerably nauseous, Jesuitism, the Machiavelism of religion, aspires after triumph on the plains of China and India, or may pursue its intrigues in our own island, the retreat of dethroned monarchs and persecuted patriots, whose open ports show the vigorous independence of its people, the fearless boldness of its middle class, which is the bulwark of the poor against the heartless domination of the rich, and the energetic defender of the rich against the angry surges raised by the selfish insolence of those who, having nothing to lose, may, in a national scramble, gain something. Brethren, amid such agitation, it is necessary to ask, Is the Church prepared to meet them? Has it the heart, is it braced, to control and direct them, to evolve order out of seeming confusion, and from the disjointed elements of society to gather its scattered portions, and construct a pile marked by imperishable grandeur, and the scene of deathless joy? What is the

Church doing at home ? Survey again the uninstructed masses of our population. Consider the niggardly selfishness of the Church, its zeal for ceremony, its carelessness for souls; the arrogant presumption of one section; the dosing, dreamy indolence of another; the sectarian bitterness, the controversial bigotry of a third. All about us teems with action, while within are graspings after sectarian ascendency or the apathy of despair; while, alas! Christ's honour is not studied, and souls die, *die unpitied*, die *unthought of*, die ETERNALLY ! Awake, awake, O arm of the Lord ! quicken thy Church, that the world may be saved. And, men and brethren, let each breathe his solemn aspiration when I present the earnest desire of the text : ' Lord be merciful to us, and bless us, and cause his face to shine upon us. That thy way may be known upon the earth, thy saving health among all nations.' Let every soul now add its amen. And may each of us catch the impelling vigour of that Spirit whose influence alone can subdue the world to the authority of God, and fill all creation with the freshness and joy of spiritual, everlasting life. Amen and amen."

In addition to the missionary journeys, and sermons, and speeches, he was often asked to preach, on anniversary occasions, and to deliver lectures throughout the length and breadth of the land. The subjects of these lectures were varied and interesting, such as—" The Crusades," " Leo and Luther," " John Wesley," " Dr Chalmers," " Hugh Miller," " Thomas Macaulay," " Pure Literature," " The Aspects of the Age, its Lights and Shadows," " The Land we live in," " Ethnology," " Media," " Italy and Garibaldi," " Æsthetics," etc., etc.

But it was in " Exeter Hall" that he achieved some of his

most memorable triumphs. That famous gathering-place of
" the tribes of the Lord," is indeed one of the " thrones of the
house of David." The " *braying*" there—to use the unhappy
phrase of Lord Macaulay—has done more for the cause of
Christ, that is, of mankind, than all the eloquence of St
Stephen's. As a centre of influence it has no rival. In the " May
Meetings " of each successive year, great and good men there
rehearse the sufferings and munificence of Christian liberality,
and the waves of its holy and heavenly strains move on majesti-
cally to the ends of the earth—yea, to the shores of the eternal
world. Dr Archer took his full share of that work. He was
generally *bespoken* as one of the speakers for months beforehand;
and he never failed, whether advocating the cause of the Jews,
the Bible Society, the Tract Society, the Ragged Schools, Anti-
slavery Society, Society for Shortening the Hours of Labour,
the oppressed dressmakers, or any of the great missionary
societies, to win the highest honours of the occasion. He
was so popular that frequently, as he appeared on the platform,
applause ran through the hall. Without any fulsome praise,
he may be said to have been a true orator; for though his
utterance was rapid, he at once took, and never lost, the
enrapt attention of the meeting. He rose to one great climax
after another, like " Alp on Alp ascending," till he had the
mass of excited mind before him completely under his spell,
and extorted the most enthusiastic cheering when he had
closed. The compiler remembers being present on one occasion when he was pleading for the Tract Society, and can
never forget the excited condition of the multitude as he concluded one special piece of eloquence, once and again and

again was the cheering repeated, so that it was with difficulty
he resumed. The passage referred to had not been written,
but had gushed out in the fulness and ripeness of his lofty imagination. His voice was at that time full-toned, and he was
heard to the remotest corner of the place. He did not, however, relish these interruptions. He sometimes motioned with
his hand to prevent them, saying, " Pray, let me go on ; and
when I am finished, you may cheer me as you like." And so
they did—sometimes even jumping on the seats and waving
their hats and handkerchiefs. On leaving the hall, there was
often a rush after him, then a hearty shaking of hands, and
warm thanks and congratulations.

He was the lecturer in Exeter Hall, on four different
occasions, before " The Young Men's Christian Association."
His subjects were, " The Unity of the Species," " The Geological Evidences of the Existence of the Deity," " The Characteristics of the Middle Ages," and " The Philosophy of the
Atonement." These were subsequently published, and their
perusal must satisfy the candid reader, that he was equal to the
discussion of such weighty themes, and that his lectures pale
not amid the many brilliant ones issued under the auspices of
the same Association. They are marked by all that clearness
of thinking, force of expression, aptness of figure, range of
reading, and power of analysis, for which, as a preacher or
lecturer, he had been so well known and so highly appreciated.

Dr Archer had a strong dislike to appear in print. Though
he had had a predilection for the " press," his numerous and
weighty avocations put authorship, to any voluminous extent,

beyond his reach. In addition to those already noticed, he is
the author of the following treatises :—

"Gaming, and its Consequences," . . in 1838.

"Lectures on Popery, Puseyism, and Protestantism," . . . . . 1839.

"Five Lectures on Palestine, Illustrating the Truth
and Meaning of Scripture," . . . 1839.

"Apostacy of Man from his Maker," . . 1839.

"Opening Address at Abney Park Cemetery," . 1841.

"Individual Accountability of Man," . . 1842.

"On the Dispersion of the Jews," . . 1843.

"Self-Culture," . . . . . 1844.

"Influence of Sabbath Observance on National
Character," . . . . . 1849.

"Life in Christ," . . . . . 1851.

"The Duke—a Sketch." . . . 1852.

"The War," . . . . . 1854.

The fifth on this list is worthy of special notice,—" The
Opening Address at Abney Park Cemetery." It was upon the
10th of May 1841 that the foundation-stone of the Chapel was
laid, and the Park was dedicated as an asylum for the dead.
The Right Honourable the Lord Mayor, Mr Sheriff Wheelton,
the Directors of the Company, and a large assembly of the
proprietors and visitors, amounting to nearly 1500 persons, met
together under a marquee erected for the occasion. After the
stone was deposited and prayer offered, Dr Archer, at the
request of the Directors, delivered the following oration, which,
for pathos and point, is not surpassed by any other production
of his pen :—

" MY LORD MAYOR—LADIES AND GENTLEMEN,

" The occasion which has called us together, and the spot
where we have met, are deeply affecting and solemn. We are
assembled to devote this ground as the resting-place of the
dead—for the undisturbed, protracted sleep of their remains;
and we are assembled where, if tradition be correct, there are
associations to bind us to the men of past centuries—and
where some now present may form links to unite this day
and place with remote ages. We commune with the dead;
their abode is our subject, and whose sensibilities does it not
move?

" I know it may be said, Why think of the temple—why
lavish ornament on it when the inhabitant has fled? when
breath—feeling—thought—MAN—has gone? The question is
cold—freezingly, unnaturally cold—as an appeal to experience,
to the heart, demonstrates. Why do we impatiently visit the
scenes of infancy—where, nursed in the affection, we have
listened to the counsels of age? Why, but because the past
is hallowed—and nature, whose impulses are stronger than the
dictates of philosophy, irresistibly guides us there? Does any
one then say, my Lord, how valueless the breathless frame!
Our appeal is to experience—not calculation; to man—not
the sophist. How do we cling to the body when the last spark
of life is fled!—stealing into the chamber where it now rests—
unconscious of our presence—its features so calm and placid
in the dim religious twilight, sympathetic with the occasion and
the emotions of the mourner—where the full glare of noonday
would offend the soul as incongruous with the sacredness of

the scene! How do we gaze upon the countenance where the traces of a wife's beauty still linger, or the expiring faint smile of parental love is fixed by death! and not till the decay and corruption of that body make its presence dangerous, and even intolerable, can we tear ourselves from its side—throwing over it, as we retire, one long, deep gaze of the soul—and then, having drunk in the vision of the loved object, permit it to be buried out of our sight! All this may appear to some the drivelling of sentimentalism; and it may be their philosophy to say, Let the dead serve the interests of the living—by promoting the ends of science. With such philosophy I have no sympathy. I know that the corse cannot quiver under the dissector's knife; but who could bear the thought of the limbs of one beloved or venerated being exposed to the rude view of strangers—or to the scientific mangling of the surgeon? Who would not feel his soul lacerated by every incision on the dead, unfeeling frame? My Lord, this may not be philosophy, but it is nature; and her voice says, Promote science as you may, but not by the disfiguration of those whose very dust is precious and sacred!

"Are we told that the condition of the dead is of no moment if there shall be a resurrection? My Lord, we know that when the figure of the Archangel shall loom on the distant sky, and the fiat shall be uttered, Arise, ye dead!—it shall fall with startling, with vivifying energy on the dull, cold ear of death. The changes of ages in the grave cannot abate its force, or prevent its accomplishment. The deep billows of ocean may have rolled over us; we may have been consumed in the devouring flame; our bones may have been rudely torn from the

sepulchre where they were first deposited, or have crumbled
into powder on the shore or desert where they fell—all shall
thrill with life and be radiant with immortality. Still, oh! still,
do we not, in the full consciousness of this inspiring and sublime vision, cling to the quiet nook where our fathers repose
under the wide-spreading arms of the cedar, or the graceful
branches of the willow? Look to the body of living death,
which the adventurer drags from the burning plains of Hindostan—happy if life remain until his shattered frame can be
laid where in boyhood he wandered—happier still if spared
once more to behold it! Behold that youth whose eye gleams
with the unnatural fire of consumption ; how earnestly does he
watch the fading outline of his land!—conscious, too truly
conscious, he never shall revisit it; but leave his body to mix
with strangers' dust, in a strange country! Who would, who
could, condemn him if the thought sadly overcast his soul?
Who would not condemn him, if, with his hopes of life, there
was not a deep tinge of this melancholy foreboding?

" It is not I, then, my Lord, that plead for the dead. Nature,
far more heart-stirring, impressive, and universal in her eloquence, pleads for the sacredness of man's remains—for the
sanctity of the tomb. If, accordingly, you follow my references,
we shall find that the state of the departed has been a matter
of consideration with almost all nations that reached any degree
of refinement.

" I am reminded by the beautiful structure that admits to
this harvest-field of death, and by its hieroglyphics so graphically describing this locality as ' the abode of the mortal part
of man'—of that people who combined a grandeur of con-

ception with a power of execution almost unrivalled. The
Egyptians [deeply respected the dead; and, ignorant—certainly without any well-defined ideas of the soul's imperish-
ability—attempted to immortalise the body. Hence their
elaborate and expensive processes of embalming; and hence,
too, in all probability, those Titanic structures, whose long
and broad shadows have fallen on the generations of forty
centuries.

"The Jews regarded the rites of sepulture as so important,
that to be deprived of them was the greatest indignity. The
hints in Scripture of their habits clearly show that the usual
places of burial were without the cities—in fields, on the mountain's side, or the bosom of their gardens. Many of these were
constructed with exquisite taste and magnificence; others with
great simplicity—some furnishing by their sequestered position
a retreat for the robber and assassin, others ministering by their
gloomy seclusion and terrors to the morbid imagination of
demoniacs.

"To behold, however, the majesty of ancient entombment,
we must visit Petra—the Edom of prediction—that city in
whose contemplation the mind is perplexed whether most to
admire the bold grandeur of a circlet of rocks, their lovely
tints, or the structure that, chiselled on their brow, seem to
rival in beauty, strength, and durability, the precipices from
which they rise. Petra, the necropolis of a nation, for a thousand years unknown even as to its locality, when discovered,
presented on every side tombs of most elaborate workmanship,
of inimitable splendour. It was 'a city filled with tombs'—
the narrow ravine through which you approach it being crowded

with monuments along its dark, precipitous sides. When you emerge from that, and the full view bursts upon the eye, temples and tombs appear everywhere around—the theatre itself being surrounded 'with death and its mansions,' all presenting the evidence of a people opulent, refined, luxurious, familiarising the mind with death, and thus endeavouring to strip it of its terrors by the gorgeousness of its abode.

" If we turn from the Oriental nations, and contemplate the more modern and not less polished Greeks, we shall find their practice consonant to the dictates of natural feeling and the suggestions of social interest. 'They exhausted,' says Judge Story, 'the resources of their exquisite art in adorning the habitations of the dead. They discouraged interments within the limits of their cities, and consigned their reliques to shady groves, in the neighbourhood of murmuring streams and mossy fountains, close by the favourite resorts of those who were engaged in the study of philosophy and nature, and called them, with the elegant expressiveness of their own beautiful language, cemeteries, or places of sleep. The Romans, faithful to the example of Greece, erected their monuments to the dead in the suburbs of the Eternal City (as they proudly denominated it), on the sides of their spacious roads, in the midst of trees, and ornamental walks, and ever-varying flowers.'

" Who has not heard, my Lord, of the Père la Chaise of the French, with its countless monuments—fantastic in many cases, as among such a people some might be expected to be—rich and elegant in others, as the proverbial taste of the French mind should lead us to anticipate—but all placed on an eleva-

H

tion, calm, commanding, and inviting to reflection by its con-
tiguity to life and gaiety! Who has not heard of Mount Auburn
of the Americans—perhaps the most attractive of all modern
cemeteries—lovely in its position, abounding in natural beauties—and losing none of its charms by grotesqueness of artificial
decoration? Or, finally, who has not heard of the resting-
places of the Turkish dead—their romantic seclusion—their
perfect repose—their almost religious calmness—in which,
under the deep shade of the cypress grove, the soul is uncon-
sciously led to thought?

" In these historical references are seen the combined, the
unanimous, sentiments of the most ancient, most refined, most
luxurious, and gayest of nations: and what produced this con-
currence but the fact that they all allowed nature to speak,
and, obedient to her promptings, at once secured public health
by burying without the city, and invited to meditation by the
united charms of nature and art?

" The propriety of this arrangement is, obvious. There is
the consideration of public health and safety—a consideration
so momentous and urgent that one is astonished at its long
neglect. On this point the most painful facts have been stated
—strongly, incontrovertibly stated. Every one is conscious of
the oppressiveness, the langour of a dying chamber; much
more of the sickly exhalations that even force us from the
corpse over which we hang in affection. What, then, must be
the effect of a multitude of putrescent dead bodies—crowded
in a narrow space—huddled under an edifice for public worship,
where no breath of heaven blows to carry away the mephitic,
the pestilential vapour? This is not the picture of self-interest.

I have no pecuniary concern in this or any other cemetery; but I have the interest of a man in my fellow-citizens' health ; and, without fear of contradiction, assert, that injury—unthought-of, incalculable injury—has flowed from the condition and locality of our churchyards. The mass of the metropolitan churchyards are a disgrace to our city and our age. For the full, the disgusting, details that would corroborate this statement, I must refer you to the 'Gleanings from Graveyards.' I may merely say, that the exhalation generated by the decomposition of animal matter is so deadly, that a light on being introduced into it is instantly extinguished, and that even recently one man was found dead at the bottom of a grave in the heart of London—suffocated by the foulness of the air ; another descended, and on stooping to lift the body of the grave-digger, 'appeared as if struck by a cannon-ball,' fell, and seemed instantly to expire — nor could the most strenuous exertion restore life ! The crowded state of these graveyards ; their position in the most swarming haunts of the poor, as if to spread contagion and death, or under churches and chapels emitting a sickly smell among the already too-heated congregation ; the fevers they are known to have produced ; the occasional removal of bodies long resting where friends consigned them, and disturbed and removed often in the most offensive manner ; all these things demand a change—demand that we should no longer throw around death horrors more numerous than its own, nor make it the instrument of mortality to the living ; demand that, while beautifying the mansion of the living body, we should prepare for it when lifeless a receptacle not gaudy or glaring, but one chastely beautiful and solemnly attractive, and which at least shall not throw over a teeming vicinity the fumes of death.

" Our churchyards are repulsive to the sensitive mind; they cannot attract the man of taste; and thus, by repelling many, they deprive the soul of that deep and holy converse with the dead that might nerve it for the duties of this world and the destinies of the next. Who, on the contrary, can doubt that, in this ground, under the boughs of yonder cedar, or of those chestnut trees, surrounded by the graves of them who shall be here interred, there shall fall upon the soul a sombre mood of thought—sombre and yet pleasant, because mingling with the appalling associations of death the cheerfulness of nature, and the imaged resurrection? What mind could be so placed without feeling itself awed, and yet invigorated, by abstraction from the world, and by self-reflection? A walk among the tombs invitingly arranged, simply adorned, throws an instructive light on the pursuits and frivolities of time, and seems to unfold the portals of immortality.

" On such principles are public cemeteries recommended, and for such purposes is this now opened; to give to the departed a quiet habitation, sacred, inviolate to the march of improvement; to furnish to friends a spot where, free from interruption and the intrusion of vulgar curiosity, they may indulge without restraint their tenderest sensibilities, and muse on the reminiscences of the past over the dust of the dead; to furnish to all a haunt of deep, of soul-felt communion; and, in a word, stripping the grave of its revolting, repelling associations, to constitute it an eloquent and impressive preacher to the living. How well fitted for these ends is this place! How still and serene ! and how likely to become much more so, when the trees planted yesterday by the hand of man shall throw their deep shadow over his grave—typifying, in the varieties of their foliage and tints and stateliness, the diversities of those who sleep beneath ! and, in the naked, the leafless desolation of winter, succeeded by the bursting vegetation and rushing verdure of spring, the full expanded beauty of summer, and the rich successive hues of autumn, imaging forth the strong probabilities and the opening glories of a physical resurrection ! Are these things without their lessons ! Can they be without them ? What heart could be unimpressed by them ? The pulpit has its voice ; but that of the tomb is more thrilling, more impressive far.

" I cannot overlook in these sketchy remarks the *moral associations* of the spot. Tradition has said, that in one corner lie the remains of Oliver Cromwell. I speak not now of the politician—I refer to the man ; and if greatness of intellectual stature, majesty of political achievement—if to rise from obscurity to be the real monarch of a great nation, to direct its thunders, to make its navies sweep the broad sea—if to throw the shelter of England's power over the persecuted of Piedmont—if these things constitute fame and glory, then do the tradition and the assumed presence of the remains of the Protector fling around this locality a lively, an imperishable interest.

" But I point now to unquestioned history. In the turret of that house were composed many of those hymns, some of which we lisped in infancy, and others of which have embodied our trembling anxieties, our ardent hopes, our rapturous joys. For years Isaac Watts lived on this spot ; the man who cou'd

write for infants or philosophers, and who, by the variety, the
elasticity of his genius, could instruct both. How often in this
locality, in these walks, has his imagination soared to heaven,
and, catching its melody, bathed in its glories, has embodied his
visions and experience in the deathless poetry that has been
the vehicle of the emotions of millions ! Here he lived and
mused and sang ; with his own hands planted many of these
trees ; and thus has imparted to the place the hallowed associations,—alas, too seldom combined !—of genius, and talent,
and piety.

" This spot, then, my Lord, rich in the beauties of nature,
richer still in moral interest, we now dedicate to the dead.
May it be sacred from foreign invasion, and the havoc of war
which even respected the grave—sacred from the hand and
changes that would disturb the bones of the departed,—and
from it may multitudes rise at the sound of the trumpet, with
holy impatience to meet their God! It is impossible in the
transactions of this day to exclude the future from our minds,
and not to think on those who shall probably be here entombed.
Let the past be our prophet, and in its light survey the next
half century,—how many shall be here committed dust to dust!
how different in circumstances and character! Here shall lie
infancy, with all its endearing prattle, its half-formed expressions of pleasure or pain, now hushed; boyhood, with its
budding hopes and ardent spirit, calmed in death; manhood,
in the maturity of its strength, and with the crowding visions
of success; old age, trembling, paralysed, sinking into second
childhood, but ripe for heaven; the husband, around whom
clustered the hopes of a family, removed when most required;

the wife, whose presence gave home its charms, and whose smile shot joy into the heart of her toil-worn partner; the manly youth, to whom both husband and wife looked with excusable pride, and as the prospective joy of their declining years; the pastor retired, now exhausted by cares, worn out in his Master's service, or arrested in a career of brilliant prospect and growing usefulness; the churchman, the dissenter, both now instructed in the truth—both now one in Christ. How many scenes of bitter grief here occur! How many tears of the crushed heart shall be here shed! How often will the orphan, the childless widowed mother, here linger by the grave of loved ones no more! and, with thoughts and anguish too deep, too holy to be seen, retire into its shady, sequestered retreats, and there, unheard and unobserved, except by God, let the soul gush forth in emotions awakened by the remembrances of the past, and only to be subdued by the anticipations of the future! Here may the Paraclete be present—to bind the broken heart—to stanch its bleeding wounds—to strengthen the bruised, the trembling reed—and to pour over this necropolis the light of immortality!

"May I be allowed one remark more strictly professional? *The dead shall live;* earth teems with the elements of future being, and, in the throes of the universe, shall cast forth from her mighty womb the germs of myriads of men. Let us, my Lord, realise the event—sublime in its own magnitude, the importance of its relations, the perpetuity of its results—and endeavour so to believe and feel and act, that, when we shall behold the distant point of light in the heavens approaching and swelling into intensity of brilliancy, until we can descry

amidst its supernatural splendour and glory the burning chariot
of the First and the Last, with the keys of Hades and Death
at his girdle, we may feel He comes to take us home—*home*
to himself, and to all that is noble, etherealised, sanctified in
mind, and refined, fresh, unfading in bliss—HOME where death
shall never separate hearts linked in deep, undying sympathy
—and from which, safe in his presence, we shall behold, in the
rushing ruins of worlds and systems, the final overthrow of
death, and the matchless conquests of Him who vanquished
death by submitting to its stroke."

As the company were moving away at the conclusion of this
address, Dr Archer turned to his wife, and said, " If you out-
live me, I should like to lie near this cedar,"—a wish which it
has become her sad duty to see gratified, as his body now
reposes very near its shadow.

Dr Archer, though sometimes requested, would never go
to the Continent as one of a deputation. He wished, when
absent, to be free of all trammels, and make up for the waste
in London by perfect brain-rest abroad. At the same time, he
did not refuse his assistance when at any time Christ's cause
could be promoted by him. On one occasion he preached in
the Oratorio in Paris, to a large congregation. It was highly
gratifying to his feelings, when the service was over, to be
waited upon by numbers of young men who had attended his
classes in Oxendon, and who were then settled in the French
capital. Before they parted, they had some very serious and
affectionate conversation, and he earnestly exhorted them, in
the midst of the gaieties and temptations of the city, never to

forget the sacredness of the Sabbath. His own life in this respect was consistent. One morning in Paris he was on his way to the house of God, when he met two friends. On saluting them, he said that he supposed they were seeking the church, and promised to show them the way, as he was going there. His friends looked rather confused, and at once admitted that they were on their way to Versailles, to see the grand water-works play—one of them adding, "No doubt, Doctor, you have often witnessed the sight." "I never have," he replied, "for when I have been here, they always have been played on the Sabbath, and I should be extremely sorry to spend any portion of this sacred day in sight-seeing. I give it wholly to Him who, in mercy to us, set it apart for His service; and surely the other six may suffice for the world, its occupations and pleasures."

Though very much of a public man, he seldom attended the meetings of Synod in Scotland. This was not only regretted by his brethren, but by his people, who felt that Oxendon should be represented in the Supreme Ecclesiastical Court. He assigned as a reason, that, as the Synod was held in May, when London was crowded with ministers and people of all denominations, and from all parts of the kingdom, many of whom he knew, and, when preaching for and to them, had received no small kindness, he ought not to be absent, but abide in town to reciprocate their hospitality and enjoy their fellowship. Assuredly, his absence from Synodical assemblies arose not from lack of love for the Church of his fathers. To that Church he was devoted, and never forgot her welfare. He did what he could for her in London, and made her known

in parts where her very name was strange. True, he had
found it hard work to maintain the cause in Oxendon, but he
succeeded. His experience, however, of the difficulties of the
situation, made him somewhat doubtful of the spread of Pres-
byterianism in England, and especially in the Metropolis.
When the Synod, in 1859, sent up a deputation to inquire into
the practicability of adding a few more places of worship to
those already in existence, he was, at the first, rather afraid
that the attempt might prove a failure, and certainly did not
give it that countenance which was hoped for. Perhaps he was
not in any error of judgment here. His reticence was occasioned, if not justified, by his own experience of the difficulties
to be incurred. At that time the munificence of Mr Henderson
of Park was not forthcoming. Dr Archer therefore pressed
the question of the necessary funds, and thought it better not
to venture too far, as matters would only be made worse
by failure. His difficulties, however, disappeared when Mr
Henderson generously offered to advance the money required
for the building of the new churches. Even before that, he
had offered the use of Oxendon Chapel in which to hold the
public meeting at which the matter was to be brought forward ;
and, failing Mr Lindsay, whose duties in the House of Commons prevented his taking the chair, which he had kindly consented to do, Dr Archer at once took his place. He thereafter invited all the members of the Synodical deputation to
breakfast with him in Hans Place ; and when the three new
churches were built, and their ministers inducted, he gave
them the heartiest welcome, and never refused either help or
counsels. The Synod's " London Church-Extension Scheme,"

has, under God's blessing, been thus far successful, and no man rejoiced more than he. It might not have been surprising, though, in the circumstances, he had felt somewhat chagrined that he had been left to bear the burden and heat of the day, for nearly thirty years, in an out-of-the-way chapel, with the most substantial of his people living far away in the suburbs, where it was proposed to erect the new churches, and into which not a few of those might be expected to pass. So far from this being the case, he from the very beginning expressed his opinion that one of these churches should be built in St John's Wood, where some of his best members resided, and that he would consent to draft off thirty or forty of these to form a nucleus. The compiler feels constrained to add that, from the day he came to Clapham, the friendship and help of Dr Archer restored to him so much of that rich brotherhood which he had reluctantly left behind him in the North. He was a friend indeed, in that he became one in time of need.

Dr Archer made only one public appearance before his Synod. The Mission Board having appointed him to speak at the Annual Synodical Missionary Meeting, in May 1850, he complied, and fully sustained his reputation as an effective platform orator. His subject was, "The Progressive Character of the Missionary Enterprise." In the following letter to Mrs Archer, he pleasantly refers to the occasion :—

" EDINBURGH, *May* 1850.

" I told you yesterday that numbers were inquiring after you most kindly. I could literally fill a sheet with the names. Old and young, from Dr K. down to J. B. J. I received from all a very kind reception, and had numerous invitations to preach on Sabbath, all of which I most firmly declined.

"For the meeting in the evening, I prepared myself well, both by study and earnest prayer, and I went to it accompanied by R. and P. When we arrived, there were a great many ministers, but few people. By seven o'clock, however, the hall was crowded, and H. R. said about 3000 persons were present. Dr K. gave an elaborate address. We had two most admirable and telling ones from Mr B. of Jamaica, and Mr M. of Paris. Then came my turn. I never felt so much in all my life. I knew that my standing as a speaker was at stake, and that great but absurd expectations had been formed. I, in my own heart, prayed to God to stand by me—and he did! When I rose, I got a good hearty cheer. Every eye was fixed upon me,—about 200 ministers of our own Church, others of other denominations, besides preachers and students, etc., forming the *elite* of our body in Edinburgh. Dr R. will tell you how I got on. He said if he had been near me when I had finished, he would have hugged me. Even Dr S. shouted '*glorious*,' and the meeting gave three rounds of applause, whilst I quietly, in my heart, thanked our Father that he had sustained me. Scores came to me to congratulate me on my success."

It only remains to be recorded, that Dr Archer's being so great a favourite was partly the result of a kindly and charitable spirit in his intercourse with society. He was never felt by his brethren to be jealous, or envious, or critically severe. He reproved fault-finding with sermons, remarking that the fault was more generally with the hearer himself than with the preacher; that, for his part, he seldom heard a discourse from which he did not derive some benefit; that in the whole course of his life he could only remember *two* which he considered to. be failures, and these were from celebrated men; and that he made allowances for these, as great minds were not always equal, and perhaps circumstances unknown to the audience had been the cause. He was equally charitable in judging of the faults of others. When appealed to by parties who had real or fancied grievances, he would say, " Look within, and, without prejudice, think how, in similar circumstances, you would have acted."

He often referred in his letters, when away from home on deputation and other duties, to the large collections he very frequently got, which, of course, was gratifying to him; but he used to remark, " his chief object was to *lodge principle*, and not merely to *get money*." Very often, after having fully explained the merits of the cause for which he was pleading, and urged the people to give "as God had prospered them," and cheerfully, for " the Lord loveth a cheerful giver," he would add, " I shall now give you the following *pithy rule* to guide you, which you can all remember, and carry with you, and which I have often given in other places :—*No man has a right to rob the Church to enrich himself, nor to rob his creditors to enrich the Church.* I shall repeat it to you," he would say, " in order to impress it well on your memories, for it is worth knowing, and I wish that it were more fully carried out."

The public labours of Dr Archer made the " United Presbyterian Church" known and respected all over England. By assuming the name " Presbyterian," the Unitarians in different

parts of the South have led many to believe that the two things
are identical. In well-informed quarters the vital difference
between them is now understood. But it is due to Dr Archer
to give him, so far, the credit of this. His evangelical sermons
and speeches, from the Channel to the Solway, have helped to
stamp out the calumny. In partially taking up the ground
which Dr Archer so long and effectively occupied, the compiler has frequently met with the most kindly references to his
eloquence and benevolence, and inquiries as to his health and
happiness. Nor does it detract from his gratification, when
visiting any of the Nonconforming Churches in the cities and
provinces of the South, to receive a welcome all the heartier
that he belongs to the Church within which Dr Archer was
such "a burning and a shining light." As he believed that his
vocation was in and around London, so he did his very best,
wherever he went, to commend the Church of his fatherland to
the sister denominations. He was too decided a Noncon-
formist to be much in fellowship with the Church of England,
yet he could number some of its clergy and people among his
friends; and on all occasions, combined so much of the Christian gentleman with his manner and spirit, as to conciliate
respect if not affection.

From this review of Dr Archer's public labours, some may
infer that the work he did was too multifarious, and perhaps
unnecessarily severe. The expediency, if not the duty, of
associating with strictly pastoral service, so much of what
seems to be extraneous, may be questioned. Certainly, if his
lectures, whether to his young men's or young women's classes,
and if his outside or deputation work had interfered with his

strictly professional obligations, he could not be justified. But it was not so. We have seen how conscientiously and continuously he prepared for the pulpit; and all his other calls were as sacredly responded to. The only one objection in his case was, the injurious effect which this extra work had upon his health. To say that his health was undermined in consequence, does not go beyond the truth; but in making this admission, we state a fatal objection to the habit. He was, in fact, the victim of a new onslaught upon the evangelical pulpit. Just when he was beginning public life, the furor for lectures on scientific and literary subjects had set in, the Christian ministry was reproved for being behind the intelligence of the age, and threatenings came from all sides, that unless our pastors detoured somewhat more frequently into other regions than those of religion, their influence should fade away. It is not to be wondered at, though many of the young and ardent yielded to the temptation. Pulpits could be bedecked with other lights than wax candles, and altars profaned with other offerings than the mass. The scintillations of mental by-play, rather than the lightning truths of God, were produced to arouse the congregations; and human works, rather than God's bleeding Lamb, became the offertory. All parties were more or less infected with this subtle poison. A distaste for the simple preaching of the Gospel was engendered, and carnal stimulants were resorted to. The consequent collapse was at hand, and the right arm of the pulpit began to be shortened and enfeebled. To keep up with the rising intelligence of the age, our young pastors had to meet, or supposed they had to meet, the new demands upon their time and talents. Some of our

finest minds have in consequence been eclipsed in the very
zenith of their usefulness. They have been led into the severities of untried, if not of unsanctioned, study, and have overtasked their physical, and agonised their mental, powers. There
is something in this to be reproved. Should ministers of the
Gospel be expected to combine in one short life the service
of God in the "Church" and that of secular learning in the
"lecture-hall?" Upon what principle of common justice
can they be expected to don the togas of the geologist, the
geographer, the chemist, the linguist, the political economist,
the almost world-wide purple of universal science? Surely the
Cross of Christ ought never to be set up as a rival to human
crucibles, where philosophy analyses and speculates. It has a
sphere entirely its own—a work exclusively its own; and while
allowing the human mind to march forward, and disport itself
to the glutting of its appetite in every direction, it commands
that mind to doff its academic insignia, and bend in lowliest
mood before its solitary, its awful, its mighty sacrifice. No
man can serve two masters anywhere,—if anywhere, never here
—never within the solemn region of the "great mystery of
godliness,"—never within the celestial walls of the university
of mercy. Let it not be inferred that we are disaffected to a
well-educated ministry. On the contrary, we glory in it. All
we plead for is a limit to the studies and anxieties of the sacred
profession.

And here it may not be out of place to notice the complaints
that are coming from all parts of Europe and America, as to
the steadily-diminishing number of candidates for the Christian
ministry. This deficiency has been variously accounted for.

Peradventure, one of its causes may be found in this same incongruous mixture of secular and sacred things, in this perpetual drain upon the strength and functions of the human brain. Too much is expected from the pulpit—then too much is attempted—then too little is effected. Had the mixed multitude of services which Dr Archer was called upon to perform, and which he performed so admirably, been presented to him in the commencement of his studies, it may be doubted whether he would have had the courage to face them. Honourable minds, at present foreseeing that, unless they are masters of all arts, they may not succeed, disaffect this grand profession. They may possibly be nauseated with the pretentiousness which such a condition imposes. They know that many of these learned lectures are simply borrowed, and that the lecturers themselves were not educated for them. The blame lies not altogether with the Christian ministry. The public taste is vitiated, and that ministry is intimidated. Let the one be purified, let the other be honest, and the evil may disappear. The liberty thus taken with the pulpit is inexplicable. Let a similar one be tried with the bar, the bench, or the senate-house, and such a hue and cry would be raised as should speedily abash its impudence. It would be resisted as insulting and oppressive, if it were demanded of the physician, that he be equally skilled in law as in medicine ; of the lawyer, that he be as ready to draw blood as to extend a deed ; of the mathematician, that he be as well posted up in the "Shorter Catechism" as in Euclid. And is it not equally unreasonable to exact from otherwise well-educated ministers, the acquirements and labours of other departments of professional life ? They ought to be left alone

I

with their own grand and peculiar work—the explanation and enforcement of the mercy of God to a lost world. The present Lord Rector of the University of Aberdeen spake weighty truth in his recent inaugural address to the students: "A large number of you," he said, "whom I see before me, intend to enter the Church, and you deserve to be congratulated, not only for having chosen a profession of such dignity and influence, but one which has this enormous advantage, that whilst all others would require you to make yourselves acquainted with a host of details which are only useful for professional purposes, the clergyman need apply himself to no study to which he would not have to apply himself, if his object were simply to make himself a highly cultivated human being. The questions with which you have to deal are of enormous and eternal, not of minor and temporary, importance."

CHAPTER VI.

HANS PLACE.

PASTORATE, filled up as was Dr Archer's with such incessant pulpit and public performances, necessarily implies a "library" of hard study, and a "closet" of unceasing prayer. The "library" in "Hans Place" could unfold a story of select and careful reading, of profound and sustained meditation, of midnight and of daylight assiduity, which accounts for the action and energy of his ministerial life; while the "closet"—the place of pleading with God—when its door was shut, and the key was turned in the lock, could testify to the agony of his soul as it wrestled for the blessing. He has, however, left no clue to this inner life beyond what may be seen in the manifestations of a pious, an ardent, and an intensely practical temperament. He kept no diary. He suspected himself too much for that, and in general disapproved of the practice. He feared the temptation that diary-keeping presents to religious ostentation, and to false or self-deceived representations of facts and feelings. He was, indeed, rather undemonstrative in this direction, choosing to be judged of by

his "walk," not by his "conversation." This reticence, however, did not set its seal upon his lip, when testimony for truth
or for Christ was demanded, or when he could unhorse calumny
and expose hypocrisy.

But his wide excursions into so many domains of literature,
secular and sacred, must have had other seclusions and starting-
points than his own private collection of books, which, though
not extensive, was select. Few dissenting ministers can afford
to purchase so largely and variously as he must needs have
done, had he been dependent on his own catalogue. But the
library of the "British Museum" supplied all his wants. Of
that magnificent collection he made most generous use. For
many years he was an unfailing and eager reader there. When
preparing his sacred or scientific lectures, he availed himself of
its treasures, as he made it a point to convince his classes and
the public, that he did not serve them with what cost him no
labour. It is peculiarly interesting to follow him, as day by
day, and week by week, he left home to bury himself for hours
in that old and historical room. On making inquiries at the
Museum, we find that some of the oldest employés remember
him as a reader as far back as thirty years ago. At that time
the apartments for reading were situated at the south end of
the Royal Library, and are now used as portion of the department of manuscripts. The books of reference then consisted
principally of a few dictionaries. The readers were few, and
the number of the books not one-tenth of what is now. The
catalogue consisted of about sixteen volumes. The reading-
rooms were subsequently changed for others of more conveni-
ence, situated at the north end of the Royal Library, In these

the means and resources of study were gradually increased ; and within the last few years, previous to the building of the present Library-room, the system of placing there a selection of the standard works on all subjects was adopted. Dr Archer had little use of the present capacious and beautiful room; but no doubt he prized its conveniences all the more from having so long known the discomforts of its predecessors. The present one is perhaps unrivalled in the world. Its dome surpasses in size that of St Paul's in London, or that of St Peter's in Rome, and has accommodation for more than 300 readers. Around the walls are ranged about 60,000 volumes of works of reference, all easily accessible. To a real student, the marvels of the place seem like the realisation of a dream. He has but to consult one of the 1500 volumes of the catalogue, write upon a ticket the name and number of the book he wishes to consult, and, in a few minutes, the attendant has placed it before him. The list of English books is almost perfect. But, besides this, the trustees have aimed at making the collection of foreign works second only to that which is found in the National Library of each nation. For example, the Russian Library in our "Museum" is only surpassed by that of St Petersburg, and the Danish one, by that of Copenhagen. In addition to its comfortable chairs and convenient desks, there is in this room a selection of about 20,000 volumes of the standard works upon all departments of literature, while the collection itself amounts to about one million of volumes. The Hebrew collection, which in Dr Archer's early days consisted of about 100 volumes, is now one of the most magnificent in the world. How great must have been the delight of his active and thoughtful mind in the midst of such increasing facilities for study. The old dingy and melancholy rooms, however, are chiefly associated with the student from Oxendon ChapeL To occupy them so often and so long as he did, said not a little for his thirst for knowledge. It is told that the literary treasures of the place were guarded by a certain insect of sharp forceps and great power of suction, supposed by Dr Owen to have been a lingering remnant of some pre-Adamite animaL This creature made all study there a real "pursuit of knowledge under difficulties," but it is now happily extinct. Yet even here, more than in the splendid building that has succeeded it, may be traced the literary glories of the National Library. Many of the most celebrated authors of the period frequented the place. It was the chosen retreat of the poet Gray, who speaks of it with affectionate reverence. In Dr Archer's younger days might be seen the Jewish, thoughtful face of the elder D'Israeli, gathering the materials for his " Curiosities of Literature ;" and the massive features of Henry Brougham, whose researches extended to almost every branch of knowledge.

There can be no doubt that here, in the quieter years of his ministry, Dr Archer gained that multifarious information which made him, if not a profound scholar, yet an intelligent, well-read man in many departments of literature. Towards the close of his life, he ceased his visits entirely. Perhaps, with all its increased comfort, the present room had fewer attractions for him. He was more often disturbed by the literary lounger or the University College student, cribbing for his Virgil or Homer. Besides, he was enjoying more and more the comforts of his own happy home, and the quietude

of his own favourite study. " Hans Place" became to him
a home at once for head and heart. Here he inwardly
digested the stores of information he had accumulated by his
sederunts in the Museum Library. With his own collection,
and with constant supplies from " Mudie's," he never wanted
for mental or moral food. He " read up" to the times, and he
read at once intelligently and usefully. He had no partialities.
He was a philosophic excursionist. He travelled with the
tourist — researched with the historian — analysed with the
chemist—hammered with the geologist—speculated with the
thinkers—soared with the poets—and dived with the fishers in
all waters. Latterly, he did not read much theology. In
young life he had thoroughly mastered " the system," as it was
called ; and in the course of years he had allowed himself an
increasing range, comprehensive of all that could gratify and
enrich the most refined and accomplished minds. One of his
great favourites was Lord Macaulay, his just appreciation of
whose merits as a historian and a statesman, is evident from the
lecture which he gave upon that eminent individual. He did
not indulge in works of fiction, though in that line Sir Walter
Scott was his favourite. He was enraptured with " Ivanhoe,"
and was in the habit of reperusing its fascinating pages from
time to time. But he was also a man of the " one Book." He
allowed no reading to supersede his daily searching of the
Scriptures. With these, his mind, and therefore his discourses,
were well furnished. His selections of texts for illustrating
Divine truth were often striking, and their application pat,
pointed, and powerful. He seldom intruded critical or ex-
pository notes in conversation ; but, when he did so, his clear

and shrewd remarks proved how carefully he had studied, and how wisely he had judged.

In society he was at once genial and gentlemanly. Not all at once was he a favourite with strangers, but a very short intimacy soon broke the crust of formality, and let in the amenities of a warm and ever-growing esteem. Those who knew him best loved him most, and those who loved him once loved him always. Seldom do we see such a union as there was in him of stern fidelity to the right and honourable, with the conciliating blandness of a true courtesy. There was no hauteur in his manner, though occasionally some bluntness; and when a display of heart was required, it seemed as if a fountain had been unsealed. No one could more than he appreciate the charms of elegant companionship, and few ever found it less difficult to be at home with the humble and the poor. He could be all things to all men. He was in an especial manner kind and hospitable. The many occasions upon which his brethren, of every sect, used to flock to London, afforded opportunities to show kindness to strangers as well as to friends. Nor was he slow either of hand to help, or of heart to sympathise. The meetings of the " Evangelical Alliance " were occasions of this kind. It seemed to enlarge his heart to gather around him "brethren," and to pour out upon them attentions of all sorts. He sometimes "kept open house," and converted " Hans Place," from its usual stillness, into the bustle of a hotel. His discrimination was seen in bringing together men of like minds and tastes, so that interchange of thought and feeling might be full and free. It was a source of delight to him to see, mingling under his roof, some of the holy, erudite, and witty men of the day, whose society he appreciated and improved ; and for many years his house was a resort for young people (during Midsummer and Christmas vacations), whose parents lived at too great a distance to allow of their going home. Joyous days and nights these were alike to old and young, but to none more than to himself. He would return in the evening, after having lectured in some distant county town, or attended some public meeting in the city, and, finding the youngsters in the height of their enjoyment, entered at once, heart and soul, into their play. He sometimes remarked, that "a good romp with the children, after heavy work, did him as much good as a trip into the country." The apostolic injunction indeed, "Use hospitality one to another, without grudging," could not have been better observed than it was in "Hans Place." For many years he kept up what were called the "Saturday evening gatherings." No formal invitations were sent out. He and Mrs Archer were expected to be "at home," and every one that came had a hearty welcome. They assembled about six o'clock; and, after tea and coffee, came music and conversation. Family worship was observed at nine o'clock. In the prayers he then offered, it was often remarked, how touchingly he referred to the peculiar situation and necessities of each one of the party present. He pleaded warmly for them accordingly. After some refreshment, all retired early. These "reunions" were not only pleasant but improving. Some who attended them, at present in good positions in their several professions, look back upon them with lively gratitude. It may perhaps excite some surprise that *Saturday* evenings should have been selected ; but they were considered preferable. Dr

Archer, as a general rule, had his preparations for Sabbath not only well advanced, but often finished, by the Friday evening. Besides, his guests were free from business at an earlier hour on Saturday, and he thought it had a good effect upon the young men especially, to anticipate the Sabbath with them in the evening sacrifice of family worship.

It was upon the occasion of one of the meetings of the " Evangelical Alliance" in London, that he, as usual, kept " open table." It was indeed a privilege to be one of the guests at such feasts of learning and of love, where Tholuck, Kuntze, and other distinguished foreigners enjoyed his hospitality. To some of his brethren from the North they were especially precious, as affording them the opportunities they never otherwise could have had, of forming the acquaintance, and even the friendship, of some of the *savans* of the day. The ruling spirit among them was Dr Archer himself. He discovered much tact in drawing out character, and in so guiding the conversation as to give all an interest in it. There was ever a flow of wit and wisdom, and all seemed to be happy and even joyous underneath the genial smiles of both hostess and host. The compiler has a pleasant recollection of one such dinner. Among other guests were Dr Harris, and Mr Philip of Maberly Chapel. It was thought that the latter, the worthy author of " The Marthas," " The Marys," etc., was somewhat prone to egotism, and often illustrated his opinions or thoughts by referring to his personal preferences and experiences. Dr Harris evidently knew this, and frequently so addressed Mr Philip as to "lead him into temptation." Some were not in the secret. They who were, enjoyed it not a little, and even laughed out-

right, Mr Philip himself being happily unconscious of thus
contributing to the glee of his fellow-guests. Dr Harris was
given to such playfulness, but he was never wicked in it. It
was ever qualified in him with the milk of human kindness.
On this occasion, however, Mrs Archer (whose name was
Martha) thought he was going rather too far, and watched her
opportunity to give him a " Roland for his Oliver." She soon
found one. The question was mooted, which was the most
amiable of the two sisters of Bethany, Mary or Martha? Dr
Archer immediately replied, " I prefer Martha for the unselfishness of her character, in being more ready to provide for the
comforts of her Lord than gratify herself."

" Pray," rejoined Dr Harris, addressing Dr Philip in a somewhat innocent tone, "What is your view? Which of the two
do you think would have made the best wife?"

"Well, really," replied the good man, "I am at a loss;
though I dare say, were I making the choice for myself, I
should prefer Mary."

After this characteristic reply, there was not only smiling,
but laughter. Mrs Archer, turning to Dr Harris, said smartly,
" Pray, Dr Harris, which of the two should you prefer?"
The author of " Mammon" was only for a moment discon-
certed, and replied, in a style which " set the table in a roar,"
" O, I think I should choose Martha *before* dinner, and Mary
after it." It was allowed that he had most cunningly fenced.

Dr Harris was one of the most delightful of companions.
In the midst of friends whom he loved and could trust, he
relaxed. His brain evidently luxuriated in the "let loose"
style which was then allowed. Sometimes, after a day of hard

study, he would find his way to " Hans Place," and brace
himself anew for work, over not only the " Falernian wine,"
but the cheering and soothing interchange of select and kindly
minds. He was much attached to Dr Archer, and was ever
ready to do him a brother's good turn, which, it need not be
said, was cordially reciprocated. He had preached in Oxendon
once, at its re-opening in 1848, when an additional gallery had
been put in to meet the demand for sittings. To repay the
debt, he requested Dr Archer to come and address the students
of the College.*

Having introduced the name of Dr Harris, no apology is
required for some further record of his pleasant intercourse
with his beloved friend in " Hans Place." In 1848 they resolved upon a trip to Scotland, where Dr Harris had never
been.   They found their way first of all to Glasgow, and
became the guests of James Mitchell, Esq. Mr Mitchell at
that time lived at " Glenarbach," a romantic country residence
a few miles down the Clyde. It is a retreat equally peaceful
and picturesque ; and so happy did the author of "Mammon"
find himself beneath its hospitable roof, and in the polished
and Christian society he met there, that he designated it " an
earthly Paradise." From Glenarbach they took several excursions into the surrounding country. " Glasgow," of course,
was keenly surveyed. He took special delight in its " old
town"—more so than in the palatial buildings of its " West
End." He was of course fêted, as he was then in the zenith
of his fame. To the exuberance of the hospitality of its

---

* The reader will find an allusion to this address in a note of Dr Harris
to Mrs Archer, in p. 145.

merchant-princes he was sufficiently alive, remarking that,
"while wide awake to seize a good stroke of business, their
hearts were ever open to the demands of benevolence and
hospitality." He expressed a wish to see "the land of Burns."
As Dr Archer had business in the city, he was accompanied by
Mrs Archer alone. He greatly enjoyed this little trip, wandering and musing around that far-famed scenery, and holding
somewhat melancholy communion with the memory of the marvellous poet who has stamped immortality on its "banks and
braes." When within the "monument" raised to the memory
of Burns, he asked the girl who was in attendance to sing to
him "Ye Banks and Braes o' Bonny Doon." She replied she
had no voice, but would find a lad who could sing. She,
however, failed in her search, when Dr Harris declared that
he would not stir an inch from the spot till he got that song.
Mrs Archer knew his determined way, and, fearing lest they
should lose the train, she proposed to sing it, for want of a
better. She did so. In thanking her, he said, "I was not
aware that my pleasant companion and guide was a 'Nightin-
gale' in the *day*-time." Having finished their visit to Glenarbach, they went up to Glasgow, where they were the guests of
Dr Robson. On returning one evening from a visit to "the
Falls of the Clyde," they were met by the good news that a
son had been, in their absence, added to the family of their
worthy host. After supper, Dr Harris asked the Doctor what
was to be the name of the little stranger, and when told that
it was to be "Henry," he immediately proposed as a toast,
"Little Henry and his bearer," in facetious allusion to the
title of that well-known book for children. His playful witti-

cisms were never unseasonable nor unsavoury. They were the expressions of a joyous exuberance—the lights that flitted about the home-circles within which he was loved, and which tended to make him a universal favourite.

With Edinburgh and its environs Dr Harris was charmed. His preferences were all on the side of Roslin and Hawthornden. The view from Stirling Castle, which was next visited, left an imperishable impression on his mind. The two doctors arrived towards evening, and set off at once to gaze upon that glorious panorama which is seen from every side of the Castle ramparts. The sun was setting at the time, and he who has looked around from these heights on such an eve requires no description of the scene. He who has not, cannot conceive of its beauty, variety, and grandeur. Mrs Archer had remained at the hotel to look after the " creature comforts," an appetite for which no sight-seeing can stave off. The night was cold — they were accommodated in " the Assembly Room "—a roaring fire had been kindled, and delicious viands were upon the table. As Dr Harris sat down, he said—" Well, Brother Archer, I am daily, nay, hourly, convinced that ' Martha ' is out-and-out the noblest character and the most estimable of all the females in the Bible ; for who else, in so short a time, could have procured such an accumulation of comforts as we have here ? I tell you, man, again and again, that your wife is an angel." " And I tell you, Harris," was the reply, " that I am very thankful she is not. She is active and light enough as she is ; but if she had the wings in addition, I fear she would be off altogether, and what could we do without her ?"

In addition to the Lakes in the West, they also visited during their tour, Perth, Dunkeld, and Inverness. They returned by the Caledonian Canal to Oban. They sailed to Staffa and Iona. They went up to Fort-William, and entered the Pass of Glencoe. Here Dr Harris was much impressed. The wildness and desolateness of the whole scene seemed to overawe him. As they were passing through it, the guard of the coach directed attention to "Ossian's Cave." "Look up," said Dr Harris to some young men who had been making themselves conspicuous by their oddities, "look up, lads; that is Ossian's Cave." "Ossian—Ossian," replied one of them; "why, who in the wide world was he? Did you ever hear of him?" appealing to his companion. "Not I," was the response; "but we had better consult "Murray." "Ossian," said Dr Harris, amused at their ignorance, "was a great poet." "O, was he? I never heard of the chap." Leaving Oban, they passed over to Inverary by Loch Awe. The fine scenery of the Pass seemed to elevate Dr Harris into the regions of poetry. He fell into musing. Nay, such was the inspiration, that he composed and recited stanzas, challenging his fellow-travellers to do likewise. Suddenly, at a precipitous part of the road, the horses became restive, and in another moment they might all have perished. When the danger was over, Mrs Archer said to him: "Your pinions have been clipped, for you were soaring aloft just now." He responded with more than his usual gravity: "We have all cause for thankfulness that we are not low in the dust; a few minutes ago I felt that our lives were imperilled."

Not long after this very pleasant Scottish tour, Dr Harris

visited Switzerland; but his letters on his return showed that the mountains, glens, rivers, lakes, hamlets, and cities of " auld Scotia" had not been obliterated from his mind, nor lowered in his opinion.

. The following brief but characteristic notes to Mrs Archer, written subsequent to the visit to the North, reveal not a little of Dr Harris in his familiar moods :—

" SANDGATE, *August 16th*, 1848.

" MY DEAR FRIEND,

" I cannot allow another day to pass without sending you *the two lines* (barely ' line upon line'), even though doomed to write them with a steel pen, which, next to an iron heart, I detest.

" My journey to London was as pleasant as it could be, considering the sacrifices which it involved. I am indebted to you for some of the happiest days I have ever enjoyed. Accept my heartfelt thanks. I can only wish you a measure of my own enjoyment. But one who derives so much happiness from the mere impartation of pleasure, is independent of good wishes, however pleasant it may be to know that they exist. Just now, I suppose you are rejoicing in the pleasures of Glenarbach; all happiness to its inhabitant and inmates! One only fault have I to find with you—that you have converted my dear child into an idolater of the image of a Newhaven fisherwoman. At this moment she is offering it the incense of her heart. You will have to answer for it.

" I need not say my love to the Doctor. He has a place

'on the box' of my heart. With sincere regards to all my new friends,—I am, my dear friend, very strongly yours,

"JOHN HARRIS.

("A malediction on all steel pens!")

"CHESHUNT COLLEGE, *Sept.* 6, 1848.

"MY DEAR FRIEND,

"I have just returned, to find your welcome letter among a shoal of others, and lose as little time as possible in acknowledging it, though only in a line.

"I hardly need say that the Continent has not obliterated Scotland from my mind—my heart: all my impressions of its glorious scenery, friendly hospitalities, etc., etc., are kept in a place apart, and are as vivid as ever. I am at this moment impatiently awaiting the advent of your beloved, to deliver his kindly promised address to the students.

"Since writing the above he has come—shone—gone. His address was all that I could have wished it to be—the very thing. And as I feel that I have not sufficiently thanked him for it, let me beg you to do so in your very best manner, and in any way which he may prefer.

"Very heartily do I thank my friend, Mr J. Mitchell, for his kind remembrance of me. I only wish I could accompany you in your expected jaunt. Happy hours to you! On your return, I shall certainly look for a full, true, and particular account of your movements, and hope you will be prepared to stand a thorough cross-examination. Dr Archer's intimation

K

of your having something in *your* eye makes my eye glisten.
Do not lose sight of it.

"I am, my dear friend, ever yours sincerely,

"JOHN HARRIS."

"CHESHUNT COLLEGE, *Aug.* 1, 1849.

"MY DEAR FRIEND,

"I am off to-night. I wish I had earlier thought of
providing something for your pet bazaar, but now it is too
late. The only alternative is to get a kind friend to purchase
one pound's worth of something, and present it in my name.
And if you would be that kind friend, I should feel obliged.

"I have just received a letter from Dr Robson, who, as
usual, is as merry as a cricket. He seems to have been
delighted with his Callander enjoyments, and invites me to
join you in October at the Evangelical Alliance. But my
duties here look forbiddingly on such a step.

"You ask where I am going. I can honestly and most
patriarchally reply that I go out not knowing whither. I have
asked 'the man in the moon' the same question two or three
times, but he looks so puzzled that I shall not ask him again,
but just be off, and chance it. At this moment I am divided
between the Lakes, Paris, and Denmark. To-morrow, by this
time, I hope to be on my way to one or the other. You say
you should like to be my companion to the Continent. I
should enjoy it much; and if I thought there were any chance
of you and the Doctor going, I would delay my trip for two
or three days. But it seems a settled thing with you both to
go to Glasgow. When you go to pleasant Glenarbach, forget

not to give my affectionate remembrances. Love to the
'Governor.'—I am, my dear friend, cordially yours,

"JOHN HARRIS."

"53 NEW FINCHLEY ROAD,
March 4, 1851.
" MY DEAR FRIEND,

" Yesterday I saw a mischievous urchin holding a
piece of bread before the eyes of a poor hungry dog, just out
of its reach. Why will you be that urchin? Why, in these
days of error, will you attempt to revive the old mythology by
turning Tantalus? Why—but remonstrance is useless. There
is no reason whatever why I should not accept your prandial
invitation, except that I cannot. This might be considered by
some, reason sufficient, but how unsatisfactory! The truth is,
I am engaged to dine at Hackney on Wednesday. I wish it
were otherwise, as I should have greatly enjoyed an interview
with your excellent visitor, Dr Eadie. *Perhaps* I may manage
a call. But if the Fates prove obstinate, I can only bewail
my loss. I have been intending, for some time past, to be a
hearer at Oxendon the first fine Sunday. It seems an age
since I saw either you or the dear Doctor. But I vow, by all
our Scottish adventures, that this estrangement shall not continue any longer. My very best regards to Dr Eadie. I shall
be able at least to pay my respects to his ' effigies' at the
artist's. But this is small satisfaction.

" Ever, my dear friend, cordially yours,
"JOHN HARRIS."

" MY DEAR FRIEND,

" This is the first letter I have written to a lady in my
new house. You desired to know when I got in. I do not
expect to have *got in* for some months, but I began *getting* in
the day before yesterday, Transferring one's goods, and transferring one's self, I find to be two things,—the latter a very
slow process. Think what a snail would feel in having to
change shells ; now I am only a snail of a larger growth.
Still, as far as I can see and foresee, I think I shall like it, and
I mean to be comfortable. But I more than ever feel how
much this depends on the sympathy of human friends, and on
the blessing of the great Divine Friend.

" Are you committed to a candidate for the Orphan School ?
If not, let me enlist your might, power, and influence for a
deserving case, which I will talk with you about. Love to the
Doctor, and love to you,

"JOHN HARRIS."

To returned missionaries Dr Archer was warmly attached
and delicately attentive. He received many proofs of their
gratitude when they had gone back to their foreign spheres of
labour. He had a great admiration for Dr Livingstone, who,
with his wife, found a home in Hans Place. The mournful
interest at present attached to that honoured and enterprising
missionary, who, it is to be sincerely hoped, still lives, must
impart solemnity to the following characteristic letter, which in
1859 was addressed to Dr and Mrs Archer:—

[*Private.*]

" RIVER SHIRE, EASTERN AFRICA,
26th October 1859.

" MY DEAR DR AND MRS ARCHER,

"I suppose there is no use in beginning apologies and explanations to you, my dear friends, for my long silence. It has troubled me more than it can have done you, for again and again have I remembered your disinterested kindness to me and mine, and felt ashamed that I had never once given you the poor acknowledgment of a letter. I do not think that a hundred would wipe out the sense of obligation I feel, nor do I desire to feel it less ; but there is a pleasure in letting one know that his goodness was appreciated, and freeing oneself, as far as may be, from the knotless-thread character. Blessings be on you and on Mrs A. for your manifold kindnesses !

" We have not been idle since we came here ; and with a thankful heart to our Father above, we have to say that his kind providence has watched over and prospered us at every turn of our path. Even circumstances which at first seemed very untoward have turned out signally for the best. It would be a long story to tell you all, so I begin at our latest feat, namely, tracing this river up to its point of emergence from the hitherto undiscovered Lake Nyassa or Nyinyesi. This is a direction in which we had no previous intention of travelling, and the result is the discovery of a cotton-producing region in every respect superior to the American. There are no frosts to endanger or cut off the crops ; and instead of the enormous toil required to raise the plant in America, one sowing serves for three years' crops, even though the plants may be burned down. The land above the cataracts is high, and disposed in three terraces of 1200 feet, 2000 feet, and 3000 feet respectively. We have, as we experienced, changes of climate within a few miles' distance of each other. The terraces are well supplied with running rills of deliciously cool water, and cotton is grown over them all. On the last terrace rises Mount Zomba, between 7000 and 8000 feet high, and cultivated on the top. Fancy Ben Ledi on the top of Ben Lomond, and a fine river running in a valley on its great top, some fifteen or twenty miles broad. This is a splendid sanatorium, and one of the great benefits our expedition will have to show, is the cure of fever, even in the lowlands, without loss of strength in general to the patient. I want the Church Missionary Society to occupy this field. They have long been trying to get into Eastern Africa. The Shire is easily navigable for a hundred miles from the Zambesi, then thirty-three miles of cataracts, and then an immense field, watered by the lakes. Tamandera we measured as ninety miles long, but no one could say how far away the head of Nyassa lay. They can come into this field—ay, that is if they have the pluck—and be at once away from the unfriendly coast tribes. The good Lord of all will assuredly occupy it by some agency or other, for it has advantages for which I have not paper to tell. Some of our friends, on hearing of this discovery, will think that I am now seeking the glory alone of discovering lakes, mountains, jenny-nettles, and puddock-stools; others will see at a glance whither my efforts tend; and perhaps it may be permitted to me to do some little to relieve our countrymen from the stain of upholding slavery by manufacturing the produce of slave-labour alone. At any rate, I shall work while life lasts for noble and Christ-like ends.

"Singularly enough, we have been without news from home since we left. Except a few newspapers given us by men-of-war's-men, and our Government despatches, which have come with great regularity, we have no private information as to how the world wags. A day or two ago, however, we heard by a man, kindly sent by a Portuguese gentleman of Senna, that a bag awaits us there. My wife was some time ago at Kuruman. We expect to ascend to the Makololo country in the beginning of next year. I hope the London Missionary Society has sent men to that interesting field, and that the men have had the sense to occupy it. When does the Free Kirk and your Kirk unite? Must death still clear the way? What a powerful body for good you will make. May the Master hasten it!

"My kindest salutations to Mrs A., and blessings be on your house and Church.

" DAVID LIVINGSTONE.

"This is written in a twenty-mile marsh, with millions of mosquitoes about. Before dark I counted ten herds of elephants feeding in the distance. My brother is here, and well, saving the mosquitoes."

In "Hans Place" generosity was the rival of hospitality. If geniality sat on one side, charity occupied the opposite chair,— Dr and Mrs Archer representing both. There many a kind and substantial scheme was concocted, and from hence issued some of the best editions of that "mercy" which is "twice blessed."

The widow and the fatherless were never forgotten, and the "shield" for the stranger was ever ready. Numerous traits of that private benevolence which only luxuriates in the shade, might be given, but the survivor forbids it. She, however, can tell of his, if not of her own. When any charitable or religious purpose asked for funds, his name was down at once for a liberal subscription, and his services were incessant in promoting the cause. It was sometimes questionable to allow him to go out of a morning with a well-filled purse. He would return in after-day, and hold it up *empty* to the eyes of his wife. He came home one evening from a meeting of Directors of the London Missionary Society, at which a communication had been received from the Christians at Madagascar, stating that the Lord's Supper could not be observed from want of a communion service. One had offered to furnish a flaggon, another a cup, etc., etc. On mentioning it to Mrs Archer, they agreed that "Oxendon" should be asked to furnish the entire service. At the meeting of the "Board" on the following Monday, he informed the Directors that it was all settled, and that his people would provide what was required. Accordingly, in a short time the money was raised, and a very handsome service of the best electro-plate was procured, which consisted of a flaggon, two cups, and two plates, with a supply of tablecloths and napkins. These were deposited in a substantial mahogany chest, also the gift of one of the congregation, and forthwith despatched. On reaching its destination, the Prince Rakotona Radama, and three of the Christians, calling themselves "Pilgrims," sent two letters to Dr Archer, of which we give an English translation :—

" To the brethren beloved of Christ, in London, the Rev. Dr Archer, and the friends in the congregation at the meeting-house, Oxendon Chapel,—

" We have received the things used in the administration of the Lord's Supper, and the new book, and the English Bible with references, which came from you. ·The whole Church rejoiced exceedingly, and gave thanks to God with one heart in the name of Jesus Christ the great Redeemer. And after we received them, the first time we used them all in a great feast with the Lord Jesus Christ the Saviour, was on the Sabbath-day, the 1st of April 1855, which was also Easter Sunday. We thanked God, for he hears our prayers through Jesus Christ the Lord. But your love to Christ is very great, though the countries are very far from one another, and the great sea is between them. You have made the land of Madagascar the object of your attachment, like the land in and about London. And let earnest prayers be made to God, in the name of Jesus Christ, for us in the land of Madagascar, for whatever trouble befalls us, we abide on the palm of the hand of the Most High, and that is the reason that we are not moved. (Psalms x. 17, xxiii. 4, xxxiv. 7, lxxi. 18, 19, cxviii. 6 ; Luke xii. 32 ; Rom. viii. 31, xvi. 20 ; 1 Tim. iii. 15 ; Heb. iii. 14 ; 1 John iv. 18 ; Rev. xxi. 8.)

" And we tell you also of the work done by the Rev. Dr William Ellis and James Cameron, owing to their love to the Lord Jesus Christ. They laboured very hard on account of their love and your pleasure. They wished to accomplish the object of their coming to the land of Madagascar. They endangered their lives by going over the sea to us and from us several times. On the 9th of March 1855, we heard that the Queen granted them both permission to come to Antananarivo; we rejoiced exceedingly, for we wished to see them face to face, for it would be like seeing you all when we see them.

" The children are continually increasing in number, for the sheep of Christ have light in the midst of darkness. The number of the people that have received the Lord's Supper are 240, and they increase continually, and there are a great many Christians besides. (Read Phil. iv. 22, 23 ; 1 Tim. i. 17; Rom. xvi. 16.)

" We, for the whole Church, present to you our salutations on paper ; and how *are you?* for we are all well through the blessing of God. May you live long, and be happy, and be blessed of God, say Rakotona Radama the Prince 13th, honour of the officers of the Palace, chief secretary, and the three Pilgrims,—Andriambahing called Joseph, and Ramanandray called John, and Andriamanantena called Peter."

"ANTANANARIVO, 18*th April* 1855.

" To the brethren beloved of Christ residing in London, the Rev. Dr Archer, and the friends in the congregation at the meeting-house called Oxendon Chapel,—

" I thank God for enabling me to write this letter to be sent to you. We wish to talk about the Word of God, for when we heard that the Rev. William Ellis and James Cameron were allowed to come to Antananarivo, we were very glad; but, as it was reported afterwards, there was a disease at the Mauritius, the Queen stopped them to come up. Then the Rev. Dr William Ellis went to the Mauritius. And as soon as we heard, on the 8th of April 1855, that they both were allowed to come up to Antananarivo, our hearts rejoiced again exceedingly, for as we now expect to see them again our joy increases. And behold this talk is among them that know the Madagasy language; and we also most earnestly wish it to be so, for a voice coming from a distant land opens the eyes of men's hearts and stirs up love. We heard of a man conversing with another as follows: ' I thank God that he did not put me in my mother's womb to be born in the land of Madagascar, for the people there are too miserable; their clothing, and their food, and their drink, and their houses are wretched, and also their service to the officers and to the Queen are very hard. But more especially those that serve God: they are persecuted; some are put to death, others bound, some put in fetters, others in chains, and others their bodies are sold to be slaves, and their wives and children are also sold, and they are perpetually reproached, reviled, and dishonoured, and compelled to do all manner of hard labour; and thus they groan under their hard bondage. Therefore, when they find the Holy Scriptures, even a very small scrap of them, they collect them to examine them, but they dare not look at them in public; they therefore take them to any place of concealment, either to holes in the earth, or in the rocks, or in caves, and as soon as they look at them to be examined, the tears flow down from their weeping eyes because they love the Word of God. These trials are too severe for any one to bear, and I thank God,' said he, ' that I have not seen such great trials as these.' But yet I thank God

even though I have experienced these trials, for every one of
them is seen by God wherever I be.

" True is the word, ' For the redemption of the soul is precious.' (Psalm xlix. 5.)   But we have this treasure in earthen
vessels, that the excellency of the power may be of God and
not of us.   We are troubled on every side, yet not distressed;
we are perplexed, but not in despair.   (1 Cor. x. 13, 2 Cor. viii.
2, 4, 17, 18.)   How true is the Word of God spoken by Paul
in the Corinthians.   (2 Cor. xii. 9, 10.)

" RAKOTONA RADAMA."

Whenever Dr Archer heard of any case of genuine distress,
his heart moved him towards it.   The great distances in the
Metropolis, and his many engagements, did not obstruct him.
It was a desperately bad case which he did not, in some
degree, try to relieve.   His wife feared sometimes that his
liberality went beyond their means ; and when she would
gently hint it, he would smile and say, " Can we not afford
to give so much ?   Are you needing what I bestow upon
others ?"   " Certainly not," she replied.   " Then, what we
have we have received from the bountiful hand of God, and
freely as we have received, so let us freely give."   In this
respect he acted very handsomely to those brethren who sometimes asked him to preach an anniversary sermon.   When the
collection was to be made on behalf of the " stipend," he made
it a rule to defray his own travelling expenses, and never left
home, on such occasions especially, without saying to Mrs
Archer, " And how much are you going to give me to put into
the plate for you ?"   " No wonder," she would reply, " that

you are so much in request, when you pay your own expenses, preach for nothing, and, in addition, contribute to the funds." One little incident may be noticed. The gathering was at a small county town; the day was fine, the congregation was large, and the collection was good. The minister offered Dr Archer a sum of money for his sermon. He refused to take it, saying,—"I never in my life took a fee for preaching on a week-day, nor on the Sabbath either, unless I had to pay for the supply of my own pulpit. My idea is, that no man has a right to make a traffic of the Gospel." The worthy pastor looked surprised. "O, sir," he said, "how different is your conduct to that of Mr ——, who preached last year. The day was wet, there were few people, and consequently a small collection. Mr —— took the guinea for his sermon, also the expenses of travelling; after which, I can assure you, very little was left for me and mine."

Everywhere, but especially in London, begging impostors are to be found. Dr Archer was sometimes ensnared. He did not, however, fall back upon this as a reason for stinting or restraining charity. It only led him to more caution in ascertaining the real facts of the case. He was one day waited on by a wretched-looking man, who was most importunate for help. He got it. He returned for more, again and again. At length Dr Archer bethought him of visiting the beggar in his own lodgings. Having got his address, he sallied forth to find him out. The lodging was in one of the lowest purlieus of Westminster. He had difficulty in finding it. A policeman to whom he applied, said—"I know it too well, sir; but may I ask what you want there?" Having told him his object, the policeman assured him that it would be unsafe for him to go alone, adding, " You can have no idea of the den into which you are going. If you please, I will accompany you." Dr Archer declined, saying he had no fear, and wished simply to know the way. Having brought him to the place, the policeman said, " I shall wait here, sir, at the foot of the stair, and if any violence is offered, just hollo, and I will be up in a minute." He then mounted a kind of ladder, which here and there wanted a step, and groped his way through darkness to the door of the apartment where the man said he lived. He knocked. " Who is there ?" asked some one. On replying, he heard a bustling in the room, and he was kept waiting for some minutes, which at once aroused his suspicions. At length the door opened, and " Come in, sir," was uttered in tones he at once felt to be feigned. He entered, and a picture of misery presented itself. There lay a man upon a bed, such as it was, and beside him sat a miserable-looking female. " Oh, sir," he feebly said, " I am very ill." He then turned down the covering, and displayed his body completely naked. As he did so, he said, " You see, sir, to what we are reduced ; I have been forced to part with my last shirt for bread. Dr Archer's quick eye detected something projecting from beneath the pillow. He drew it forth, and found it to be a good shirt. As he held it up, he said, " What is this ? I perceive you are an impostor! While I was kept waiting at the door, you stripped and got into bed. You have had relief from me at various times, and have eaten the bread you did not deserve. I came, intending to help you, but now I shall give you nothing." The man was speechless. The minister left the room. He descended the perilous ladder, and, on reaching the street, the policeman congratulated him. "I am so thankful you are safe," he said ; "I have been trembling for you ever since you went up, and was beginning to fear that something had happened." Dr Archer related the interview. "I am not surprised," was the reply. "It is no uncommon thing, sir, in these sinks of iniquity, for deeds of violence being done to charitable visitors like you. It must have been your manly bearing and fearless looks that daunted the wretches."

He carried the same sympathising spirit with him wherever he went. Once, when travelling on the Continent, he reached Chambery late on a Friday evening, intending to remain till Monday, and then cross Mount Cenis into Italy. Next day, Mrs Archer proposed to go out to the market and buy a good-sized basket-full of grapes for the journey. "And you," she added, "will rest quietly here till I return." "No," he said, "I must go with my '*mouth-piece*'" (referring to her proficiency in the Continental languages), "as I wish to see the market too." They found their way to the place where fruit was sold, and there saw large baskets full of the most delicious grapes, just newly brought in from the vineyards. Buyers and sellers were crowded together. There was also a company of soldiers, whom Dr Archer saw eyeing the fruit most wistfully, but, having no "*sous*," could not purchase. He immediately turned to Mrs Archer, and asked her to give each of the soldiers a goodly bunch, adding, "We can buy for ourselves afterwards." The men looked pleased, but astonished, when she explained how it had been done at her husband's desire. Later in the day, when strolling about, they occasionally met the same parties, who saluted them with smiles and courtesies. "How delightful," he remarked, "it is to do an act of kindness! If such a trifle as the distribution of a few bunches of grapes has given such pleasure, how grateful should we be to have had it in our power to give them." "I feel that, too," replied Mrs Archer, "and wish that more who have the power had, like you, the heart to part with it." "I have no pleasure," he said, "greater than that of pleasing and making others happy."

Indeed, Dr Archer could scarce go to his chapel on a week evening without being beset with people pleading their distresses. The deserving he relieved at once; but after the scene in the upper-room in Westminster, he was chary of what seemed doubtful cases. From such he got their addresses, and promised to call and inquire. Sometimes the question was put, "When will you call, sir? He specified an hour, and went. Once, upon an occasion of this kind, he was rather behind time. The person he expected to see had left. He was told that she had hired the room for one hour, expecting a gentleman to call, but that, as he did not come, she had left. This is no uncommon occurrence among beggars in London.

CHAPTER VII.

CARDIPHONIA.

MAN, it has been said, is known by his friendships. The heart of a man may be known from his letters, especially from letters to his wife. We have, unfortunately, few other specimens of Dr Archer's letter-writing. He was not a letter-writer at any period of his life. He disliked it, and generally left such business to her who was ever but too ready to relieve her husband of any onerous duty she could properly undertake. To her, however, when absent from London, as he often was, he proved in this respect sweetly attentive, and the following "excerpts" are given to supply what must otherwise have been a defect in this Memoir. 'The reader will, of course, make the most ample allowance for the confidential frankness which they discover, and the occasional playfulness of style, which might seem to border on conceit. No one, however, who knew the writer, would for a moment charge him with it. While he could gratefully appreciate well-earned applause, he never failed, in looking within and around, to humble himself. In these "excerpts," too, we have abundant confirmation of what has been advanced in other portions of this volume, as well as illustrations of such traits of character as have been touched upon.   In short, they are all that remain of what, had he kept a diary, might have been pronounced *autobiographical.* Unfortunately, he was not always in the habit of dating his letters.   He simply notes the day of the week on which they were written.   This circumstance will sufficiently account for any inaccuracies of arrangement.

LETTERS TO MRS ARCHER.*

" My DEAR FRIEND,

" I gladly avail myself of this opportunity to express my deep sympathy with you in your present affliction.   Expecting to have seen you yesterday in your usual place in the chapel, I only learned, at the close of the morning's service, of your uncle's severe distress—by me unexpected and deeply lamented.   Ever since I came to London he has been a kind friend to me.   To whom was he not ?   Would to God that I were able to see him now !   However, he is in good hands ; and although far from home and its comforts, he has got the society of his friends, and, above all, has the presence of his best and last supporter to maintain him in the hour of his need. It is all for the best ; and well do I know your uncle's desire and intention to take a trip abroad, expressed to me so kindly when in Ramsgate.   How mysterious are God's ways ! and how little of his purposes do we see in the forming of our plans !

" I rejoice to see, from your last letter, that your good uncle's

* Mrs A. was at this time in Paris with her uncle, Mr Gray.

mind is calm. I expected this. Never keenly excited in prosperity, his soul will be comparatively at peace in distress, and
the religion of his heart, like all his conduct, always sincere
and never ostentatious, will, I believe, sustain him. If in the
land of the living, may God be with him! and how cheering
His presence! And if, alas! no more, may we imitate his
virtues, his humble retiring piety, and prepare to meet him
in heaven, never, never to part!

" Your affection for your best earthly friend could alone bear
you up in your present sorrows and toils. May the angel of
God's presence console and strengthen you still !

" Excuse these lines—hurried—but the sincere expression of
my feelings and wishes.—I remain, yours truly,

" THOMAS ARCHER."

"QUEEN'S ARMS, LIVERPOOL.

" Here I am, after a passage the roughest and most disagreeable that I have ever had. We had first a heavy ground swell,
pitching us from side to side. This motion was then relieved
with rolling from stem to stern, and all increased in misery by
the roaring wind and continued showers. I suppose there were
hardly any free from sickness. It was wretched, unspeakably
wretched, and sufficient to make any one, however sea-hardy,
to say that, if Britannia *rules* the waves, it is a great pity she
does not rule them straight. I rose at half-past nine, and was
glad to return to my berth at ten, where I remained until half-
past seven this evening, and have tasted nothing but a biscuit
the entire day. I have ordered my supper, and hope to get a
good night's rest. As we did not arrive in the dock until half-

past nine, I could not go to my old quarters and kind friends in Catherine Street, but I purpose joining them at breakfast to-morrow morning.

"We had a glorious sunset, the like I have scarcely ever witnessed. It was enough to arouse the most insensible and fire the least poetic.

"I am too tired to write long; you shall hear from me from London. May God keep you and cheer you in my absence; and O that your residence in Scotland may materially minister to your health!"

"18 HANS PLACE, *Monday.*

"I went to Catherine Street, as I told you I would, and in time for breakfast, where, I need scarcely say, I met with the old kind welcome. All so glad to see me, and so anxious to please me in every way; but from your note they expected me the day before to dinner—some mistake. Well, I had such a happy meeting yesterday with my dear people in Oxendon. Such joy depicted in their countenances when I ascended the pulpit, and such warm congratulations when the service was over! There seemed but one drawback to their happiness, and that was, I was *alone.* So many inquiries about you, and so much sincere regret that you were still too delicate to return to London. We must wait His time, and trust that ere long you will be mingling with them again. It is so sweet to me to hear them speak as they do of *you.*

"I have had a thoroughly good morning's work at my action sermon, of which, perhaps, I will send you a sketch."

"We had yesterday a very pleasant service in Dr M'Kerrow's in the afternoon. In the evening the congregation was not large, owing to the weather, but we had a very good collection, amounting to £94. This morning we have had a most delightful party to breakfast, and every hour of the day will be fully occupied. You cannot imagine what an intelligent and kind host I have; I quite enjoy his society. I do just what I like, and I know that would suit you. *All* are kind to me; not only the head of the house, but those who serve.

"I hope to be home on Wednesday, unless I stay to hear my dear friend Dr Harris, which, you will allow, is a great temptation."

"MARGATE, *Sept.* 24, 1840.

"A thousand thanks for your dear epistle. It is you—your heart—your shrewdness—your life—all but your living body—and, small as that is, it cannot go by the penny post.

"Mr S. drove me this morning to Ramsgate, where I met a great many of my own flock, who seemed truly glad to see me; and so warm were the greetings, that one would have imagined we had been parted for months instead of only a fortnight. How sweet it is to live in the hearts of my people ! Since my return I have been pleading the cause of Missions before a goodly number, and have travelled in Africa, to Greenland and Labrador—among the American Indians and West Indian negroes; in short, almost in every place where the seed of the Gospel has been sown by the Society; and I trust the hearts of my hearers have been touched for their own good, and enlarged with a strong desire to give of their substance, as well as their prayers, for the spread of the truth among the benighted heathen.

"All here are as kind to me as can be. *Nothing—nobody* could be more so. I begin to fancy, by all the attentions I receive, that I must be a great man, but one glance within says '*No.*'"

"STOURBRIDGE.

"I was so late in arriving here last night that it was quite impossible to write to you. I left Stratford-on-Avon the night before; had a most miserable congregation, and an equally small collection. I arrived in Birmingham after a very pleasant drive of twenty-two miles, and took the opportunity of strolling through that famous place of smoke, &c. It contains some beautiful buildings, and is full of bustle and life. I was to leave per coach for Stourbridge at a quarter before two, and went, accordingly, exactly in time—to be too late. Owing to some difference in the clocks, the coach had started two minutes before I reached the office, and I had no alternative but to walk a distance of twelve miles. It was for the first *six* very pleasant, but then I came among the signs of manufactories and misery. For a considerable distance, on both sides of the road, were houses filled with forges, at which men and *women* were indiscriminately employed making nails. All had the appearance of abject wretchedness and the deepest poverty; and as I had it not in my power to alleviate it, I was glad to escape into the minister's house here, of whose great kindness and hospitality I had often heard, and, I can assure you, the reports were not exaggerated. Everything is done for my comfort, and I am as happy, and, I may say, happier than many would be under the circumstances, for I had last night as wretched a congregation as can well be conceived. I really do not think there were more than ninety persons, but I felt *His* presence with me, and I do earnestly trust I may have done some good; and if I have been the means of lodging some truth in even *one* mind, that will take root and never lose its power, my sermon will have been a great boon here.

"Small as was my audience, I have no reason to complain of the collection; and, in addition to it, I got seven new annual subscribers, and these are a greater help to the Society than collections, because they can always calculate on them for current expenses. The more I have to do with the Moravian Mission the better pleased I am with it. I preach here again to-night, and if the weather be fine (which, to present appearances, is not likely), I may have a larger audience.

"I am happy to say that as yet I have caught no cold, which is marvellous, considering the wettings I have had. You will, I know, attend to all the notices. See after the supply for the pulpit, and write to all the parties I mentioned to you yesterday. I feel, however, it is quite needless to *remind* you of what you have to do for me.

"I must tell you before I close, that to-day I have been over an immense iron-work. I never saw anything like the machinery for *power*. They have a knife that cuts through bars of iron two inches thick with one blow, and the machinery for elongating the iron when red hot, by putting it through a

succession of cylindrical rollers, is truly wonderful.   I shall
look about me, see all I can, and give a full and faithful
account to you when we meet.   Until then, and for ever, may
Heaven's best, *richest* blessings rest on you!"

"LIVERPOOL.

"Just a line to tell you of my safe arrival here.   I passed
through the Trent valley, and did not therefore go through Birmingham.   The guard, who was very civil, *for a shilling* (oh,
bribery and corruption, how universal, how omnipotent, from
a railway guard to a J—— B—— !) kept the compartment of
the carriage for myself, allowed me, if I liked, to smoke a
cigar, and gave me six minutes at Crew for refreshments.   On
we went, and when I got to Catherine Street, I found my dear,
kind friends waiting dinner for me.   I went afterwards to the
lecture in a car, and the place was '*choke full,*' as our friend
Mr R. described it.   By some mistake, the bills were issued
that I was to lecture on the 'Inquisition.'   I showed the
Committee their own announcement, at which they marvelled,
and I said it proved that they did not belong to the Infallible
Church.   The lecturer was received with great enthusiasm;
and as I proceeded with my work, the audience began cheering at every other sentence, so I begged them to be quiet and
allow me to go on, which they tried to do, but it seemed with
difficulty they restrained themselves.   Now I can fancy I hear
you exclaim, 'What egotism ! what vanity !'   Well, the lecture
was an hour and a half in length, and was followed, at its
close, with rounds of cheers.

"I had my old, comfortable quarters last night, and had a

good sleep, but I cannot say I felt refreshed, for I was very tired. Travelling that long distance, and lecturing in one day, were too much. I have been out, had a good, sharp walk, and a voyage across the Mersey, but I was well wrapped up, and I feel all the better for it.—All here send their love to you, and I add mine, changeless and deep."

" 18 HANS PLACE.

"I know you will be anxious to hear what I preached on yesterday, so, before I begin my day's labour, almost every hour of which is marked out, I will tell you. In the morning we had more than a good—we had a capital congregation; and I experienced, from a great many who could speak to me, a very warm welcome home. Numerous kind inquiries about you, and when should they see you back, etc., etc. I preached on Christ the example of the Christian's life, and the following was my plan: My introduction was intended to point out the erroneousness, and trace the origin, of the opposite and opposing opinions of the Socinian and the Antinomian on the subject. The one maintains that Christ is *only* an *example*, and nothing more; the other, that he is an atonement, and nothing else. After displaying the true view, that *he is both*, I proceeded to remark :—

"I. That an example of the Christian life is *highly desirable*, in order to invest the Gospel with the charms of embodied truth, and to show that the precepts of Christ are *practicable*.

"II. That Jesus Christ was *designed* to be the example of the Christian life, and this was shown by a reference to his own words, 'Learn of me,' the language of the apostle, 'Be ye followers of me,' etc.

"III. That Jesus Christ was FITTED to be an example of the Christian life: 1. He was *man*, and therefore could act as we should; 2. He was in similar condition and circumstances with us, and therefore could show us practically how we should act; 3. His conduct was perfectly *intelligible* and *clear*—no disguise—no ambiguity about it; and 4. His conduct was perfectly *uniform* and *even*.

"IV. That it is *practical Christianity* to adopt Christ as the example of the Christian life,—religion not consisting in the belief of certain opinions, or in the making a certain profession, but in the imitation of Jesus Christ.

"V. That heaven is the perfect adoption and following of Christ's example,—a state of likeness to Christ. I closed with stating that the subject,—1. Furnished *rebuke to the unbeliever*, for the character of Christ was so singular—so beautiful—so consistent, it must have been *real*, that is, *divine;* so that, with Rousseau, we might conclude—if not real—if a fiction—the inventor is more wonderful than the hero. 2. Warning to the *mere professor*, who, if he believed in Christ's atonement, was bound to follow Christ's example, or to act on the force of Alexander's appeal to a person of the same name, but a great coward, 'Either *be* like me, or renounce my name.' 3. Encouragement to the true disciple; for there is no condition in which he could be where his Master had not been, and where He could not or would not help him.

"Now, Mrs Critic, mount your chair, look grave and wise, and give me your opinion of the preceding sketch.

"Our congregation in the evening was good, although, on account of the threatened rain, not so full as in the morning.

"I am, in the first place, going to see some sick persons, of whom I have a great many just now. Miss C——, I think, is sinking. She looks to me like the inhabitant of another world, —so fleshless, so transparent, so placid. The visits of Mr M—— are a great comfort to her; and I trust I have been able to take some trouble off her breast."

"18 HANS PLACE.

"We had a thoroughly November day on Sabbath, so foggy that we were obliged to have the gas lighted in the church, which was far better filled than I expected. In the morning I opened my course of exposition on the Spirit of God, namely, his Personality—his Divinity—and contingent characteristics. I sincerely hope the course will do much good to my dear people, as well as to myself. In the evening we had a remarkably good congregation, and I preached on the elements of the Church's prosperity. If I have time to-morrow, I will perhaps give you the *heads;* the HEART of the ideas spoke from my lips, and is now gone.

"I have so many things to attend to this day, I scarcely know which way to turn, and not having you here to help me, makes the burden doubly heavy.

"You think I do not speak in sufficiently warm terms to our dear friends at the Glen, for their great kindness to you. All I can say is, that I feel very grateful, and I depute you to say for me just what your own heart dictates, and that will convey my feelings in stronger and warmer language than my *Northern* tongue can command."

" BATH.

" I cannot tell you what a warm welcome I got here, how charmed I am with that dear old man, Mr Jay; and, what do you think, he seems very well pleased with me! He thanked me last night repeatedly for my sermon, and to-day, after my morning's discourse, expressed an earnest desire to see both of my sermons in print. Don't you consider that an honour? You know, however, my dislike to publishing, and my opinion that, if those persons who are so fond of appearing in print were to live and to read their own productions ten years after they had come before the public, they would, in many cases, have reason to be ashamed of them.

" You will be pleased to hear we have had a full meeting. It was an experiment, being the first held in the evening. I hope it may be profitable in every way.

" Mr Jay asked your name, and when I said 'Martha,' he remarked, 'I am particularly fond of that name,' and presented me with three volumes of his sermons for you, and has written your name in them.

" Remember me kindly to all your visitors, and may Heaven's best blessing rest on you ! "

" PLYMOUTH.

" Instead of being now on the breakwater, the water is breaking on us in the shape of continued and heavy showers, accompanied by rough wind. We had everything arranged,

—our company and our times; and the superintendent of the gigantic works had ordered his four-oared boat, but, alas! it was in vain for to-day. I have two or three chances yet, and I confess I am most anxious to see this wonder of our age. We had very excellent meetings last night. Dr L—— and I were the only speakers, with the exception of a few local friends, who were brief, and wisely left the evening to the deputation. After I wrote to you in the morning, I went over the victualling offices, which are incomparably finer than those at Deptford. I saw some of the most magnificent machinery for grinding corn that I have ever seen. These are pleasant recreations, and do one good in the midst of work.

" I fear I cannot be home before Saturday, but I have been preparing for Sabbath. One of my sermons will be from the text, ' To him that overcometh,' etc. My divisions: the Conflict—the Conquest—the Reward. If all be well, you will hear it, and then you can tell me whether travelling about has interfered with my preparation for my own pulpit."

" 18 HANS PLACE.

" Well, I had intended sending you a long letter to-day, giving you a full account of my visit yesterday, and the place; but I find it will take up too much of my time, and break in too much on my studies, in which I have been immersed since nine o'clock this morning; and I have had a glorious day's work of thought, the results of which I will give my people on Sunday. Besides, this letter cannot reach the Glen before Sabbath morning, when you will have abundance of more important topics to engross your thoughts; and whether you spend the day in the sanctuary, or pass it in sweet retirement with that dear, delightful, holy man, Dr Mitchell, I pray that the presence of the Master may be with you to cheer and bless you."

"I told you that, last Sabbath morning, I was to preach to young men; and I did so, to an overflowing house. All the pews and aisles were closely packed, and numbers were standing. My subject was—'The danger and sin of being ashamed of Christ;' and I have heard that my discourse told most powerfully. God grant that the effect may be lasting, and that those who heard me, when mingling, as many of them do in their houses of business, with scoffers at religion, may have grace given them to stand firm in the faith, to live the Christian, and speak boldly for the cause of the Redeemer.

"Mrs H—— called last night, and I wish you could have seen the joy that illumined her countenance. She came to tell me that such had been the effect of my lectures on Popery, etc., on her husband, that his heart had been touched, and his mind so enlightened, that he had renounced his former faith, and become a Protestant, and, she added with such energy, 'All through *you;* yes, all through *you.*' I endeavoured to lead her to look higher for the mighty change, and to bless God for the teaching of the Holy Spirit. I have been very busy all the forenoon, preparing for Sabbath, and am getting on thoroughly, most comfortably, and, I trust, will prove usefully, with a sermon from the text, 'It is good to draw near to God.' My other discourse is on 'Reconciliation with God,' to which I purpose to devote all to-morrow.

"You tell me, in your last letter, to think of you often. You need never repeat that suggestion, my own Martha. I can't take a step in the house, or a look at the church, or kneel before our God, without thinking of you."

"18 HANS PLACE.

"If your charming letter, received this morning, had been fifty times the length it was, I would not, could not, have tired of it. It came to me quite refreshing, after a very heavy Sunday's work and a restless night, and it cheered and warmed my heart. How thankful ought we to be for our friends' safety, and I rejoice with them that you were not on board the steamer, for you are a thorough *coward* on water—a *heroine* on land. Give my kindest regards to them, and express my anticipation of the pleasure I shall have in 'my brief visit to them. Would it could be longer! I preached three times yesterday, and feel fagged to-day. Last night, after the evening service, I called to condole with Mrs W——. She was at the Communion last Sunday week, and her husband was then quite well. On the following Wednesday he was dead, and she is left with three children. May He who has promised to be the husband of the widow, and the father of the fatherless, protect and keep her!

"Your *article* of yesterday was a real treat, it came so opportunely. M—— brought it into the vestry after the service, and it inspired me with new life, for I was thoroughly exhausted, having preached three times on Sunday, and preached yesterday morning at Wandsworth, and last evening in Oxendon ; but when I had read all your interesting information, I went home with joy and glee to supper and home duties.

"I am not surprised you enjoyed Mr J.'s sermon, on Sabbath. He is a warm, large-hearted man, has been much blessed by his Master, and, I have no doubt, will continue to be so, as long as he is spared to labour. You say you did not find any *originality* in him. Alas! who has it? Do we not almost all live by feeding on the brains of others? The text he preached from is a glorious one, and has been the subject of many an appeal. May we all drink of that full, free, and precious Fountain to which it points!"

"*Monday.*

"I cannot tell you how much I enjoy the society of my dear friend, Dr Harris, in this journey: he is such a charming companion, so full of wit—his conversation flowing with such brilliant ideas, clothed in such exquisite language, that it is enough to inspire one—and his heart so warm ; and perhaps I love him the more because he speaks of you in such glowing terms. I hear he gave a splendid sermon yesterday morning. Of course I did not hear him, for I was preaching elsewhere ; but he heard me in the afternoon when I preached, and at the close of the service he said, 'I tell you what, Doctor, I never heard such a sermon, and delivered, too, with such life. You are well named *Archer*, and you shoot with such unerring aim, that I am sure many a heart must have been pierced this afternoon. Why, man, who would suppose, to hear you, that you had been firing away this morning, and I am told you did it in superlative style ; and I will answer for it, you will come out again to-night, fresh as a daisy, when I feel done up, and good for nothing.' I was told he gave a brilliant discourse in the evening. All he does is *first-rate.* This will be a memorable day in London. I wish it were well over. I trust no serious evil may occur by the gathering of the Chartists. It is now raining, and Dr Harris says, ' Every drop will be as good as a *special constable;* and, in that case, we shan't have a drop too much.' Is he not droll ? "

" 22 HIGH STREET, HULL.

" On Sunday we had most capital collections, as I told you in my article of yesterday, and a noble meeting on Monday evening, after which I was really fagged, for I made a very great effort, and my labour was not in vain, for my speech told in every way.

" You know from experience the great hospitality of this house, and the kindness shown to me by all parties. Miss J—— is extraordinarily thoughtful, and everything is done for my comfort, but deputation-work in Yorkshire is something fearful, and I could not stand the riotous, rackety system long, for it is eat, eat, drink, drink, speak, speak, from morn till night—mind and body both overdone ; but then, after all, I enjoy the thing amazingly, for everybody is so kind, so very kind ; they do all they can, not only for our comfort, but make plans for our recreation.

" Yesterday morning we had a large and delightful party to breakfast, after which we started in a carriage,—with a pair of fine horses, and such a splash postillion that would have flabbergasted Ascot, to Beverley,—where we had a meeting in

M

the evening, and where, of course, I spoke. As soon as I had finished my work, I rushed off to see the Cathedral—a little gem. The screen is a miniature of the one at York, and lovely. You know I have a great deal to do on this tour, but you shall have a notice daily, however short, of my proceedings.

"All here send (M. says) *oceans* of love. I add mine to swell the mass."

"PLYMOUTH.

"The journey here was very frosty the first part, and thoroughly wet the second; so I had a variety, and glad enough I was when I reached its close. However, a very warm reception and good refreshments revived me; and I went invigorated to a thoroughly good meeting, and where, I imagine, I must have made a very good speech,— at anyrate, one that told well, for three gentlemen were to speak after me, and all they did was to come forward and bow, and would say nothing,—so you see that, if my speech *electrified* the audience, it *mesmerised* the orators. Eh! do you see? I retired to rest, awfully sleepy, about half-past ten o'clock, and had a capital night. I have walked about this place for three hours this morning, and am somewhat tired. I start again at two to the opening of some new wash-houses, then a dinner-party at half-past four, and afterwards my lecture on 'Leo and Luther,' which will close the day; and I trust my labours here will prove a blessing."

"18 HANS PLACE.

"In case, my dearest Martha, I may not find time to write to you from Hitchen, I drop you a line to say I got through yesterday's services pretty comfortably, notwithstanding I was

not very well. I preached from the words in Rev. xvii. 14,
—' They that are with the Lamb are called, and chosen, and
faithful.' In the morning ' CALLED,' in the evening ' CHOSEN,'
and I intend next Sabbath forenoon to take ' FAITHFUL.' I
have not time to give you the divisions now. You can think
over the subject for yourself—there is abundance of food for
thought."

" ROCHDALE, *Monday.*

" I drop you merely a line, to say I got here safely on Saturday. Yesterday was lovely. We had a very large gathering
in the morning. In the afternoon I addressed the Sabbath-
school children and teachers—in number about 500—and I
greatly enjoyed the service."

"18 HANS PLACE.

" Most heartily thankful am I that you are better, and I
hope and pray that you may continue to gather strength, and
return to our dear home vigorous, as you once were.

" This is Monday, and I am Mondayish. Besides my usual
prostration and lowness of spirits, consequent on an attack of
my old enemy the bile, I have the misery of a pelting, dull,
boisterous day. The rain has been pouring in torrents; its
constant patter, patter, only interrupted by the wild blast howl-
ing through the trees! How I am to reach Ivy Cottage is
more than I can tell, unless it be by two omnibuses—one to
the Mission House, where I must go, and then another to St
John's Wood. I know your anxiety about me, and so I shall
be careful. I shall take shoes and socks in my pocket, and

if my feet should be wet, can make myself comfortable there. A. looked better yesterday, and your aunt is fresh and vigorous. She was very anxious for my company to-day, and so was dear A. Both unite in kindest regards and love to you.

" Mr S. leaves to-morrow for the North. I received a note last Saturday, stating that his family were very anxious to hear him again, and *hinted* they would like me to ask him to preach yesterday morning in Oxendon, but I said I *could not*, as I had been absent four Sabbaths from my own people, and I am to be in Cambridge next Sunday. I took measures, however, for his preaching in ——, and I hope they were successful.

" Yesterday morning I preached from Galatians i. 15, 16,— 'It pleased God to reveal his Son in me, that I might preach him among the Gentiles.' I began by referring to the simplicity of the Apostle's language in describing the mightiest change of which man was capable; that the *conversion* of a soul was the most momentous and glorious in the universe; that Paul's was *peculiarly* so; but that, after all, it contained the same *elements*, although differing in degree, of the conversion of the poorest and humblest child of God. For,

" 1*st*, In the conversion of every soul there was *illumination* on Spiritual truth equalling a REVELATION. These discoveries related to GOD—his LAW—our own *hearts*, and the *judgment*. The discoveries were a revelation *relatively*, not *literally*. Nature existed, the grass grew, the flowers bloomed, the stars shone, although the blind man did not see them. The difference was in *him*, not in *them*.

" 2*d*, In conversion, grand discoveries *refer to Christ*. It was *His son* whom he revealed. He is the grand object of attraction, who sheds light on all others, and makes them *attractive*, not terrible.

" 3*d*, The discoveries are direct and *personal* in ME,—not to those around, but to myself.

"4*th*, The discoveries are direct and *internal* IN me. This is the great distinction of the call of the Gospel : it goes home to the *heart.*

" 5*th*, The discoveries are the result of DIVINE power. GOD revealed his Son in me.

" 6*th*, The discoveries are the objects of the Divine APPOINT-MENT—PLEASED God.

" 7*th*, These discoveries are given, not for ourselves, but for *others*, that *I might preach Him* to the Gentiles.

" The congregation was extremely good. Not so at night, for an hour before our time it rained very heavily, which made our audience thin,—I mean thin *comparatively*, for there were twice as many last night as I have seen eleven or twelve years ago in the fullest of our congregations.

" After service I called at your uncle's, and then went home. Had worship, and sat down to think."

" SCARBOROUGH, *Saturday Night.*

" I started yesterday, after despatching my wee note to you, for a ramble with my landlord, who is an extremely intelligent and prudent, as well as a kind man. I enjoy his society very much, and he seems to enjoy mine, so that we are very comfortable, indeed, together. His wife seems very amiable, and his children are quite friends with me.

" This town is beautifully situated. Its most prominent

object is the remains of the Castle, which is built on a tongue of land—rather awkwardly placed, as the broad part projects instead of the narrow, to lick the sea when it comes against it. The Castle, which must once have been a place of immense strength, is now quite in ruins, yet bold and commanding. The town itself is like most sea-bathing places—a singular, almost fantastic, combination of the old and new, the steep and plain, the narrow and wide, the dirty dingy alley, and the elegant open terrace. It has no harbour or buildings to compare with Ramsgate, but the sea is bolder and more animated. The streets were crowded in the evening, so was the neighbourhood of the Spa. Masses of well, even elegantly, dressed people, were moving in all directions, when the band ceased to play at nine o'clock. There was a blind man, accompanying his own beautiful voice on the violoncello, in ' Sound the loud Timbrel.' In the adjoining square was a party of glee singers, while the next street was regaled with the musical glasses and the human voice divine. All this liveliness, and the fineness of the evening, contributed to make my congregation very small. This morning I was waked up at *four* o'clock to see the sun rise. I arose! and what a sight! The hues were endlessly diversified—green, blue, red of every shade and degree of intensity, fringed with living gold, and throwing it out in over-whelming gorgeousness, all pillared on a boundless sea. But I wax poetical ; so off to my bed to finish my nap. Well, only think; when I arose at seven, all was changed—all was not—breezy, misty, as miserable as could well be. However, about twelve it cleared a little, and we started for a stroll along the beach. After we had got about two miles, the storm gathered

and burst; one clap succeeded another. The lightning went
zig-zag, and played along and off the sea. The rain came
down in torrents, from which we got shelter in some caves in
the rocks. The finest sight I witnessed was a light veil of
mist, almost snow-white, rising on the rock, and wreathing in
beautiful softened tracery the old ruins, while beyond and
through it you could see the flashes play. It was the most
striking contrast with the calm glory of the daybreak. On
returning home I got your two letters—many thanks for them.
Dark prospect for to-morrow. I fear, indeed, that my trip
here, although pleasant to myself, will not be very profitable
to others. It is certainly pouring now, but it may be fine to-
morrow.

" Mr R. tells me that where I am appointed to preach I am
not likely to get more than £5, and he has known the collection to be as small as 30s.; but I shall, with help from above,
do the best I am able, and you shall hear the result on Monday, if all be well."

" 18 Hans Place.

" I suppose you will scarcely have finished reading my last
long letter when you receive this. Well, this will be very short
at anyrate, because, in the first place, I have nothing to say,
and, secondly, if I had I could not spare time from my studies
to tell it. I preach three times next Sunday. In the city in
the afternoon; therefore I dine with Mr B. in Old Change.

" On Monday, this is the programme :—The Mission House
at nine o'clock; then I go to C—— Square to examine a
catechist for the West Indies; then to Hans Place to get your

letter, which I feel sure of, as I had *none* to-day; then off to Brentford, where I preach in the evening, first meeting some people at dinner. Pretty much, you will say, after three sermons on the previous day; but I always have strength given to me, simply, I believe, because I ASK it."

" I do not understand why you did not receive a letter from me on Saturday, for I certainly did write on Friday, and gave you a full account of the numerous callers who hindered me with my preparations for Sabbath, so that I was late at my work in the evening. Saturday there were numerous disasters in the house, which you will hear about some future time, for I am now going to speak of yesterday. I begin with telling you that we had a good, extremely good congregation, which quite cheered me, and I preached with spirit.

" In the morning I lectured on Joseph in the pit, and in the evening I preached on Christ the 'Plant of Renown' (Ezek. xxxiv. 29). My plan was this :—A few remarks on the natural love of flowers—on their poetry—and the imagery they had furnished to genius — and the exquisite comparisons in the sacred volume derived from them.

" 1*st,* Some plants are famed for the *beauty of their appearance,* — the LILY — its delicacy — its height, reaching in the East to 4½ feet—its elegance. Now, Christ, the plant of renown, was the *altogether lovely*—view him in the constitution . of his person—the properties of his mind—the actions of his life.

" 2*d,* Some plants are famed for the *exquisiteness of their* *fragrance,*—the ROSE. The title given to Christ is the 'Rose of Sharon.'

" 3*d,* Some plants are famed for the *deliciousness of their fruit,*—the VINE.

" 4*th,* Some plants are famed for the *depth of their shadow,*— the OAK ; but especially the SYCAMORE, which is sometimes forty paces in diameter.

" 5*th,* Some plants are famed for their *medicinal qualities,*— the SPIKENARD—the BALSAM. Now Christ is *Jehovah Rophi*— the Lord our Healer.

" 6*th,* Some plants are famed for their *transplantibility.*

" 7*th,* Some plants are famed for their *durability ;* but they fade at last. Christ never dies.

" 8*th,* Some plants are famed for the *combination of their various perfections.* All these meet in Christ.—Then closed with a few remarks on *the* Plant of Renown being UNCHANGING —created objects being sometimes fickle and capricious in their love. UNIVERSAL, not *local,* but extends over all the earth. EVERLASTING, not *temporary,* but goes into eternity.

" No *change* here—no *flaw*—no exhaustion of its beauties, etc., etc.

" You will, perhaps, hear the discourse some day preached in full ; in the meantime you can think over it, and cultivate the growth of this Plant of Renown in your own heart."

" 18 HANS PLACE.

" I was very busy all yesterday forenoon preparing an essay on the present distress of the country, its causes, and the conse- quent duties of the Church regarding it. It caused me some pains in hunting out statistics; and its principal object was to trace the connection of present suffering with national sins and the displeasure of Almighty God. I delivered it in the evening at Dr L.'s, to a crowded audience, and all the ministers present tendered me their greatest gratitude for it. I half think of sending it to some magazine, but my utter aversion to appear in print says ' No.' "

"BRAINTREE.

" We had last night a very small meeting, as almost everybody was engaged with the harvest. The place of worship was large, so you can imagine the miserable appearance that about eighty or ninety persons made in it; but I did my best, and got what was considered a capital collection for the few who were there. You know I do not need the excitement of numbers to stir up my energies, for I can preach as well to fifty as when I address five thousand.

" My earnest prayer is, that some good seed has been sown, and that *many* out of the *few* may reap everlasting benefit."

"18 HANS PLACE.

"No letter from you, my dearest Martha, to-day. Well, I could scarcely have expected one. Still, still, it would have been a joy to have received it by surprise. I felt yesterday so low and wretched, suffering fearfully from bile, that you can hardly imagine the joy your delightful letter gave me. It was, as you knew, my birthday, and I had no one here to wish me many happy returns. The past rose before me. Six-and-thirty years of my life gone, and gone in doing what? and gone from a line of years at the verge seventy, on an average but ten years more than I have lived. Well, it is past. Oh, that the future may be more devoted to the service of my Master, in labouring more assiduously for the salvation of souls, and may He bless my efforts!

"Now for my journal. On Sabbath morning I preached on a text made up of two clauses,—1 Timothy i. 18, and 2 Timothy ii. 3,—the good warfare and the good soldier. After an introduction derived from Paul's circumstances,—imprisoned, on the brink of the grave, his heroism, and the value of his testimony to the reality of religion while the shadows of death were gathering around, the fires of judgment flashing in his sight,—I described the warfare as *good*.

"1st, Good in its *objects*, to crush sin, the world, death, etc.; contemplating nothing ruinous, immoral, and therefore redeeming itself, vindicating its grandeur, even if it should fail, by the nobility of its purpose. Howard unsuccessful would have been much more illustrious than Napoleon triumphant at Borodino.

"2d, Good in its *weapons*, nothing carnal, no crime, no circumvention. Its weapons are good, because spiritual, *forged in heaven*, complete (not like the invulnerability of Achilles, who, supported by his mother's hand by the heel, was there untouched, and there struck by an arrow, which killed him), and *tried, proved* weapons.

"3d, Good, because its *Leadership* is good. The magic of a great name inspires soldiers. Here the greatest of all, Jesus, and best of all,—for (1st.) he knows every movement of our foes; (2d.) his resources are infinite; (3d.) he shares all dangers with the humblest of his soldiers; and (4*th*) he never dies—no casualty can touch him.

" 4*th*, Good, because the *results* are good; triumph over evil, accompanied by the richest glories in heaven, and all certain, and full, and everlasting. The good soldier I portrayed as having these qualities—*vigilance*, never to sleep on his post ; *obedience*, regular and uniform; *firm* and *unflinching*, *patient* in suffering, etc.

" The sketch of my evening sermon you shall perhaps have to-morrow.

" I felt awfully fagged on Sabbath night, as I was so poorly. I had large audiences both times, and my people seemed much pleased. They were profoundly attentive, and some spoke to me after each service, and thanked me for my discourses. I have a meeting of Presbytery at Albion at four o'clock, and from thence back to Oxendon, to meet communicants. To-morrow I preach at Isleworth, but you shall have a line before I start."

" 18 HANS PLACE.

" After leaving Hackney last evening in an omnibus, to the bank, a storm arose of almost unexampled severity and grandeur. The whole heavens were one sheet of flame, darting with intense vividness from numberless points, and converting the darkness of night into the splendour of day. The flashes were so bright, and so quick in succession, that horses could hardly be governed, and no doubt many accidents must have occurred. I stood for about twenty minutes at the Post-office, gazing on St Paul's, now resting in sombre majesty, its magnificent dark outline seen in gloom, and then all bursting into glory and lustre on the eye. The light was tinged with blue, which added to the grandeur of the scene. By this time, a quarter-past eight, the thunder awaked, and leaping from point to point, uttered in its deep roll the voice of the Eternal. Everything was awful and soul-moving. Never have I seen so much that was so truly sublime, or been more subdued *without terror*, since one evening, on the Round Tower at Windsor, when the lightning was running along the slopes, and playing on the bosom of old Father Thames. I referred on Sunday evening to the omnipresence of God, as displayed in the minstrelsy of ocean, the streaks of the lightning, and the solemn music of the skies. But what expression can approach one clap—one gleam! Well, now, the rain began to pour with such fury that, along Cheapside, you could see it spring up from the stones at least two feet high. I intended to walk home, but that was out of the question, so I watched for an omnibus, and at last succeeded in getting a place.

"When I reached home, poor M—— was in a sad state; you know how terrified she is at thunder. She trembled so, that she could scarcely stand, and she seemed more dead than alive; but I gave her something to do her good, had worship, and sent her off to her bed at ten o'clock. I went off early to mine, but no sleep could I get, for the wind howled most furiously. To-day it has rained incessantly, and I got very wet in visiting some people that I had promised to see. I am now going to dine, and I mean to remain at home this evening, and try to dispel the dulness of the day and of the *house* without you, by thought for next Sabbath.

" Speaking of lightning, you may think it is dangerous to go into a vehicle in such a storm.   This is Barham's last joke —he is the author of the ' Ingoldsby Legends:'—'Where is the safest place in a thunder-storm ?   An omnibus !—Why ?   Because it has a *conductor !'*   That's good,—is it not ? "

.*" BRITISH MUSEUM, 2 P.M.*

" Here I am, my dearest Martha, amid the Monads and Triads of Egyptian mythology, endeavouring to ascertain whether the Triads of the East indicate a trinity of the Godhead, or refer to a trinity in the Noahic succession.   I have been boring away at Berosus and Sanchoniatho, at Nimrod and Vishnu, at Demi-gods and Typhons, for the last three hours, and I am just about as wise as I was when I began my studies this morning.   Oh ! what a fine thing is learning ! and yet what a labour to attain it !   I am determined that much shall not make me mad.   I will turn an intellectual *homœopathist,* and take learning in infinitesimally small doses.   So now I shall take a pause in my researches, and write to you, my darling wife—better far than all the beauties of Pharoah's court, or the ladies that revelled in the mythology of Greece ; and then, as I purpose to remain here until seven o'clock, pursuing my labours, I shall take my letter to the post-office, and get my dinner.

" My sermon to-morrow morning is on ' The Omnipotence of God.'   I begin with a reference to the storm of Wednesday night, and the impression produced by it.   While a single flash might have struck me dead, none could touch me without the permission of Him who wields it. What, then, must be his energy, who guides all in its fitful coruscations, and succeeds in a moment the tempest by the lovely tranquillity of nature. What his power, whose whisper-sound is the thunder, and the glance of whose eye is the lightning's beam! This brings me into my subject. I proceed to show the mysterious *nature* of power generally—and especially of Divine—mind acting on matter—creating it—moulding it—a breath evolving a world into beauty; yet while inscrutable, it is a *fact*, a reality. I then proceed to distinguish between *moral and physical* power. I illustrate it in this way:—A man has a knife to stab a friend. Physically, he can do it—morally, he cannot; his arm is strong enough, but his soul shudders from the act; his inability to do it arises from strength of affection, and to say, therefore, he cannot do it, is merely putting it in the stronger form, he *won't* —and so on—and so on. After this I get out of the region of metaphysics—that delightful sea of mud—and come to the text:—Power belongeth unto God—*power* in opposition to weakness—*power* adequate to his will, and hence the source of joy—for the correspondence of will and ability is pleasure— and belonging to him, not derived nor contingent.

"This power we see in *creation*—immensity—variety spring- ing *from nothing*, for each layer of earth has the imprint of his tread—and deeper and deeper we go to reach the period of non-existence—and the *ease* with which all is called into being —his repose never being broken.

"In Providence—its countless objects—*infinite relations—sim- plicity* of movements—call them laws—yet displaying his power —because they are so fixed, all moves with noiseless regularity

—and he is not required visibly to interfere to rectify disor-
ganisations.

"So much must suffice for the present. The rest I reserve
for another opportunity. Seriously, you must be tired of reading this scratch; so, farewell; and may that Power ever shield
you."

"I do not know that the sketch of my sermon will be more
edifying than that of the K—— divine, but I think you will
regard it with a more favourable eye and heart. I told you
that I preached in the evening on Ezekiel ix. 3, 4. After
sketching the scenery of the preceding chapter, which formed
the burden of the prophet's instruction, and of the Divine
indignation, and referring to the aptness of the genius of
Ezekiel for such terrible imagery,—his mind and style being
alike impetuous and sternly, darkly sublime,—I alluded to some
of the phraseology requiring explanation. The glory of the
Lord being the emblem of his presence in his own house, and
its position having being removed from the cherub or mercy-
seat to the threshold, where it still lingered, indicated how
reluctantly, yet how necessarily, God withdraws from scenes of
pollution and dishonour. The man with the inkhorn we find
in the Turkish secretaries of modern times, who carry an
inkhorn in their girdle where other Turks wear a poignard.
'The mark' probably refers to the brand on the brow of
slaves to denote their ownership; and this suggests the reality
and visibility of God's interest in his people. This opens up
the text:—

"I.

" *The resemblance of ancient Jerusalem and our own land.*

" 1*st, Contempt of God's authority,* viii. 17.—Putting the branch to the nose being the symbol of contempt.

" 2*d, Idolatry,* 5th to 11th verses.—Ours being much—Idolatry of wealth — Influence — *Intellect*—to the exclusion of moral character.

" 3*d, Infidelity,* verse 12.—Ours seen in the vulgar ribaldry— Material, grovelling socialism of the times, and the practical atheism so widely prevalent.

" 4*th,* Widespread corruption of manners—The land filled with violence, verse 17.—Ours with crime—All classes—agricultural, embraced in ignorance—Mechanical, stimulated into unhealthy volcanic excitement—The mercantile keen, unscrupulous in business—The aristocrat rolling in luxury amid the sufferings of humanity, etc., etc.

" II.

" In times of greatest profligacy and declension there are always some to lament over their wickedness. Noah in the antediluvian epoch, Lot in Sodom, David in Jerusalem, Elijah in Israel, furnish illustrations.

" To be genuine, this grief *should be secret* as well as public, otherwise we may be seeking a character for personal virtue by condemning public vice.

" It should be connected with *individual sins*—severe against our own—accompanied by endeavours to reform and reclaim; and, finally, should be displayed in most *perilous times.* This

N

demands not eloquence, but moral heroism,—the spirit of the Scotchwoman, who, when asked many questions by her minister on application for Communion, could not answer one ; and on retiring, by his advice to learn something, turned to him, and with tears on her cheeks, said, ' Sir, sir, I canna *speak* for Christ, but I can *dee* for him !'

"III.

"However obscure and unnoticed by the world these men are, God *knows* and *owns* them. Elijah lamented the solitariness of his grief. God pointed to seven thousand uncompromising servants. No one escapes his eye—no tear—no sigh—all are before him.

"IV.

"God is often pleased to spare the men who weep and sigh when he pours out his judgment on others—Lot—Noah—Israelites, and the destroying angel—the flight of the Christians from Jerusalem to Pella, in the siege, furnished illustrations.

"Ordinary calamities we must expect, but in signal interpositions of wrath, we may anticipate equally illustrious displays of protection, etc., etc.

"Now, my little petticoated-theologian, pray, what think you of that? Give me your criticism.

"Yesterday evening I went into the vestry to meet applicants for the last time this Communion. We have seventeen joining now, a goodly quota, but not more than we need to make up for the constant fluctuations in our Chapel ; so many young men coming from Scotland, and elsewhere, to get an insight into London business, and then after a time returning. I found, when I reached home, a note from our kind friend Miss G., stating that the Rev. John Clayton was to lunch to-day at the Gore, at one, and wished me to meet him; and I think I shall, and enjoy an hour of his cheerful company, as well as the society of that genial circle."

"I steal a short time before breakfast, to write a few lines with an atrociously bad steel-pen. I know of hardly any case more pitiable than that of dear J. K.'s. In the flower of his age, with so many natural and acquired distinctions and powers,—in the midst of a young, numerous family, and among a people who deeply love him,—to be laid aside, like a withered, sapless, useless trunk, is truly melancholy. No consolation remains but two,—that even now another climate may brace for a season his exhausted frame, and that he may be spared a little longer; and, let the worst happen, it does happen under His authority who directs His power with wisdom and tempers His judgment and severity with mercy. Let us then commend him to the faithful guardianship of his Father and God, and pray that his sun, pale and cold as even now is its light may not go down at noon. May He have mercy on his wife and babes!

"On Monday evening I preached in Oxendon to a good audience, who seemed to relish my address very much. We had a meeting of the School-committee after the service. Our collections will be next Sunday, and our service next Monday

evening, in connection with the schools. I have pledged myself to some of the teachers (*D. V.*) to be present, and I must
endeavour, by a double measure of attention and kindness, to
make up in some small degree for your absence. What do
you think Mr —— said the other day, when speaking of you,
and the loss your absence would be to the social meeting?—
' That the sight of you always cheered them. The sound of
your voice was so sweet, and you always uttered some words
of encouragement and kindness ; and even though you did not
speak, your look of approbation did them good, and the smiles
that passed over your lips were bright as sunbeams, and filled
their hearts with joy and gladness.' Now, don't you consider
that a compliment? I am wrong—not a *compliment*, but the
honest outpourings of the sincere sentiments of a heart that
loved you.

"I told you of my drive to Tonbridge Wells. Do you know,
I should like hugely to spend a week or two in that place. It
seems a most delightful and glorious spot. I was told, on my
arrival there, by the friends of the Mission, that I need scarcely
expect to get anything, but, much to their astonishment, and
to my own satisfaction, I got what was considered a large
collection. I rose yesterday morning at half-past *five !* Only
think of such a feat for me ! Had a long walk, breakfasted
at seven, and started at half-past seven for Maidstone. The
drive was truly grand. A month or six weeks ago it might
have been richer, when the hops were in flower, but as we had
the *poles*, my fancy supplied the hops, and what was wanting
by their absence was compensated for by the intensely-beauti-
ful and boundlessly-varied tints of Autumn. I dreamed on

through the scene in true enjoyment. I had to wait two hours and a half at Maidstone ; and as I felt hungry, I thought I might as well dine there as at Chatham, which I did, and was all the better for the diet, for although I had had much food for the mind, there was a vacuum in the body which yearned to be filled. I reached Chatham between three and four o'clock, met with a very warm reception, but heard many complaints as to the badness of the times, no trade, etc., which was as much as to say,—' Your collection for the Mission will be a failure.' These hints, you know, never discourage me. I go forward to the work in real earnest, and if I obtain an attentive audience, although the numbers be small, I trust and pray that lasting benefit to the souls of my hearers may be the result, let the money collected be ever so trifling. I was told the collection last year was £3, 12s., but I must not be disappointed if it did not reach that sum, as there was so much distress in the country. I made no remark, but after my sermon I simply told for what Society I was pleading, and how much good was done by their instrumentality, and the collection amounted to £8, 3s., besides which I expect some annual subscriptions.

"As I was walking along the streets, an officer addressed me, one Dr M——, whom my mother knew, and I went with him up to and over Pitt. This morning I am to inspect the dockyard and some large ships, and I start at one for Faversham, where I preach to-night. Town to-morrow, where I used to think and feel all my journeyings and turmoils ended happily when I received a kind greeting from you ; but, alas ! that pleasure does not await me now. That time, however,

I trust, will come again, and may be soon (if He wills it), when the sunshine of 18 Hans Place will be all the brighter for the temporary cloud that has hung over it from your absence."

" The Session met last night, and we had a long sederunt, but a very pleasant one. There is to be an election of elders on Monday three weeks, when I hope God may direct the people to a wise and suitable choice. I am very sure that nothing would more facilitate my labours, or augment my ministerial comfort, than the presence and support of a number of active, intelligent, pious men, in whose judgment I could repose confidence, and who could command some time to work with me.

" The missionary collectors met, and I did your work as well as I could. I will keep the lists of the names of the contributors till you return. The meeting at the service was not large. I delivered an address on ' The Lord the Believer's Portion.' May we seek that most inestimable of all possessions! Seek Him earnestly *now*, for our time may be short—so many of our friends have lately been removed, and our home-circle is becoming much diminished.

" When I had finished my service at Oxendon, I went to ——, and gave a speech at a Bible Society meeting. Mr S. and his *better half*, according to vulgar parlance—' the *weaker vessel*,' according to Scripture—sent their fond love to you. You may suppose I was rather late in reaching home, and somewhat tired; but I am quite well to-day. I tell you this, to keep your mind easy, for I know your great anxiety about me when we are parted. I will now only add my affectionate regards to our kind friends, and the earnest hope that your present sojourn with them may be the means of restoring you to perfect health, so that you may ere long light up our ain fireside again.—Ever yours,

"Thomas Archer."

CHAPTER VIII.

RECREATION.

N 1851, Dr Archer had a very serious illness. He had been all his life the victim of a biliary disorder, and the laborious duties of the pastorate, acting upon such a temperament, caused him frequent indispositions. It exalts such a man in our estimation, when we know, that very often, under severe suffering, he appeared in the pulpit and conducted the services so that no one discovered it. Once engrossed with his subject, the very sense of debility left him. When he was able to take walking exercise, his enemy could be kept in subjection. He enjoyed a long walk much, and frequently had twelve miles of it daily, especially when in the country, or at the coast. The illness referred to greatly prostrated him. He had been out on "deputation work" for nearly three weeks. He had been overwrought, and, on his return on the Friday evening, looked jaded and sad. His head was pained, and his spirits were low—a very unusual thing with him. He would not listen to the proposal of having supply for Sabbath. "If I once get into the pulpit," he said, "I am sure to be able to preach;" and he did preach, morning and evening, to the surprise of all who heard him, and especially of those who knew the state in which he was. He preferred to walk home after the evening work. Mrs Archer, who was at home an invalid, waited his arrival anxiously. At length, the well-known knock was heard. She opened the door, and there was Dr Archer, and with him a gentleman, who told her that he found him lying in a faint near "Hans Place." Medical assistance was at once obtained. The doctor assured Mrs Archer that, but for some medicine he had taken on the Friday evening, which had to some extent relieved the liver from a surcharged state, the preaching of that Sabbath must have induced an apoplectic fit, and he might have died in the pulpit. The Lord's Supper was to be dispensed on the following Sabbath. He was anxious to preside, but it could not be. He was too weak for that. In lieu of himself, the following letter was read to the congregation :—

" MY DEAR FRIENDS,

" I had fondly hoped to have been a partaker in your holy feast this day, though not dispensing it; but the cause and effects of the event, which providentially befell me near my own door, confines me, and for a few days longer must confine me, to my bed-room. At this I do not murmur, and my absence this day may turn to future good. The accident, which might have been more serious, or even fatal, has developed the origin of that mental prostration under which I had been suffering for some days,—to wit, utter biliary derangement and overflow of blood to the head ; while by *stringent* medicine and entire cessation from labour, I hope to be raised to a state of health which for years I have not enjoyed.

" To my own heart its most beneficial result is this : I have been seized from the whirl of excitement in which I have too long been—have been thrown on and into myself ; and, in spite of medical orders *not* to think, have been led to reflect deeply and seriously.

" I have surveyed my ministerial history, and the one point in it to which I now allude, is the exciting engagements in the religious world to which I have referred.

" How I entered on them is not necessary to inquire.

" I can solemnly say, it was not for the love of *lucre*, nor for the thirst of *fame ;* and had it been for either, and both been gained, they would have been dearly purchased by the tear and wear of the body, and the feverish racking of the mind.

" My bed-chamber review on this subject has solemnly deepened the resolution at which I had arrived in Scotland, not altogether, but almost entirely to abandon that line of action, and to withdraw in a large degree from travelling and deputation labour, with all its excitement and exhaustion.

" The advantages I anticipate from this course are,—1*st*, more time for calm thought and reading, and more matured preparation for my pulpit, and that thus I may be more thoroughly furnished for the exposition and enforcement of God's Word ; and, 2*d*, and above all, that I shall be enabled to live more than I have done with and among my own people.

" Here I say no more, than that your regrets on that point are not deeper than mine.

" My earnest desire is to spend, and be spent, among you ;

and by husbanding my resources for you, engaging in schemes of practical usefulness, and walking in the intercourse of love, to promote your holiness and advance my own peace. I must, however, for this purpose, beseech your earnest co-operation, as well as *Divine* aid.

" I ardently entreat a deeper place in your hearts and prayers than ever; and if you so act, blessed as my ministry has been in many cases, it will be more largely and lastingly blessed still. Farewell! May your God and the God of your fathers have you all in his holy keeping !—Yours most affectionately,

"THOMAS ARCHER."

As soon as he was partially recovered from this attack, and before his strength was restored, he was anxious to fulfil the engagements for which he was pledged, as he disliked to disappoint his friends. He was urged not to undertake so much, and he resolved he should not; still it was not easy to escape from the vortex into which he was drawn. He had frequently more than fifty engagements on his book, as it was no unusual occurrence for applications to be made six, nine, and sometimes twelve months before his services were needed, in order to secure them.

About three years after this, in 1854, he suffered much from varicose veins. This was a severe trial to him, as it prevented him from taking his usual walking exercise. The consequence was, his health suffered materially; but his willingness to labour never abated. In 1858 he had been travelling on deputation work, and could not have the necessary home attentions. On his return to town, his leg was in a fearfully swollen state. His

medical adviser forbade his attempting to stand, and prescribed perfect rest. At this time he sent the following letter
to be read to his congregation :—

"MY DEAR FRIENDS,

"Little did I think last Sabbath, when I was urging
the duty of prayerful preparation for the feast of this day,
that I should not be a guest. Even on Friday night I expressed a hope of being at the Communion, although not
preaching.

"A consultation with my medical adviser forbids all such
hope. He prescribes perfect bodily rest for a few days, and I
must submit.

"Some of you may be naturally and kindly anxious to know
what is the matter. To this with pleasure I say, that it is not
connected with my bodily health, which is now much improved,
and better than it has been for a long time. My present
illness is caused by a bad leg, from which you may have perceived I have been suffering for a considerable period, by my
lameness, but from which I trust speedily to recover. There is
much pain connected with the limb; and irksome as it is for
me to be confined and deprived of my usual walking exercise,
yet I must bow with submission.

"Deeply do I regret my absence from you this morning;
but this is of the less moment if, while the servant is absent,
the Master is doubly present.

"My earnest desire and hope is, that you, and my old friend
who preaches to you, may have a large measure of *His* blessing

and favour; and that, when as I hope to see you next Sabbath, our voices shall be those of congratulation and praise.

"My prayer this day will rise in my *Patmos* on *your* behalf. Let yours, in your *Zion*, rise on behalf of *me*.

"May God be with you, and bless you for ever.—I remain, your most affectionate and faithful pastor,

. " THOMAS ARCHER."

These severe illnesses gradually undermined his naturally robust health, and necessitated occasional absences from home. He, consequently, made the best use of his holiday. He required recreation, and he took it; but the recreations of a London pastor are somewhat different from those of a country parson. Like the swallow, the latter while working can rest on the wing, whereas the other knows no rest till he has taken flight, when summer comes, to the " shady retreats," or across the Channel, to the "abandon" of Continental travel. Dr Archer, while in London, found no rest either to foot or tongue. He was oft wearied and worn, and nature demanded a halt. In spring he sometimes took " the minister's week," leaving early on Monday and returning, after one Sabbath's absence, on the Saturday following. Paris was generally selected for these short trips. It had been the first Continental city he had visited in the spring after his marriage, and he liked to renew former enjoyments. If he took his holiday after the July Communion, he selected some quiet and beautiful scenery, where the long summer day could be spent amid the pictur-esque or sublime. If after the September Communion, he visited the cities abroad. For several years he went alternately to Scotland and the Continent, but when his relatives had died he confined himself to foreign lands. Mrs Archer invariably accompanied him; and in this way, during many years, they frequently visited France, Belgium, Holland, Germany, Prussia, Austria, Bohemia, Bavaria, Switzerland, and Italy. He had his favourite spots and scenes, and to these he would more frequently resort. He particularly admired the Tyrol. Its magnificent scenery reminded him of some of the beauties of his loved Scotland. It was not unusual for him to call attention to them by asking, " Is not that Scotch ?" His favourite rivers, besides the Rhine, were the Moselle, for its varied and imposing scenery; the Danube for its bolder, romantic shores. The Rhone and the Meuse he also much admired. In Italy the lake he loved was Como; and in Switzerland he preferred Geneva, Thun, and Lucerne. As these tours drew from him some of the few letters he ever wrote, and as these letters are as descriptive of himself as of the scenes to which they refer, the reader is asked to accompany him during a few of the last of them.

In 1860 Dr and Mrs Archer visited the Tyrol, and from thence they entered Italy. Verona was the first city at which they stopped. They lodged in the hotel " Due Torri," where the splendour of the rooms, with the marble floors and pillars, greatly surprised them. As they took possession of their gorgeous apartment, he said to his wife, " You have often sung,

' I dreamt that I dwelt in marble halls,'

but here we have the *reality*." Here they visited all the marvels, and were principally struck with the marble amphitheatre, but not less so with the ugliness and deformity of numbers of the women, in a land where they expected only the beauty of the Italian face. From Verona they proceeded to Venice. Having hired a comfortable gondola and an intelligent gondolier, they saw many schools of painting and private collections unnoticed in guide-books, and many gems of churches and palaces, all rich in paintings, frescoes, sculptures, and mosaics, but not mentioned in the usual list of sights. On their first Sabbath in Venice, they worshipped in the morning in one of the ancient palaces near the Rialto, and heard a good sermon from these words—" Woe is me, that I dwell in Mesech." It was announced that the place would be shut up for two months, as the clergyman was leaving. The afternoon and evening were consequently spent in retirement. One of their great enjoyments was crossing the Lido, and strolling for hours on the shores of the Adriatic. There, as also on the shores of the Mediterranean, did he sketch some of his most telling discourses. When lounging one evening on the Piazzo St Marco, and admiring its mingled beauties, he suddenly said— " This is undoubtedly a splendid place, but it is a city of the dead, borne down under the iron yoke of oppression; my belief however is, that in a very few years it will be free, and then, what a different aspect will everything wear! We must come and see the change, if God spare us both." Having left Venice with regret, they went next to Milan, and ultimately found their way home, his health greatly improved. When asked why he had not visited Rome, he replied—" I will never do so while the Pope is there;" and he never did, though on one occasion he was within a few hours of the " seven-hilled city."

He was preparing for his tour in May 1862, when he was requested to delay the time of his leaving till after the anniversary of his ordination. The intention was to make him a presentation ere he left. The thing was kept a secret from him; and great, therefore, was his surprise when, after tea, a magnificent time-piece was brought in and placed on the table in front of the pulpit. W. S. Lindsay, Esq., M.P., then took the chair, and, in asking his acceptance of the gift, delivered a beautiful address, which moved all present, and especially the pastor. The reply was in keeping with the occasion,—meek but ardent, feeling but firm. Mr Lindsay had thereafter to leave to attend to his duties in Parliament, and the chair was occupied by John Geikie, Esq., one of the elders, who had been in office for forty-eight years, and has only recently passed away, loved and respected by all. This proved to be one of the last of such happy meetings in Oxendon. The time-piece bore the following inscription :—

"Presented to
The Rev. THOMAS ARCHER, D.D.,
in affectionate recognition
of Thirty Years' faithful Ministry
and kindly Social Intercourse,
by the
Congregation of Oxendon Chapel,
May 5, 1862."

Immediately after this he revisited Italy, and from Genoa addressed the following letter to one of his elders :—

" MY DEAR MR ——,

"We leave this place to-day at one o'clock, travel all night, and hope to reach Florence to-morrow about two o'clock P.M.

" This city is one of the most magnificent we ever saw. We arrived in it on Thursday, and every hour, or walk, or drive, has only brought out new beauty or grandeur. It is situated on a gulf of the Mediterranean, whose waters are as blue as the sky above, and clear as the air is light and free. It forms a crescent. In the centre is the harbour, of which I have a view from our windows, where I write. Around are hills, covered to their tops with rich villas, and the most exquisite groves, and flowers, and foliage. One street is composed almost entirely of palaces and great government offices, and at the end is a church—not a cathedral—the like of which I have never seen. Its floors are of marble, and so are its numerous pillars, crowned with the richest gold ornaments; and its ceiling crowded—not confused—with the most glorious pictures, in the brightest colours. In short, we shall leave Genoa with great regret, and, not least of all, leave our apartments with regret, they are so magnificent, and would be so useful if we were Roman Catholics, for one of our rooms contains an altar—no doubt used when this house was not an hotel, but a palace.

" The heat here has been awful. It was so in Turin, from which we came to Genoa ; but there you have always a shelter

—its wide and vast streets having on each side a piazza like the Old Quadrant, but much wider, having coloured blinds before them, which exclude the sun so, that, in the hottest hour of the hottest day, you can walk with perfect coolness. There is nothing of that kind here ; so that you get, for six or seven hours, the merciless beams of a fierce sun upon your pate—the consequences of which my poor Martha has felt, in a violent attack of ———, which, I am glad to say, is now abating.

"In coming here we crossed again the Alps by Mount Cenis. Wonderful !—wonderful ! beyond all language—beyond all thought ! Its summit is 6780 feet above the sea, which we reached, drawn by a succession of ten mules and two horses— all sturdy creatures. It forms one continuation of zig-zags, and at every point you get some new view. The sun is burning with a strong glare—the snow is now lying above you, now below you, in vast sheets, and just *white* as *snow*, and—I can say no more. Underneath it are forests of green trees, and below them fields of corn—ripe-yellow, and stacked or stocked ; amid them, gardens of grapes, peaches, almonds, and melons —does it not make your mouth water ?—while at the foot runs a rapid, brawling, mountain-stream. When we reached the summit, the mules were taken away, and down we rushed, with a succession of two horses, through gorges and ravines, and roads not much wider than two omnibuses, at the rate of twelve or fourteen miles an hour, 5000 feet above the valley, which stretched in surpassing grandeur and variety as far as the eye, aided by our powerful glass, could reach.

" We had thirteen hours that day, from six in the morning

until seven P.M., and such a day we have never spent, and, in all likelihood, shall never spend again. We return from Italy by another pass into Switzerland, down the Rhine, and then home. You will be good enough to announce, on the last Sabbath of the month, that I shall, all being well, be in Oxendon the following Sabbath, to meet applicants for admission to the Lord's Table, and to distribute tokens. I have not much time for writing; the morning is so lovely and inviting, I cannot stay longer in the house—so, farewell.

"Very truly yours,

"THOMAS ARCHER."

Mrs Archer thus refers to what remains of this happy tour :—

"A letter from Florence, written about a week after the above, shows that, as they proceeded, their impressions of Italy, so far as the buildings and the galleries of the fine arts were concerned, were more striking and startling. Dr Archer said that, ' notwithstanding he had formed such high conceptions of Florence, it surpassed his most sanguine expectations.' But there must be some alloy to every pleasure, and the constant sight of so many objects of squalid misery, which were continually crossing their path, was most depressing and sickening. Dr A. remarked, that three classes of persons abounded in every part of Italy—*soldiers*, *priests*, and *beggars;* the latter the most importunate and impudent, and sometimes so filthy as to be really revolting."

When they left Flórence for the shores of Lake Maggiore,

they settled down there for a rest at Arona, an enchanting place, combining in one landscape everything that goes to make a perfect picture. The delight, however, must be felt to be appreciated, for it cannot be expressed in words. He and his companion revelled in sensation of luxuriant repose, when seated in their pretty apartment, away from the noise of a busy city. He was a lover of the fine arts, and during his travels had thoroughly examined all the galleries of Paris, the Hague, Munich, Dresden, and Florence ; yet here he remarked, "What a sight is here before us—how sublime ! I confess I do not care if I never see another painting or another piece of sculpture, for, however magnificent in design or exquisite in execution the works of *man* are, yet they pall upon the senses." And as again he cast his eyes over the lake, he said, "Who could ever weary with gazing on the glorious works of the Great Creator, in which there are endless varieties of beauty, and always something fresh and lovely, sublime and exalting ?"

Upon the second day of their stay here, they went to the market to see what was to be sold. Mrs A. missed her husband for a short time. On his return, he said, "Whilst you have been busy at the fig and peach stalls, I have been patronising one, the sight of which has cheered my heart, and gratified me more than all the wonders and beauties of this country that we have witnessed." His wife was all curiosity to learn what had pleased him so much, when he informed her that it was a stall with *Bibles* for sale, and that they seemed to be eagerly bought, for there were several customers. And "Oh !" he added, "I pray that the teaching of the Holy Spirit may accompany the reading of the Word; and what a glorious land will this be, with all its natural advantages, when it becomes not only *politically*, but what will be far better, *religiously* free !"

His health was greatly benefited by this tour; but having again overtasked his strength, he became very ill in the spring of 1863, and left London for Margate, from which place he wrote to his people thus :—

"MARGATE.

" MY BELOVED FRIENDS,

"When we met on Sabbath week to unite in heart-felt thanks to our Heavenly Father for our common mercies, and solemnly to commit ourselves to his tender care for the future, I mentioned that I would take an opportunity of writing what I could not utter—some expressions of gratitude for your great, your untiring kindness in my recent illness. This I now do, very briefly, but very *cordially*. But, first, let me mention my great and rapid improvement since I came here. The change of scene, the fresh breezes, the freedom from excitement and close study, light mental amusement—all have promoted this. Of course I need not say I am not yet myself. An illness so severe as mine, and of which my physician tells me I have no notion, produces results which it takes time and care to remove ; but for this I look with confident hope, that I shall recover from the present, and be stronger for work—at least for a time—in the future. Whichever way I turn, I can only speak of mercy. It is plain that my illness has long been coming on, through an overworking brain, which demands more equable labour hereafter. The lesson, therefore, though severe, will, I trust, be salutary, and you, I pray, may reap the benefits of it.

"Allow me now to thank you for your constant inquiries after me during my confinement to my room, for your many expressions of kindness, and for your earnest prayers on my behalf. I cannot write to *each*, and therefore I address this catholic letter to all. I cannot trust myself to speak, for my feelings would overpower me, and almost, if not altogether, befool me. I therefore adopt the seemingly colder but not less affectionate mode of writing to you.

"God bless you all, my people! The Lord make his light to shine in your houses, and strengthen your roof-tree! The Lord bless you and your children from henceforth and for ever. Think of me and *her*, at your family altars, as we think of you at ours.

"Farewell till we meet again in our sanctuary-home. Love to all—old and young, rich and poor.

"Your grateful and loving

"THOMAS ARCHER."

"*P.S.*—I am not quite sure whether I shall be in old Oxendon next Sabbath. Much will depend on the weather. But whether or not present in the body, we shall meet in spirit around the cross, the grave, the throne of the loved One."

In July thereafter he revisited some of the old scenes on the Continent, particularly in Austria and Bavaria, and then returned by the Rhine,—a river with which he was thoroughly familiar, having often explored its varied beauties, ascended its mountains, examined the ruins of its castles, and wandered through its valleys and glens, of which he never seemed to weary. The store of health which he brought home with him, carried him through his autumn and winter work both at Oxendon and elsewhere. He again drooped in spring, and in May 1864 he treated himself to a fortnight in Paris. There he was taken alarmingly ill, but recovered sufficiently to resume work on his return. But it was now painfully evident that his strength was weakening by the way. In the month of July he and his devoted partner started again, and, for the last time, for Switzerland. They had to travel very leisurely. They rested for some days in Boulogne, then again in Paris, and at length they reached Geneva. His vigour was gradually returning, his spirits were good, and his hopes revived. He addressed the following graphic and touching letters from Geneva :—

"GENEVA, *July* 27, 1864.

"We have now been, my dear friends and brethren, a week in this charming spot, on the borders of the Lake Leman, which our room commands and overlooks for many a mile. The spot is one for lingering—enchanting by its endless drives and walks. Along either side of the lake (itself quiet, yet noble) run lines of towering mountains. It is a gem of the sweetest and serenest, most brilliantly and boldly set, where neither gem nor setting eclipse each other, but both display the grandeur of their common Author. These all indeed tend to fix, elevate, yet soothe the mind ; and it were sad if they did not touchingly, sensibly, melt the heart into holy awe and love.

" But other, though inferior and varied associations, cluster around Geneva and its neighbourhood. I may mention only two representative antipodal men, Calvin and Voltaire. We went to Ferney yesterday, the residence of the latter, and most certainly it is a lovely spot; but its former lord,—What was he, and where is he, and what has he done? A life incessantly, absorbingly devoted to one end, marked in its course by terrific volcanic flashes of success in France, closed in defeat; while the body of the philosopher of Ferney rests not there, nor in the *Pantheon* of Paris, but, stolen from its last place of sepulture, has been long purposely destroyed.

" Now, very true, Calvin's grave is not well and surely distinguished here. A little stone with his initials marks the conjectured spot where he lies. He despised the pomp of monument. Perhaps he sought for *that* in more than *marble* grandeur, in his writings—in their effects; above all, in the testimony of Him whose cross he exalted and whose law he maintained and vindicated.

" It is a glorious lesson, and in this age of assault, in various forms, on the Cross and the crucified One, furnishes a blessed hope and encouragement to the humble disciples of the Redeemer.

" You will hardly then wonder—I am sure you will be glad to hear—that, in such scenery and circumstances, we are both much better. Our health has certainly improved, and our spirits are much freer and more elastic. I do not see that it could be otherwise. I am sure that when, from the roof of my hotel, we looked last evening on Mont Blanc, just tinged with a soft golden hue of the setting sun, it was enough to cheer and give new life to the man. But with all this physical magnificence and loveliness are associated the hallowed thought that we are not forgotten by you—you are not by us. We leave this on Saturday, only to continue our Swiss rambles ; but, wherever we are, *home* affections are uppermost and tenderest. May I just express my hope that, in this time and season of wandering, you are keeping close by Oxendon, paying respect, by your attendance, to the ministers who occupy my pulpit, and thus paying respect to my ministry to you ?

" Again, may God smile on you all, and largely bless you.

" Ever your own true and loving

" THOMAS ARCHER."

The day after, he wrote the following letter to a friend, one of his congregation :—

" GENEVA, *July 28th,* 1864.

" MY DEAR MR S.,—In a letter which I wrote for Oxendon, I referred to a glance which we had on Tuesday evening of Mont Blanc. Last night we had an overwhelmingly grand view. After dinner, we went to the belvedere on the roof of our hotel, and we waited quietly for sunset, and were amply, more than amply, rewarded. The giant himself, and his clusters and ranges of peaks, were in full view, though forty-five miles off. They appeared successively in the most varied lights and hues —now silver grey, now light and delicate golden tinted, now warm in the rose glow, and, finally, as they ceased to catch the last rays of the dying day, in the cold, bright whiteness of their native snow.

" It was a sight never to be forgotten—to be seen only in

silence, and which would force upon the most undevout mind that looked upon the surrounding Alpine rock-waves as but the dust of His feet, but now all bathed in beauty and glory, —' Thyself how glorious then !' We lingered and lingered, till time bade us retire to our chamber. We propose to-night, if favourable, to repeat the pleasure. I say, if favourable, for ' Murray' tells us that the giant only condescends to show himself sixty days in the year. If so, we are special favourites, for he has condescended to show himself to us two nights out of six. It is such things that cast a spell around *Leman.* Some, indeed, care not for these things,—they are unromantic, tasteless Gallios. Such a person addressed us at dinner this week, wondering how we could stop so long in Geneva,—what was to see in it? *Faugh,* the clay-souled Cockney!—I was born in Scotland !

"We remain here till Saturday, when we remove farther up the lake, and our Sabbath will be spent in Lausanne—we hope in the company of Dr Macfarlane's daughter, who is there at school. We shall likely pass the Monday there, visiting Chillon, and on—on—Tuesday—reaching Zurich on Saturday, where we shall wander about for a few days reviving old memories, and laying the foundation of new ones. After leaving Switzerland, we shall get on the Rhine, and take it very quietly, as is our wont in this pilgrimage. Everything has been hitherto pleasant,—delightfully so, the weather all we could desire,—until to-day, which has been terribly hot; but where I write, we have a delicious breeze from the lake. My wife is busy at her window knitting, but finds time to send to you and your wife affectionate regards.

"Many thanks for your papers,—*Scotsman* came to hand this morning, *Telegraph* yesterday,—they are a great treat. Any you forward to me after this, address,—

"Poste Restante
"à Zurich.

"Be good enough to tell my friend Mr B——, with thanks for the *Times* received this morning, that we get that paper at all the hotels, and, if he sends me any paper at all, the *Daily News* would be a greater treat. But I forget that *beggars must not be choosers.*

"I think, my dear friend, that I have exhausted my budget, —probably exhausted your patience. Don't forget us to your neighbours. May every blessing rest on your own house!

"Ever most truly yours,

"THOMAS ARCHER."

The following was written to his congregation:—

"ZURICH, *August* 10, 1864.

"As by the time this reaches you we shall have left Switzerland, it may be best, my dear friends, to send you the last loving epistle on this part of my present furlough. Zurich, from which I write, is a most lovely and interesting locality. I write on the banks of its quiet and pastoral waters—crowded along their shores with white Swiss cottages and mansions, and villages rising from and peering among endless vineyards and fruit groves. The town is occupied by a most active, energetic, and prosperous people; and when I have said *Protestant* people, I have explained the fact. The spirit of Zwingle, their head, still animates them; his fiery sword-bearing spirit is not

extinct, though modified. Luther, Melancthon, Calvin, Zwingle
—how much the same, yet how different! The same in love
to the truth—how different in the agencies of its promotion!
Strong, earnest appeal ; soft, gentle pathos of love ; acute,
polished, classical scholarship, or the use of physical power in the
contentions of the age and the land. But however misguided or
ill-judging, the undaunted champion of Zurich has consecrated
and perpetuated, in his own blood on the battle-field, the independence and advance of Fatherland. Another view, however, must be taken of the Canton. Its spiritual condition is
sad in the extreme. It is lamented even by remaining, lingering Zurich piety. Pious men here feel that they can *do* no
more. All that is left is to pray for souls around them, and
they ask *your* prayers; and will you not give them for a country
whose motto is destined again to be realised after a long spiritual eclipse—'After darkness comes the light?' The fact seems
this, that in too many lands, certainly *here*, the Reformation
gave and secured to the people an eagle-eyed and eagle-hearted
independence of thought. Its dove-like purity and tenderness,
and genial love, were not attained, scarcely aimed at. Zwingle's
blood nurtured Swiss manhood. A *nobler*, shed on a *nobler
field*, is needed to originate and nurture Swiss sainthood ; and
in answer to the prayers of the Church, that, too, shall be
poured forth, and applied universally.

"We leave this to-morrow (Thursday) for Constance, the
scene of the martyrdom of John Huss. Every spot, indeed,
of this land is rich with the memories of the past; is it Utopian
to imagine that it is the teeming cradle of a more glorious
future, and that this mountain-girt land of lake and waterfall is

destined once more to sound to Europe the watch-cry of liberty and the Cross?

" From Switzerland,—which I leave with regret, as who would not who has rambled in it as we have done, quietly and happily? —we pass on to the Rhine, and then to our *two* homes—Hans Place and Oxendon.

"I have not space enough to give my regards *individually*, but to all I beg to send the feeble expression of the sincerest esteem. My earnest desires are,—

" That in all our relations we may abide in peace universally and for ever:

" That the elders may continue with myself, as we have hitherto done, in Christian counsel and concord:

" That the managers, president, treasurer, and secretary, and all, may act prudently and affectionately:

" That the Sabbath-school teachers may be cheered amid all their arduous and self-denying labours by His blessing and presence:

" And finally, that in every house and chamber of this church, God's covenanted blessing may rest, closely, practically, and savingly.

" Meantime, my dearest friends, I bid you the farewell of your sincere friend and minister,

" Thomas Archer."

On their way home they remained some days at Boulogne for sea air, which always benefited him, and reached Hans Place on the 26th of August 1864.

Before closing the sketch of his Continental tours, it deserves

special notice that he was a most conscientious observer of
the Sabbaths when on travel,—and all the more so when he
saw that blessed day utterly disregarded. He always sought
out (if one could be found), a Protestant place of worship, and
in general expressed himself satisfied with the service.   On
one occasion, in Chamberry, the landlord of their hotel sent
" garçon " along with him and Mrs Archer to show them a
French Protestant chapel. " Garçon " guided them to a Roman
Catholic church; and when remonstrated with, declared that
he knew of no other.   On returning, the landlord gave them
more specific directions, and by and by they found themselves
standing before a *cabaret*—a drinking-shop—upon which their
conductor expressed his surprise that a house of prayer should
be found in such a place.   They ascended to the top, and
found about sixty persons, several of them soldiers, engaged in
worship.   The minister was praying,—after which a psalm was
sung, and then the 14th, 15th, and 16th verses of the 10th
chapter of John were read and expounded in a very simple,
truthful, but telling manner.   On concluding, he called upon
one of the soldiers to pray, which was done in an impressive
style.   On descending, Mrs Archer said, " Surely this has
been a most solemn service, and the place the house of God
and the gate of heaven.   When sitting in the apartment, I
could not help thinking of the 'upper room' in Jerusalem."
" The very same thought," he replied, " passed through my
mind." On inquiry, they found that they could not enjoy a
similar treat in the evening, as that service was conducted
in the Barracks, exclusively for the military.

On Sabbath the 28th August he occupied his own pulpit,

and seemed so much improved in health, that all present were cheered, and fondly hoped that their beloved pastor would be spared to them for some time; and warm indeed were the congratulations he received. On the 11th of September was the Communion. He preached in the morning from John i. 29,— " Behold the Lamb of God, which taketh away the sin of the world!" combined with 1 Corinthians v. 7, " Christ our passover is sacrificed for us," following up the subject in the address at the table. The solemnity of the discourse, and the touching pathos with which it was delivered, will not be soon forgotten by those who were privileged to hear it. In the evening he preached from 2 Corinthians v. 14, " The love of Christ constraineth us,"—a discourse which was remarkable for its intense fervour.

On the 27th of September he and Mrs Archer went to spend a few days with their kind friends at " Randall's Park." He seemed to enjoy the visit very much, and derived benefit from it, as he preached twice the following Sabbath with considerable vigour, and without being over-fatigued.

He had been applied to by some of the brethren to know if he would accept the office of Moderator, at the meeting of the English Synod, which was to be held in London on the 10th of October, but he declined, saying, "He wished that compliment paid to his friend Mr Redpath, who was the senior minister in London." When the Synod met, he had for his guests in Hans Place his two old and beloved friends, Dr Crichton of Liverpool, and Dr Skinner of Blackburn. He greatly enjoyed their society, though he was all the time under great suffering. With difficulty he managed to go and hear the Moderator (Dr Crichton) preach the "Synod Sermon," which was to him as "waters to a thirsty soul." On the following Sabbath, Dr Skinner supplied his pulpit, that he might enjoy a rest; and he did enjoy one. He could only attend in the morning. The preacher and the hearer have both, since then, entered upon the everlasting rest of the saints. "They were lovely and pleasant in their lives, and in their death they were not (long) divided."

CHAPTER IX.

THE ENDING.

S we approach the few remaining days of this pleasant, busy, and useful " Life," the desire becomes strong, not only to know how they were spent, but to glean as much as we can from the lips and services of the now evidently dying pastor of Oxendon. So firmly had his soul grasped and luxuriated in the sublime service of preaching, that he almost in agony relaxed his hold of the pulpit. He was now so feeble in the limbs that he could not ascend farther than the desk; but when he was once in, and fairly begun, the usual fervour and eloquence appeared. He has but three more Sabbaths in which to work. It will be alike interesting and instructive to watch the ending of such a pastorate.

His text on the morning of the 23d October 1864, was from Revelation xxii. 1,—" He showed me a pure river of water of life;" which he divided thus:—

1. What the river is.
2. Whence the river flows.

3. Where the river runs.

4. To whom the river comes.

5. What does the river do?

He spoke on these topics as one who himself stood on the brink of that river of which he so beautifully discoursed. He did not preach in the evening, being necessitated to remain at home.

Next Sabbath (30th October), his morning text was taken from Revelation xxii. 2,—" The tree of life." After the introduction, he remarked that the text contained a figurative representation of the Cross,—*first*, as a tree; and, *secondly*, as the tree of life. The division was as follows :—

I.

Let us contemplate the Cross under the *figure of a "tree."* Its resemblances :—

1*st*, Progressive development—oak—acorn.

2*d*, Preparation for its appearance. Husbandman chooses and prepares the soil.

3*d*, Some trees there are which derive their flourishing and strength from the application of *blood*—the VINE. This plant of renown springs from a soil saturated with blood—the blood of Christ.

CONTRAST (1.)—This tree is *universally transplantable*, suited to all climes.

(2.)—Perpetually flourishing—no storms, however frequent or severe, can hurt it—its umbrageous arms are ever spread for the shelter of all who repair to it.

II.

Let us now contemplate the Cross under the idea of the
"*tree of life :*"—

1st, The Cross is *life-inspiring.*

2d, This tree conveys not only life but HEALTH.—Ezekiel
xlvii. 12—" Leaves for the healing," etc.

Moralists, philosophers, toiling in unreality, are weak and
tottering, but here is health.

3d, Nor is this all; it provides for the nurture of vigorous
health. It is *laden with fruit.* (Ezekiel xlvii. 12.) Not like the
fruit of the Dead Sea, but rich in nourishment.

4th, Its transition opens a *source of pleasure*—fruit sweet.
(Song of Solomon ii. 3.)

INFERENCE :—The fulness of Christ for every condition.

III.

Now, of this tree thus defined, the passage asserts some
prominent *characteristic facts :—*

Its central position.—Its accessibleness.

1st, Its productiveness is *uniform* and *constant*—other trees
bloom for a season—this every month—perennial.

2d, Its productiveness is *boundlessly profuse*—its endless
variety—all manner of fruit, for the healing of grief, ignorance,
disease, sin, death.

3d, Its productiveness is derived from its *proximity to the
river of life.*

4th, Its productiveness is ALONE.

REFLECTIONS :—

1st, Contrast the perpetual richness of this tree with the

short life of those who sit under its shade—they are gone—
the tree is here still.

2*d*, Joys of heaven.

3*d*, Contemplate its future destined expansion.

His last working Sabbath now dawned—6th November 1864.
As if under presentiment, he arose earlier than usual, and gave
himself to prayer and meditation. It had ever been his custom
to retire with Mrs Archer, before leaving for the house of God,
and implore the Divine help and blessing for the day. On the
morning of this particular Sabbath, his partner was unable to
rise. She had been for some weeks laid up under sore trouble.
When he entered her room, she was weeping, not for herself,
but for him. "This is the heaviest trial," she said, " the
Almighty has ever inflicted upon me, to lay me aside when I
see you so much in need of my help." He replied, " Pray do
not weep ; you will break my heart if you do. The affliction
is indeed severe, but it is His will, and we must bow with submission: we know that He afflicts none willingly, and this blow,
heavy as it is, is dealt by the hand of a kind and gracious Father.
Let us both *try* to say in sincerity, ' Thy will be done.' " He
then added : "The Searcher of hearts knows what I have suffered on witnessing your sufferings, but you must look to that
Source to which you have so often led others for comfort.
Our faithful Friend will support and raise you up in His own
good time. He has given you wonderful patience, and we
have both good reason for thankfulness that you are still alive
and somewhat better." Before he left her, she hinted at her
purpose to leave her bed that day, and receive him on his

return from Oxendon. She said she had, during that night, agonized in prayer to be so enabled, and she believed she would be. He affectionately besought her not to rise, as the physician had assured him of the danger she was in. He then told her of the subject upon which he was going to preach, and said: " I am well prepared, and I feel that strength will be imparted to me. Oh ! is not the subject a glorious one; and I trust that this morning's service may be blessed to all who shall be present." Having prayed with her, he left, saying, " You know, dearest, you will not lose the sermon, for I can give it to you when I return. You must pray for me in your retirement, as I shall do for you in the sanctuary, and we may rest assured that our prayers will be heard." One of the elders having kindly‧ called to accompany him, he took his last journey to the pulpit. His text was from Rev. xxi. 23,— " For the glory of the Lord did lighten it, and the Lamb was the light thereof." He had written this sermon more fully out than was his usual, as if his last offering on the altar should be as golden as he could make it. His introduction was on the nature and importance of light, it being essential alike to animal and vegetable life—also to health. He then drew some vivid pictures of its effects on scenes he had witnessed in his travels. These were his divisions :—

1. The light of heaven is original and supreme.

2. The light of heaven is universally diffused.

3. The light of heaven equally and uniformly acts.

4. The light of heaven is perpetual.

5. The light of heaven reveals and shines on the purest scenes, only to bless them.

Having finished one of the most heavenly discourses he had been ever heard to preach, amid the tears falling and the prayers rising of many who listened, some of them, impressed that they should hear his voice and see his face no more, pressed forward to speak with him and shake hands. He left old Oxendon behind him, and went home to equip himself for another temple and another service. Mrs Archer had risen, as she had resolved; she was anxiously awaiting his arrival; she heard the sound of wheels; she was seated at the window above, and looked out; she saw the elder and the coachman lifting him from the carriage. Having been confined to bed for three weeks, during which time he had, untold to her, become gradually weaker and weaker, she had no idea that his strength was so far gone, and was accordingly greatly distressed on his account. When she asked how he felt, he replied, " Oh, pretty well; but I should be much better if I could see you suffer less." He had with difficulty got up to her room, and after being seated for a while, he said, " I earnestly hope you may not be thrown back by this exertion." He then put into her hand the outline of the sermon he had just preached, and said, " Though I say it, I don't think I ever preached a more effective sermon, and I believe my own people will long re-member it. They listened with the most profound attention, seemed deeply touched, and I saw the eyes of many suffused with tears." A witness states that the whole of that morning's service was unspeakably solemn, and that in one of his prayers especially he seemed to be carried beyond himself, as he wrestled with God for the eternal salvation of his people.

He did not leave the house that week. He told a friend who

called, that he was taking rest to be fit for the Communion service on the coming Sabbath. When alone, he said to Mrs
Archer, "Do you remember what day this is?" She replied,
"It is Thursday." "Oh!" he rejoined, "I mean the day of
the month." She said, "It is the 10th." He then with some
emphasis asked, "Well, dearest, but do you not remember what
particular day this is?" "Yes," replied his tender wife; "but I
did not wish to refer to it: this is the anniversary of our
wedding-day." He then added, "I have been thinking a good
deal about it; we have been married twenty-eight years to-day."
Mrs Archer tried to say, in a cheerful tone, "Yes, I have
served 'you four apprenticeships." "You *have*, indeed," he
said, "and a *faithful* serving it has been."

Much to his sorrow, he was too weak, when the Sabbath
returned, to go to his beloved Oxendon. The Communion
service was conducted by his kind friend, Mr Redpath, who
read from the pulpit the following address:—

"November 13, 1864.

"To my own people, only the more endeared by affliction
and sympathy:—

"When these few lines are read to you, you will be seated
around His table, where I had fondly hoped to be your companion and friend, but to Him it seems better otherwise; and
my communion with you will be in your own pews this morning, where my heart will point out every one of you.

"Your thoughts, no doubt, will be addressed to that death
on which I meant to have pondered with you in reflections
which were suggested at Geneva, and matured for Oxendon.

That death, let me beseech you, consider in its origin and its personal moral results; beginning in love, it originates, sustains, and inflames it in the saint. Let me implore you, therefore, in the name of the Cross, to love Him who bore it, to love Him growingly, to love Him practically, and never to stop in your advancing love until you can answer the question, 'Lovest thou me?' by the simple reply, 'Lord, thou knowest all things, thou knowest that I love thee.'

"My beloved friends, this love to Him will extend to all His; to the lambs of His flock; to your dear little ones; to the aged disciples who have watched over you with the tenderest affection; to your middle-aged companions who have fought the battle of life with you, and who, after many a hard pull, have reached the summit-level, and must soon turn their faces homewards to heaven. Such love will hallow every relation, mitigate every difficulty, soothe all cares, and breathe a Bethel-spirit over your firesides.

"I ask not your love for me, for I know I have it; its proofs are far too numerous and too constant for me to question. I can only add, most humbly and most sincerely, 'Oh, that I were worthier of it!' However, continue that love and your prayers for the present—a brighter time of strength and health and usefulness may be in store for me; and even now, over your Table, may be rising that Sun that shall cast over our future its most bright and glorious light.

"May God grant it. Amen, and amen."

"For a few days after this," Mrs Archer writes, "there was no apparent change. He read and conversed, was cheerful and happy, but was unable to leave his room. He often spoke of the mercy of God in dealing so kindly with him, and in giving his wife sufficient strength to be beside him ; but towards the end of the week, a person injudiciously told him of the dangerous illness of Dr Macfarlane of Clapham, which distressed him exceedingly. It seemed to weigh heavily on his mind, and depressed his spirits, and he would repeatedly say, ' What will my old and dear friend, John Macfarlane, think of me for not going to see him when he is so ill ? I wish I could manage to get to Clapham to speak a word of comfort to him.' His wife endeavoured to calm his anxiety, by saying she was sure Dr Macfarlane would not wish him to make the effort in his weak state, and could not expect him if he knew how ill he was."

On Sabbath the 20th, his elder called as usual, and this attention gratified him very much. After some conversation, he gave him the following letter, to be read to the congregation :—

"*November* 20*th*.

" My Beloved People,—My last letter was written by my wife's enfeebled hand. The effort was, in *itself*, painful and injurious. The present is written by a fast friend to the Church and to myself; but whatever the pen that writes, the letter itself is the *heart epistle* of Thomas Archer to you, my loved and loving ones.

" I confess, when I preached last, that I had no idea of my own feeble state, long creeping on. At last my illness quickened its speed. The power of a man was gone, and to the bowed

down one was given the impotency of a child. Of this I became terribly aware, when, grasping the arm of my living staff,
I had but to crawl across my bedroom. Thus God has been
pleased to bow me down. I begin to feel slightly better; but,
alas! at my time of life we cannot remount the hill so rapidly
as we have been driven down it. Much patience and care are
demanded, and must be given, and, God helping me, shall be
employed. I cannot say that I expect to be the man I have
been, but still I cherish a hope, fond though foolish, that there
is still some work in me for Him and for you. Meantime, I
must throw myself on your continued forbearance and your
constant prayers. Keep together, my dear people, in love,
although the centre should be such a poor one as myself. Our
duty, our prosperity, our future, our present, all depend upon
this.

"I need not say my afflicted wife unites with me in deepest
gratitude for the marks of love shown to me in my present
affliction.

"I remain, my dear flock, yours affectionately in Christ,

"THOMAS ARCHER."

No apparent change seemed to take place, but he said that
he thought he felt a little better. On Wednesday the 23d, his
wife's aunt called very early, before he had risen. She was
urging the necessity of having a nurse, seeing how jaded and
ill Mrs A. looked, and said, "If you continue, as you have
been doing, to sit up night after night, I am sure you will sink
under the fatigue, and then what will be the consequence to
both!" Mrs A. implored her to desist, and, at anyrate, to

speak softly, lest her husband should hear the conversation. He had heard it.

When he rose, and had prayed with the family, he walked for some time about the room, leaning on his wife's arm. "We are a feeble pair," he said, "for I feel you tottering when trying to support me; but you are certainly better than I once thought you would be. I feared you would not recover, and oh! what reason we both have to be grateful to the Giver of all good, for His continued and multiplied mercies. We can raise our Ebenezer, and say, 'Hitherto hath the Lord helped us,' and let the past be a token to us for the future. He is all-sufficient. Let us trust and hope, and pray on." In the afternoon, when they were sitting by the fire, he said, "Do you mean to get a nurse for me, as I heard your aunt propose this morning?" She replied, "*Never, never,* so long as our gracious Father will give me strength to wait upon you." He said, with much warmth, "*Just like you, just like you!* my own loved one; I felt sure you would never allow a hireling to touch me."

On the following evening, the 26th, when he had dictated the letter to be read on Sabbath, he complained of exhaustion, and said he thought he would lie down on the bed for a little; but his wife, knowing it would fatigue him to rise again to prepare for the night, suggested that he should take some refreshment, and then rest for the night. When he was comfortably in bed, Mrs Archer said, "I trust God will give you a good night's rest, my all on earth." He turned, and, fixing his eyes lovingly upon her, replied, "I may well call *you,* 'my all on earth,' for what should I have been, and what could I do

without you now? God will reward you for your undying
love to me, and your unwearied attention. I never can repay
you." She replied, " The richest reward the Almighty can
bestow on me is to restore you to health."   To which he
said, " If it be His will to raise me up again, to preach His
glorious Gospel, I shall be grateful ; but if my work here is
finished, and He sees fit to call me home, I am ready to
depart, and I can say, with deep sincerity and submission,
' Thy will be done.' "   He had a sweetly calm night, and on
the following morning, when his elder called, he told him he
was no worse.

Among other matters, he mentioned that he should like the
198th Hymn to be sung, and then gave him the following
letter, to be read to the congregation :—

"18 HANS PLACE, *November 27th.*

" If, my dear friends, you are not tired of hearing, I am not
tired of dictating an occasional epistle from my solitude—quite
the reverse.   Shut out for the present from you by the mysterious providence of God, we are cut off from that intercom-
munion of sense, the play of voice and ear, the interchange
of the eye melting and reciprocating the kind-hearted glance ;
nothing then remains but the expression of the letter of affection.   I fondly trust that I need hardly assure you that you are
very deeply on and in my heart.   I am sure I am very much
on yours.   I had a belief of this long ago, but of its depth I
only know now.   It is only, my beloved ones, when trials like
that which has now befallen me occur, that we get the test of
our faith in His fidelity, and our brother's heart.   Our faith

how strong, His faithfulness how unchanging, and how wisely it waits its time for action ! And our brother's soul, which may often have seemed cold and indifferent, is now pained with anxious care, melts with liberal love, and soars with dove-like swiftness from the bedside of the sufferer to the throne of the sufferer's and supplicant's Friend and Saviour.

"All these I have often felt, and feel doubly now, and they act like a balm upon my sad, and, alas! impatient spirit—impatient to be at work again—impatient at the burden which, by my forced inaction, I impose upon you and your resources. But still I feel that this must continue for some time, that all this I must bear, and you share with me ; and that meantime our common duty is to say, with our Redeemer,—but alas! at what a distance of patient faith,—' *Thy will be done!*' It is in this spirit and temper I would urge on you and on myself the one peculiarity in His case and ours, well worthy of consideration. My Master had no friends; when He suffered, the storm drove them all away. My affliction has brought them out, and brought them near.

"'Bless the Lord, O my soul, and all that is within me, be stirred up to bless his holy name.'

"I cannot close without expressing my gratitude on behalf of my afflicted wife and myself, for your continued inquiries and prayers. Individual thanks would be invidious ; they are due to all, and are hereby offered to all. To my elders, managers, Sabbath-school teachers, and Sabbath scholars,—in short, to every one of the fellowships of Oxendon, the attendants of our common house of prayer and praise.

"Thank God, I feel myself still improving, and hope by and

by to make more rapid progress. Meantime, pray earnestly and agonize for your afflicted friend and pastor,

"Thomas Archer."

"This Sabbath," writes Mrs Archer, "was spent very pleasantly, though not in Oxendon." He read a considerable portion of it to himself, and his wife read several chapters to him which he selected, and made some beautiful remarks upon them. His mind was in a most holy frame, and he conversed a good deal on the joys and bliss of the future state. He sat up that night, and conducted the family worship, and mentioned several persons by name whom he wished especially to commend to the care of his heavenly Father. The parents of a babe that was born that day came particularly under his notice, and his petitions for the infant were most touching and earnest. He seemed to *yearn* for the salvation of the little stranger. Whilst he was praying, his wife noticed that he placed his hand upon his chest, and she feared he felt pain there. He assured her he did not, but had a little soreness in his throat. When the time drew near for retiring to rest, he said to Mrs Archer, "Do you think of lying down to-night?" She replied, "I did say that, as you did not need anything last night, perhaps I might try and take a short rest." He made no reply, which took her by surprise. She asked, "Would you like me to sit up to-night?" and he answered, "It seems an act of cruelty to ask you to do so, after so many nights' vigilant watching." She immediately replied, "Not at all; I am quite able to sit up; and if it will be any comfort to you, I shall be glad to do it." He said, "*Perhaps you had better.*" Few as these words were, they spoke volumes to her, for she knew he felt ill, although he would not own it. He went to rest, and she took her wonted seat at his bedside, with a sinking and sorrowing heart. He slept calmly for some hours, and when he awoke and saw her, he said, "What! still in the same place, my sleepless, faithful watcher." After taking a warm drink, he fell asleep again, and did not awake until after the post was delivered on the following morning. Hearing his wife's pen, he said, "To whom are you writing?" She replied, "I am answering a letter that came from Sneinton this morning." He inquired its purport, and she told him it was an application for him to preach for the schools. They had made the same request last year, and then she had told them he was in very delicate health, and could not do it, but, if spared, and more robust, he would be glad to serve them at some future time. He said, "But what have you said *now?*" She answered, "I have said that you are still very delicate, and therefore you cannot make any engagements so far distant as May 1865." "*Quite wise, quite wise,*" was his remark; "because, you know, after our May Communion, if it be His will, we purpose going *abroad.*" (*Two days* after this he was AT HOME with the REDEEMED.)

When Mrs Archer gave him breakfast this morning, he said, "Do not press me to eat, for I feel just as I did when I was in Paris last spring. It is a miserably wet day, and the weather has a great effect upon me; but I shall be better by and by." His wife begged him to allow her to send for the physician; but he said there was no necessity, for that her love made her over-anxious, and she thought he was worse than he really was,

Q

and he felt sure the slight pain in his throat would soon wear away. She then urged that it would be a great satisfaction to *herself* to hear the opinion of the physician, who might prescribe something to give him relief, but he seemed so unwilling to accede to the proposal, that she ceased to press it.

He rose at the usual hour, and, when dressed, read to himself, but did not converse much. His wife avoided conversation purposely, thinking it might irritate the throat, and read aloud to amuse him. This day passed, the hour of rest again came round, and he slept sweetly and soundly the whole night. On the morning of Tuesday the 29th, when he awoke, he was really cheerful and chatty, and spoke without difficulty ; there was apparently a marked change for the better. He made an excellent breakfast, swallowing with ease, and when he had finished, he said, " You see, my own, how much better I am to-day ; I told you I thought I should. God has been kind to us ; let us now give him thanks for his tender mercies to us both." After the prayer, which was remarkable for its comprehensiveness and fervour and pathos, he proposed rising, as he felt so much better. " I am always ready," she said ; " I have no other occupation but to attend upon you, and all you have to do is to say '*when*,' and I will be at your side." "I think *now*," was his reply, "for the morning is bright, and all things look so cheering, I must not remain in bed." Some months before his death, he had said to her, " There are now only two petitions regarding this world that I constantly and earnestly offer up : the one is, that you may be spared to me as long as I live, for what a poor, helpless creature I should be without you ; and the other is, that when 'the Master' sees fit to call me home, He will not lay me long aside from my work." In great mercy both of these prayers were heard, and were now being answered.

He now attempted to rise, and while being assisted to do so, he was seized with a violent shivering. In great alarm, Mrs Archer instantly sent off for a dear friend. When she told her husband what she had done, he said, " All I need is rest, and I am very comfortable." He expressed his pleasure that his kind friend should be with him, remarking, " What a holy, consistent disciple he is, so like the Master and the beloved disciple, his namesake."

Mrs Archer sent also for Dr S., the physician, who, after examination, pronounced the disease to be inflammation of the membranes of the heart. He prescribed, and ordered medicine and nourishment to be given every hour alternately, which was done. Dr Archer was perfectly sensible during the day, and through the night, and took everything that was offered to him, until eight o'clock on the morning of the 30th, when his wife noticed he did not swallow so easily, though not appearing to suffer pain. He was perfectly calm, and held his wife's hand, which he frequently pressed. She then noticed a sweet smile passing over his face, telling of great happiness. She was thus steadfastly looking, her hand still locked in his, when the physician entered. She withdrew to the sofa. In a minute or so she felt a hand on her shoulder, and Dr S. said, ' Thy Maker is now thine Husband, the Lord of hosts is his name.' The spirit of her beloved partner had fled. There had been no *sigh*, no *motion* to indicate the moment of the change. Perhaps, when that smile was seen, the angels were around him, ready to convey his soul to the house of many mansions, the abode of the blessed.

His passing away was a translation from earth to heaven—from time to eternity. What a *glorious change* for *him!* What a *desolate* state for *her!*

Thus lived and died a marked man in his sacred profession —a man of good intellect, of varied information, and of sterling piety; a man who knew his place and kept it, who knew his duty and did it, who loved his Master and served Him faithfully; a man of unwearied powers of application to study and to work, who never shirked either a debatable question or a disagreeable task, and whose whole soul was poured out in tenderness upon the flock he fed, and in devotedness to the Lord he loved; a man without ostentatious claims of any kind, but of firm adherence to what he knew was due to and from him; a man, in short, who, in the undying love of his people, proved his title to their confidence, and in the appreciation by the religious world of his talents and services, his superiority to sectarian partisanship. At the very first he took the right measure of his position in London. With a marvellous adaptation to the solemnities of the situation, he soon gained general respect, and unwaveringly made his way up to the eminence whereon he died. He left his impress around him, a sweet savour of him remains wherever he was active, and his name shall long be remembered, not only in the precincts of Oxendon, but in many English hearts and homes and holy places, where his sunny influences drew affection, his manly bearing commanded respect, his genial manners conciliated differences, and his fervid piety secured confidence.

It only remains to be added, that his funeral took place on Thursday the 8th December 1864. His body was laid in Abney Park Cemetery, at the opening of which, in 1840, he made his celebrated oration. His voice is heard there again, but it is the voice from the tomb, which says, " All flesh is grass." On the Sabbath following, funeral sermons, alike solemn, discriminating, and eloquent, were preached to his bereaved and mourning congregation, in the Oxendon Chapel, by the Rev. Mr Redpath in the forenoon, and by the Rev. Dr Edmond in the evening, by both of whom warm tributes were paid to the worth and work of the deceased pastor. The compiler may here use the privilege of saying that, had God willed it, he too should have taken part in the obsequies of his bereaved friend; but at that time he was supposed to be on his own deathbed, and Dr Archer had been gone a month before the sad account could be communicated to him. He has lived to perform this service of love and admiration, though with a somewhat weak and trembling hand; and now commits it, with all its imperfections, to that gracious Lord with whom is the spirit of the departed one, and who can turn to his own glory the humblest efforts of them that serve him.

Shortly after Dr Archer's death, a marble tablet to his memory was placed by his people on the wall to the right hand of the pulpit, which bears the following inscription :—

INSCRIPTION ON TABLET IN OXENDON CHAPEL.

Sacred
TO THE MEMORY OF
THOMAS ARCHER, D.D.,
FOR THIRTY-THREE YEARS
THE BELOVED PASTOR OF THIS CONGREGATION.

Powerful in Intellect, Genial in Spirit,
and Masterly in Speech: Devout in Personal Religion,
Earnest in Evangelical Doctrine, and Faithful in Ministry:
He laboured with diligence and success in the cause of Christ,
And he lived in the hearts of his People.

Born at Perth, 12th September 1806; Ordained 3d May 1832;
Died 30th November 1864.

His Memorial is expressed in the Text of his First Sermon, Prov. xi. 30.
His Rest is described in the Text of his Last, Rev. xxi. 23.

HIS CONGREGATION HAVE ERECTED THIS TABLET.

A beautiful monument has also been placed above his grave, in Abney Park, an illustration of which is presented.

In the concluding chapter, the reader may peruse some of the private and public expressions of regard for the deceased pastor of Oxendon.

INSCRIPTION ON MONUMENT IN ABNEY PARK CEMETERY.

ERECTED

BY HIS CONGREGATION

IN MEMORY OF

THOMAS ARCHER, D.D.,

FOR THIRTY-THREE YEARS THE MUCH LOVED PASTOR
OF THE UNITED PRESBYTERIAN CHURCH, OXENDON STREET.

BORN IN PERTH, 19TH SEPTR. 1806.
DIED IN LONDON, 30TH NOVR. 1864.

A FAITHFUL MINISTER OF THE LORD JESUS CHRIST,
AN ATTRACTIVE PREACHER, AND AN ACCOMPLISHED PUBLIC SPEAKER,
HE LONG HELD A HIGH PLACE AMONG THE ABLE AND ELOQUENT
CHRISTIAN PHILANTHROPISTS, WHOSE AIM IT WAS TO MAINTAIN
THE CAUSE OF LIBERTY AND TRUTH, AND TO PROMOTE THE BEST
INTERESTS OF MEN OF ALL CLASSES AND CLIMES.

HE WAS PRE-EMINENTLY

THE FRIEND OF YOUTH.

HE THAT WINNETH SOULS IS WISE.

Prov. XI. 30.

MONUMENT IN ABNEY PARK CEMETERY.

CHAPTER X.

LAMENTATIONS.

E read in Scripture that "devout men carried Stephen to his burial, and made great lamentation over him." It may be so recorded of Dr Archer. The mourning over him was not confined to the silent chambers of "Hans Place," nor to "the inky cloaks" that draped the worshippers of Oxendon Chapel; it extended itself to the "Board Rooms" of religious and philanthropic societies, and to many of the sanctuaries of the land. In the body of this Memoir have been placed some, not all, of the public testimonials he received in his lifetime. We select a few out of the many that have been awarded to his memory since he passed into heaven. It is meet that we present, first, the reminiscences of one of his most beloved and valuable friends, James Mitchell, Esq., Glasgow, son of the late Dr Mitchell, one of the ministers of Glasgow, and one of the Professors of Theology to the United Presbyterian Church. The sketch will be found as worthy ot the parentage of its writer as it is of the subject of which it treats :—

" No one could see Dr Archer without being impressed with
the thought that he was a man of character and energy, possessed of qualities that were peculiarly his own, creating for
him a distinctive individuality. His broad, firm forehead, his
expressive mouth, and his well-knit frame, were indications of
a vigour which shone out from his dark eye, sometimes amid
the vehemence of his utterance, sometimes in the flashing of a
bland and loving smile of attachment." Manliness and affection
may be said to have been the main features of his nature.

" In early life he mingled with the foremost of his school and
college companions in their games and their frolics, perhaps in
their practical jokes too ; and in later life the same vigour
showed itself in the steadfast prosecution of the work he had
on hand, and especially in the work of his high calling ; and
towards the close of his ministry, when his strength was weak-
ened, and his end was approaching, it was signally blended
with the mellowing influences of a spirit of trust in God and
love to man.

" The ministry of the Word was, in his estimation, the high
vocation, and to it he devoted his earnest attention. Accomplished for it by his early studies at college, and in the Divinity
Hall of our Church, under Dr Dick and Dr Mitchell, he took
his own place as a preacher of mark, and soon acquired a position in the estimation of the congregation of Oxendon, and of
the religious world in London, which he ever afterwards retained with growing acceptance and usefulness.

" The services of the sanctuary were his chosen and constant
employment. Few ministers have been seldomer out of their
pulpits, except when bad health induced absence ; and few

have prepared themselves for their work with greater assiduity or ardour of purpose. To him study was habitual. He frequently repaired to the British Museum, and spent whole forenoons in reading recent publications on the subject of his lectures, especially those which he was writing for his class of young men. Thus he instructed them in the discoveries that had been made in Egyptian hieroglyphics, and in Assyrian inscriptions and monuments; defended the Bible against the supposed contrariety of modern science, and our holy religion against the corruptions of ritualism and the seductions] of sceptical speculations. His lectures were therefore at once instructive, edifying, and monitory, and their value was recognised by large numbers who attended them, and by whom they were highly appreciated. For his stated congregation, his study was as earnest, although it did not require such preparatory reading. Possessed of the materials for unfolding the subject which he had chosen, he mentally revolved them until he had formed his plan, and settled his course of illustration. He had the power of mental control in rare measure, and possessed the faculty of directing and exercising his strong intellect wherever he was and howsoever employed—whether in his own room, or in walking out, in riding on an omnibus, or journeying in a railway carriage. His powers of observation were unusually good; and there is reason to think that, during his opportunities for observation, he was employing them to study human life and conduct, and lay up materials for exhibiting its phases and its principles, and illustrating and enforcing the doctrines and precepts of Scripture. Certain it is that his discourses abounded with such illustrations applied to the condition of men and of society; and that the preacher and the platform speaker were supplied with telling allusions and pointed applications, whether for reproof, or correction, or instruction in righteousness.

"Thus furnished by reading, study, and observation, with materials orderly arranged in his mind, ordinarily committed to paper only as notes of leading ideas, and all unquestionably bathed in the spirit of prayer, he occupied his pulpit from Sabbath to Sabbath as a workman who needed not to be ashamed. His were no perfunctory services. His opening prayer was usually full of the utterances of a heart that felt the realities of life and knew the exigencies of his people, and sought to lead them all in supplication and intercession to the throne of the Eternal, and to educate and train them by a 'manly faith' in the way of obedience, of thankfulness, and of trust. None could listen to these prayers without finding something that was suitable to his case, promotive of his hope in God, and directive of his way. His lectures were truly expositions of the passage—not verbal so much as philosophical and practical, bringing out the truths that were taught and the lessons that were inculcated. Like the discourses of the generation of ministers under whom he had studied, the lectures of Dr Archer were fitted to make men wise through the knowledge of Scripture, to impress their minds with its authority, to instruct them by its teachings and examples, as applicable to all times and all circumstances, and to make them strong in its faith and its hopes. Such practical bearings and tendencies especially characterised the evening sermons, which not unfrequently pointed to prevailing errors or forms of evil. Under his ministry, no week could be begun without fresh instruction being conveyed, and a fresh impulse given in the faith of the Gospel and the path of rectitude. The Cross of Christ was ever the great theme of his preaching, the grand central truth for the heart and the conscience of man, the animating motive for entire consecration to God.

"All his discourses were clothed in a Saxon style. His diction was, like his intellect, masculine and powerful. He did not emulate elegance or the mere graces of speech; his language seemed to be chosen for its appropriateness and its force. And so was it in reference to his speeches from the platform of religious and philanthropic societies. These were always pertinent and effective, and they usually presented a view of the cause, and pleaded it from a standpoint, which were peculiar to himself. They were the compound result of his own convictions, and of his sense of the prevailing taste and character of his audience, or his estimate of the feature most prominent at the time, of the society or cause which he was advocating. In this department of public usefulness he was quite distinguished, and was everywhere received with much acceptance and favour. And so highly did he appreciate its importance, and so conscientiously did he adhere to engagements which he had made, that no disappointment marred the expectation of those who had invited his aid, and no journey needful to afford it was allowed to prevent his fulfilling his part, however much it might have encroached upon his rest or his strength. Fidelity to engagements, and tenacity to friendships, eminently characterised him.

"His manliness of spirit did not desert him during the last

year of his life, when his strength sensibly declined, and the
shadows of evening and the harbingers of change came over his
spirit—making his discourses more pathetic and his appeals
more admonitory and more tender. The writer of these notices
heard him officiate during several Sabbaths of that year, and
the very subjects of his discourses showed the fervency of his
spirit and the yearning of his heart. Thus, on a Sabbath in
May, he lectured from John xv. 16,—'Ye have not chosen me,
but I have chosen you, and ordained you that ye should,' etc.;
and in the evening he preached from Isa. ii. 17,—'And the
Lord above shall be exalted in that day,' etc. On another
Sabbath in the same month the subject of lecture was
Heb. iv. 1,—'Let us therefore fear, lest, a promise being left
us,' etc.; and in the evening it was 1 Cor. iii. 11, compared
with 1 Pet. ii. 6, etc.,—'For other foundations can no man lay
than that is laid,' etc. On the first Sabbath of June, he lectured from a kindred subject in Psalm cxviii. 22, 23,—'The
stone which the builders refused is become the head stone of the
corner,' etc.; and in the evening he discoursed from 1 Pet. ii. 5,
—'Ye also, as lively stones, are built up a spiritual house,' etc.
Perhaps the most touching of these services were those of the
Communion, on the second Sabbath of July, when his action
sermon was taken from John xvii. 24,—'Father, I will that they
also whom thou hast given me, be with me,' etc. The address
before the Communion was at once explanatory and hortatory;
and in the evening he preached from the admonitory words in
Heb. iii. 12,—'Take heed, brethren, lest there be in any of
you an evil heart of unbelief, in departing from the living God.'
A prayer meeting, in view of his departure for six weeks on a

Continental excursion to seek for health, and, as it was hoped, to obtain invigoration, closed the solemn services of this day, on which a farewell was for the last time to be uttered at parting with some whose fears mingled with their hopes, and their sorrows with both.

"During all the services of these Sabbaths, and of others that preceded and followed them, although oppressed with weakness and suffering from pain, his mental energy never deserted him. He had a work to do, and, like his Master, he did not go back. His tones took the tenderness of his frame, and both conspired to touch the hearts of those who were interested in him. His voice was plaintive, but his understanding was strong. His countenance wore the hue of his delicate health—such as we have seen in other cases of approaching change—but there was no faltering of his faith, or his hope, or his energetic performance of duty. The mellowing power of things unseen and eternal, more impressively felt amid the decay of nature, was more touchingly exhibited to the people of his charge and his affection. It spoke in his appearance, and thrilled in his voice.

"His letters were pointed and suggestive, rather than detailed or illustrative. But they breathed, and as it were embodied and concentrated, his strong affections. They were always vivid, and even yet bring him personally before the mental view.

"Thus, in May 1862, writing the day after the presentation meeting of his congregation, he says, 'I could not leave without mentioning to you, first of all, that there was a social meeting at Oxendon last night. Mr Lindsay was chairman. There was a fine gathering, and oh, much love!' In the same year, he writes:—' Oh for half-an-hour with you, to interpour mind and heart!' And to a house, mutually dear to their recollections, he refers as 'a very Elysium of hospitality and geniality.'

"On 1st January 1863, he writes:—' It is too late to wish you formally a happy new year, for by the time you receive this note, its inauguration will have commenced and budded. But in heart I earnestly desire and pray that, to both of us, '63 may be an advance on its predecessor in every point,—health, happiness, usefulness.'

"In March, in the same year, he writes:—' If you see Mrs Alexander again, will you give her our kindest regards. Hardly did I ever meet an American minister whom I more promptly loved, and more truly and kindly remember, than Dr Alexander.' —the late admirable Dr James W. Alexander, of New York. And, in the end of the same month, he says:—' I find that I have preached in Oxendon about sixty sermons since I returned from our trip, besides week-day discourses, etc.'

"On his return from his Continental excursion, in 1864, he thus writes:—

"'*September 6th.*

"'MY VERY DEAR FRIEND,—You have heard, if I remember right, of and from us at Zurich, where we realised, as who would not? a few days of enjoyment in the soft and beautiful, and occasionally sublime, scenery skirting its lovely waters; and then left for the Rhine by a somewhat circuitous but new route to us. Our object was to see and sail upon Constance, and visit

the town ever memorable—rather, ever infamous—in its association with Huss and Jerome. After Lucerne and Zurich, the
lake was nothing. It was prettily pastoral, but tame, and,
besides, the day turned out very damp and cold, with rain ;
and what we expected was to turn out one of the pleasantest
days of our journey, proved one of the least pleasant, and
almost the only blank one, and so we were glad on the morrow
to push on to Mayence by the early and fast train. It went
no farther than Manheim that day. . . . We moved on to
Boulogne, in which we spent a few days, and then to our own
Hans Place—thankful to Him for all his protection and
refreshing blessings, in a journey to me the best I have ever
made. We had glorious weather—a little too hot at times.
I was blessed with sound sleep, with a voracious appetite,—the
result of improved health, of change of air and scene and diet,
—and, not least of all, by mental rest and idleness. We had
everything to make us happy ; we had none of the little things
which are in a London life too often a trouble ; we were alone.
And thus ended our '64 summer Continental ramble—begun,
continued, and closed with peaceful feelings—with the happy
resolve to be happy—and with grateful dependence on Him
whose presence we sought, and, I doubt not, found.'

" In the following month (October), Mrs Archer had an
attack of rheumatic gout, with fever, and her illness aroused all
his sensibilities, and affected his strength. He writes—' Again,
my dear friend, you will be surprised to see my hand, and not
the hand so fluent, and pointed, and loving, and so loved. The
fact is this, my Martha is in bed laid up with a terrible attack

of rheumatic gout and fever. She has been completely over-done, and that for a long time. She has struggled against all—and, oh! for me! . . . Everything that can be done shall be done, and I fondly hope daily to see some improvement and abatement of her pain. She bears all with wonderful patience. May God our Father continue it. I am sure my dear . . . . I need not ask your prayers for her. Give me, oh give me, a share in them!'

"His next, and as it turned out, his last letter to the same friend, contained these words:—'I am glad to say that my wife's pains are somewhat mitigated. To say that they are gone were incorrect. That will be a matter of time and patient suffering. Meantime, her present stage is a matter of devout and loving gratitude. Continue with me, my dear, my very dear friend, in prayer on her behalf.'"

William S. Lindsay, Esq., M.P., kindly contributes the following loving and discriminating notice :—

"There is one feature in the character of Dr Archer, which at all times was very striking: he was one of the most unselfish men I ever knew. Though he enjoyed the good things of this life, all his conduct was that of a good pilgrim on a journey to another country, who had not much to do here beyond pre-paring for a hereafter, and inducing others to accompany him to that happier clime, of which he seemed to have the most lively and vivid impressions.

"I often had the pleasure and honour of presiding at those annual meetings in Oxendon Chapel—better known, perhaps, by the name of 'tea-gatherings,' but nevertheless of the most pleasing and instructive character. On such occasions he so frequently referred to the end of his journey, that I was often disposed to think that he wearied for its close. The venerable elders and members of his congregation who had ' finished their course,' were often referred to ; and when he spoke of the time when they should all meet again, his face was radiant with joy, as if he actually saw them ready to meet him in their mansions of bliss. But these displays were with him no mere figures of speech. He spoke as if heaven were opened to his view, and as if he really saw departed friends and brethren around the throne, where the Lamb that was slain sits enthroned in glory. This was generally the case with him. He never spoke unless he was in earnest—so thoroughly in earnest, that he could hardly fail to make an impression on every one who listened to him, especially when speaking from the platform, or addressing himself to young persons.

" To those youths who had come from the country, and were just commencing the great struggle of life in our counting-houses or shops or warehouses, his mode of conveying instruction was peculiarly happy and attractive.

" His week-night lectures in Oxendon, which were numerously attended, produced, therefore, the most beneficial results. These lectures, I am certain, saved many a youth who would otherwise have been led astray by the numerous temptations to vice with which, in this mighty Metropolis, they are constantly surrounded.

" But, apart from his public lectures, there are hundreds of men now in London who could speak in the most affectionate terms of his kindness, and the great service he rendered by his

R

advice to them in private, at that period of life when they stood most in need of a true friend and a Christian minister. Amongst those who came from Scotland to push their fortunes amongst us, his name was like a household word. Whenever they stood in need of advice or assistance, they invariably found their way, on an evening, to the little vestry-room in Oxendon Chapel, or to Hans Place, where he lived, and where one of the best and most devoted of wives adorned his household. There they would receive a kind and hearty welcome, and there they never sought in vain the assistance they required, or the advice of which they stood in need. If about to be led into temptation, a quotation from the old family Bible, and a word in his own rough and homely way, about the misery that any deviation from the paths of rectitude must inflict upon those friends from whom the young man had so recently parted, would save him from that fatal step which the Doctor saw he was about to take.

"'*What would your auld father and mither think?*' I once heard him ask a youth whom he knew was being led into temptation. Twenty sermons could not have produced so happy a result. All the associations of home, and parents whom he had fondly loved, were instantly awakened. The theatres, with their gaudy grandeur, and the fascinating scenes of those night-saloons, where thousands of young men have been for ever ruined, lost their charms when compared with the home of purity he had left, and which the simple question had brought vividly to his recollection,—'What would your father and mother think if they saw you there?' I saw by the looks of the youth that the words had made a deep impression upon him, and I am sure, from that time forward, he was not again tempted to cross the threshold of those glittering dens of vice.

"There was also another very fine feature in Dr Archer's character worthy of note: he never reproved in anger. Though somewhat rough in his style of speaking, he was always the gentleman—not polished, but nevertheless a thorough gentleman in all his sayings and actions. When he found fault, it was with a countenance radiant with a smile, and beaming with benevolence, but yet so full of anxiety and earnestness, that his words could not fail to produce the desired effect. Though he would not speak soft words when the occasion required him to reprove, I never heard him say anything with which any person could be offended.

"His style of public speaking was admirably adapted to the platform, especially when addressing large masses of the people. On these occasions I think he was more effective as a speaker than he was even as a preacher. Almost every one of his sermons contained some bright flash, or some original idea, which could not fail to awaken and impress the hearer; and perhaps those sermons which he had studied least, contained most of those striking passages.

"As you are aware, he was one of the most liberal-minded ministers of our Church, and did not hesitate to express his displeasure when he heard any one teaching narrow-minded doctrines in regard to the road to heaven. On one occasion, when discoursing on the subject of religious sects, he came out with one of those bright flashes of eloquence which is as fresh on my memory now as when it was spoken ten or twelve years ago. 'Some men,' he said, 'expect to be saved because they

are Episcopalians; another class because they are Presbyterians; others, again, see salvation only through the Methodist,
or the Independent, or the Baptist chapels; and, I dare say,
there are some people here who think the only road to heaven
is across the threshold of the United Presbyterian Church.
But away with all such dogmas as these; the mere profession
of any creed will not help you over the crystal battlements of
Emanuel.'

"He had also at times a quaint and forcible mode of expressing himself. I remember, when the Duke of Wellington died,
Dr Archer, in the course of his sermon, remarked on his
death, that he would never have thought of noticing the matter
because he was a duke, but when 'the Duke—the *Iron* Duke
—had gone,' it was another striking warning to us of our frail
mortality.

"As a whole, Dr Archer was no common man, and our Church
sustained a great loss when he was called away from amongst
us.   He was peculiarly adapted to the field of labour on which
his lot had been cast, and in his day and generation was a
happy instrument of leading, I doubt not, many souls to Christ."

Extract from a letter to Mrs ARCHER, *from the*
Rev. HENRY RENTON, *Kelso.*

"KELSO, *October* 16, 1865.

" MY DEAR MRS ARCHER,—

"I am sorry, and not a little, that I cannot
comply with the request which is the object of your letter.
Alas! all I can supply, at this distant date, is but a brief
reminiscence.

"It was in May 1840 I spent some eight or ten days under
your roof, and experienced from yourself and your husband an
amount of kindness and attention I can never recall without
lively gratitude. He was then in the zenith of his powers,—
full of health, of spirits, and of energy. It was the season
of religious anniversaries, of much company, and, to popular
preachers and platform speakers, of much work. In this class
he then occupied a prominent place; and I was amazed, not at
the demands made upon him, but at the number of them he
complied with, and the facility and vigour with which he performed whatever he undertook. So far as my recollection goes,
within these ten days—of which his kindness led him to give too
large a portion to my gratification, in the forenoons snatching a
few hours for sights out of the common reach, and, when no
engagement broke the day, accompanying me in excursions to
Windsor and other places, where his intimate conversance with
the objects visited, and his genial conversation, immensely
enhanced their interest and enjoyments, while the afternoons
and evenings were all filled up with meetings or private engagements—he delivered three public addresses in London, the
most memorable being the inaugural oration at the opening of
Abney Park Cemetery, the second at Exeter Hall, the third at
a Methodist chapel, and preached an anniversary sermon at
some place forty or fifty miles distant, which took him a night
from home. The first of these addresses was written out, and
formed the one grand attraction of that day's imposing assembly.
For the other, I had reason to think that his only preparation
consisted in some premeditations, for he had acquired the
habit of selecting and arranging his ideas on any subject he

was to treat, and trusting to the occasion for their expression and expansion. And certainly the addresses I heard had all the characteristics and success of natural and vigorous eloquence— exciting the expectation, rivetting the attention, enlisting the sympathy, and carrying along with him the sentiments and feelings of the large audiences he addressed. On learning what had been his pulpit 'and platform engagements for some weeks before, and what they were for some weeks after, it seemed to me that, had he been without any pastoral charge, the professional advocate or official representative of any society, he would have been reckoned a very busy and hard-working labourer in the public cause of religion ; and I marvelled that, with so many engagements, and so much work of an extraneous, exciting, and exhausting nature, he should prepare so fully as he did for the pulpit, and keep up his pastoral visitation, and maintain his congregational classes, with such efficiency. But the nature of his powers, the character of his eloquence, the variety of his attainments, and the multiplicity of his labours, others far better competent have already described."

Extracts from a letter from the Rev. Mr Hogg,
of Jamaica.

"Newport P.-O., Jamaica,
6th April 1865.

"My Dear Mrs Archer,—

"Far away in Jamaica here, we thought much and spoke much of your sore bereavement, when we learned from the public prints that 'a prince and a great man in Israel had fallen'—and *he, your husband!* And though I have long delayed giving expression to our feelings, it may even yet be not unacceptable to you to have a few lines from one who experienced very much of the friendliness and generosity of the justly-lamented Dr Archer, as well as your own.

"In looking back some twenty-two years ago, I often wonder and feel ashamed at the very great and constant kindness, on so munificent a scale too, which I experienced at 18 *Hans Place.* That kindness, it would say little for me, if I could ever forget, and I regret that I have never had the privilege of testifying the grateful feelings of my heart other ways than by words. It was my great happiness and privilege to be often an inmate of your house—than which in London there could be none more hospitable; and I had every opportunity of observing and admiring the *private worth*—the amiability and love to make every one around him happy—as I had frequently the privilege of admiring his intellectual gifts and acquirements, as well as his uncommon powers as an orator *in public,* both on the platform and in the pulpit. To the latter excellences the public press, I rejoice to see, has done something like justice, in referring to Dr Archer's death. The Church and the religious world must long feel the blank occasioned by this sad event; and I trust that some permanent memorial of the talents and varied worth of your admirable husband will ere long be given to the world; but it is *you,* my dear Mrs Archer, who must daily, hourly, and oh how deeply! feel the greatness of the loss his removal has occasioned, in the desolateness of the *heart* and of the *dwelling,* of both of which (to you) he was the light and the joy! To know all that you have suffered, and still suffer, in the withdrawal from you, even to the 'better land,' of one who for so many years could scarcely separate himself from you for a day, and who, when separated, was never himself till by your side again—of one of so much worth, so much wisdom, so much affection, and, in his best days, of such uniform joyousness and sprightliness of spirit,—one must experience what you have suffered in such a loss to appreciate its severity. And yet, my dear friend, no 'strange thing' has happened to you: it is 'common to men,' to our Queen on the throne, and to the humblest of her subjects; but, what is more important, your loss, in all its magnitude, is well known to God. He knows all about this great and sore trial, and 'like as a father pitieth his children, so the Lord pitieth them that fear him.'

"I believe, my dear Mrs Archer, that when you live over the past, as you will often do, you will see cause for praising God that in his providence he gave you so excellent a man, and a minister of Jesus Christ, as your husband; that he spared him so long to you; that he gave you so much happiness in each other, and rendered him so honoured and useful in London, in England, and in the Church; and that he made you both such blessings to Oxendon, and to an ever-widening circle of acquaintances, to whom God put it into your hearts to do good. And now that, in the judgment of Him who is infinitely wise and infinitely kind, he has finished his work on earth, and 'served his generation according to the will of God,' you know well it is becoming, however difficult, to say, 'He hath done all things well;' 'not my will, but thine, be done.'

How much cause for thankfulness is there that Dr Archer was fit for public service till the very close of his life; and how delightful to see that on his last Sabbath on earth he was penning to his beloved flock, who were no more to hear his voice, words of comfort and counsel. You have the unspeakable comfort of believing that his is the blessedness of those who 'die in the Lord;' and you will remember the words of our compassionate Saviour to his sorrowing disciples: 'If ye loved me, ye would rejoice, because I go to the Father.' Your beloved husband is only 'gone before;' and all who are united to the one Redeemer and Saviour shall ere long meet again in a brighter and happier than any earthly home, which is only the place of our pilgrimage, and you meet to part no more for ever. And to look back on it from the eternal world, how very short will the interval of the separation seem? And then, too, we shall know what we may very dimly see now, that the separation, though so sad and so sorrowful, was in love designed to make reunion more sweet—was only part of our needful discipline to be made 'meet' for the holy happiness of heaven, for the 'inheritance of the saints in light.'

"I need not remind you of what I believe you have experienced,—the preciousness of our Saviour's sympathy and grace. I trust he is ever near you, ever with you, comforting your heart, brightening your hopes of heaven, and ever disposing you, so long as he sees meet to spare you, to be as zealous as before, and even far more zealous, for his glory and the good of his Church and people. It is thus, you know, my dear friend, we are taught to expect that an entrance shall be ministered to us abundantly into the everlasting kingdom of our Lord and Saviour Jesus Christ. What else is worth living for? And to all of whom it can be affirmed, 'To me to live is Christ,' of them too it shall be added, 'To me to die is gain.'

"I am inclined to believe, my dear Mrs Archer, that you will be pleased to get a few lines from one of the very many who were wont to share the kindnesses and hospitalities of 18 Hans Place, and of the lovers and admirers of Dr Archer and yourself. A few lines at any time from yourself would be highly valued. I am desirous to know if any volume of Dr Archer's remains are to be published, and under whose editorship; and I confess I feel a deep interest in the future of *Oxendon* Chapel; but, above all, I am anxious to hear how you are sustained under your sore bereavement."

His widow since his death has received many letters of the deepest sympathy. She has found those of them to be most soothing that have come from persons who have dated to his faithful ministry their saving knowledge of the truth as it is in Jesus. Extracts only from some of these can be given.

D. W. states: "I attended the winter classes from the first of my coming to London, and acquired much useful instruction, as well as felt my principles of thought and action greatly established thereby. The course on 'Moral and Intellectual Improvement' has been of the greatest use to me, and I have always associated it with any success that has attended me. When I came to London my mind was inclined to *question*—a state that often leads to infidelity or something bordering upon it,—and owing to Dr Archer's practical, powerful, and earnest illustrations of Divine truth, great and, I trust, lasting impressions have been made on my mind. I thought I could not

better mark my feelings at the loss of the departed than to
express those long-cherished sentiments, which I felt would be
more acceptable to you than any other expressions of condolence that I could offer."

W. R. writes: "I have seen to-day in the papers an an-.
nouncement of the death of your dear husband, and my dear
friend. I am exceedingly grieved to find that one to whom I
owe so much has thus gone. Alas! such sorrow is but too
common. I do indeed owe the Doctor a great debt for taking
me by the hand when I was inclining to what was dangerous
in thought and feeling, and for impressing me with the greatness and majesty of Gospel truth,—more even by the manliness
(or to use his own word, the *robustness*) of his personal character than by his words. The Doctor always seemed to be
the incarnation of massiveness and courage, and his very bearing acted as a mental tonic on me. The last time I saw him
at S——, I was much struck with the change in his appearance.
Alas! he is now gone; but if gone from us, gone to his everlasting recompense and rest."

H. L. writes: "How deeply do I deplore the loss of the
dear departed, and how I shall ever revere his memory; for it
was through his faithful preaching, and the blessing of God,
that I was brought seriously to think of religion, and see my
need of a Saviour. Ah! how often have I thought of the kind
way he used to address his flock, and how very impressive his
sermons were. I shall have reason, as long as I live, to thank
God I was brought to sit under the teaching of such a great
man as your dear departed husband, for I did indeed feel
real delight, and so truly happy, when from Sabbath to Sab-

bath I had the privilege of listening with so much pleasure, and, I believe,'great profit, to his preaching ; and I hope never to forget him, nor lose the serious impressions he made on my mind," etc.

Others of the congregation have called to express in person the great benefit they and their families have reaped by the kind and faithful ministrations of their dear departed pastor —some mentioning instances of mere children being led to inquire, from the tender and impressive manner in which he pictured the beauties of holiness to their young hearts, and who were early induced to give themselves to the Lord. Mr N. mentioned, with much emotion, that his daughter, at the age of *twelve*, was so seriously impressed with what she heard, that she became a decided Christian, and has ever since, through the blessing of God, been kept a faithful follower of the Lamb. He added: " No words can describe what we owe to the teaching of your dearly-beloved husband and our best earthly friend."

S. F. R. writes : " The lectures on ' Popery and Puseyism,' delivered by your husband, were the means of drawing my attention to the Holy Scriptures, being a sceptic at that time ; and I ascribe my entire change of views and feelings, under God, to the earnest ministry of Dr Archer. It is now twenty-three years since I first entered upon the work of an Evangelist; and I look back with thankfulness, that for so long a period I have been enabled to testify to the grace of God, preaching Christ from house to house, being engaged the whole of that time either as a city or home missionary ; and I am fully assured that there is no happier life on earth than to be so employed ; and I can never feel sufficiently grateful for the mercy that I was thus early constrained to devote myself to so glorious a work, and the name of Dr Archer will ever be venerated by me as the instrument by which it was accomplished."

In addition to these, the widow received most consolatory letters from the elders, managers, and Sabbath-school teachers of Oxendon, all lamenting the heavy loss the Church had sustained. At the first meeting, after his death, of his own Presbytery, the following resolution was unanimously adopted:—

"PRESBYTERY OF LONDON,
12th December 1864.

"*Resolved*, That this Presbytery receive the announcement now made of the decease of the Rev. Dr Archer with deep regret, and desire to record their sense of the great loss sustained in his removal by this Presbytery, and by the congregation to which he had ministered for thirty-three years ; and at the same time their appreciation of the high qualities of mird and heart with which he was endowed, and of the important services which he rendered to the people of his charge, to the United Presbyterian Church in England, to the cause of Christian Missions, to the interests of education, and to schemes of benevolent enterprise,—all of which he often advocated with great power, both from the pulpit and from the platform, in many parts of the kingdom.

"*Resolved, further*, That a copy of the foregoing be sent to Mrs Archer, with expression of the warmest sympathy of the members of this Presbytery, under the still heavier and irreparable loss which *she* has sustained in the death of her gifted, devoted, and beloved husband."

The Rev. H. M. MacGill, the able Home Secretary of the United Presbyterian Church, thus beautifully refers to Dr Archer, in the Report of Church Extension in London submitted to the Synod in May 1865 :—

"One solemn event of the past year the committee would note. The Rev. Dr Archer has been removed by death from his chosen and much-loved sphere of service in Oxendon Chapel. To his memory it is due to view the fact, that seldom has a minister in any sphere had a deeper hold on the individual hearts and personal affections of his people. His distinguished gifts, his fervid temperament, and his effective eloquence, served for many years to make our Church known in not a few quarters of the Metropolis and of England, where otherwise it would have escaped observation. His comparatively early death carries in it admonition to all his brethren in the ministry, reminding them that the 'night cometh when no man can work.'"

The various societies whom he had so long and so usefully served were not behind in their expressions of condolence. The Secretary of the Society for the Conversion of the Jews writes :—

" Dear Madam,—

"At the last meeting of the committee, on the review of the past year, the members recorded on the minutes, with heartfelt and unanimous regret, the decease of the Rev. Dr Archer, one of the earliest friends of the British Society for the Propagation of the Gospel among the Jews. They recall to mind the very valuable and efficient services which he so cordially rendered to the cause on every occasion. They can only now acknowledge their obligations, and hope that in the presence of his and our God he will for ever witness the fruits of his ready services in this portion of his Master's vineyard."

The Secretary of the Moravian Society writes :—

" I have much pleasure in bearing testimony to the character and services of our late and much-lamented friend Dr Archer, for whom I always entertained great esteem and respect, having had the privilege of much communication with him on the affairs of the Moravian Mission, in which he took a lively interest, and was ever ready to plead its cause when requested, provided his own engagements would allow him."

The following was received just after he had preached the jubilee sermon of the " Sunday School Union :"—

"SUNDAY SCHOOL UNION,
July 16, 1853.

" MY DEAR DR ARCHER,—

"It gives me much pleasure to be the medium of conveying to you the following resolution, adopted with great satisfaction by our committee last evening :—

" ' That the cordial thanks of this committee be presented to the Rev. T. Archer, D.D., for his able, eloquent, and most interesting jubilee sermon, preached at Surrey Chapel, July 12th.'

" That you may long be spared to preach such spirit-stirring discourses, and ever have an audience as intelligently interested, and who listened with almost breathless attention on that occasion, is the sincere desire of,

" My dear Dr Archer, yours very faithfully,

"W. G."

For the London Missionary Society, the venerable Dr Tidman writes :—

" MY DEAR MRS ARCHER,—

" As a fellow-labourer with your late beloved and deeply-lamented husband in the service of the London Missionary Society, for the long period of twenty years, I had abundant opportunity of appreciating his Christian character and ministerial usefulness, and I have seldom had an associate so much to be loved and trusted. The discharge of his duties as a director of this Society was unremitting, and his devotedness to the interests of Christian Missions, as a public advocate, was exemplary and generous.

" The ministers with whom he officially co-operated in the Society have nearly all passed away, but I am sure that those who still survive share with me in sincere respect and affectionate remembrance of his character and worth.

" Trusting that, in the sorrow of your widowhood, you enjoy the sympathy and consolation of the Holy Spirit,

" I am, dear Mrs Archer, yours faithfully,

" ARTHUR TIDMAN."

DISCOURSES

BY

DR ARCHER.

DISCOURSE I.

THE SPIRIT OF GOD IN THE CONVERSION OF THE WORLD.*

"Not by might, nor by power, but by my Spirit, saith the Lord of hosts."—ZECHARIAH iv. 6.

THE primary allusion of these words requires no explanation. The temple of Jerusalem, which was associated with the proudest and holiest feelings of the Jewish heart, now lay prostrate in the dust—its glory departed, its music hushed. The ground on which it stood had been profaned by the tread of the stranger; while the descendants of earth's noblest aristocracy, the world's patriarchs, wandered as exiles, sighing over the bondage of their Fatherland with a poignancy of regret that no humiliation could quench, and panting for restoration with a yearning desire which amounted to a passion, nay, formed part of themselves. Now, however, when they had been emancipated from Babylonish thraldom, and the temple was to be rebuilt,

* Preached in the Tabernacle, Moorfields, before the Directors of the London Missionary Society, May 14, 1845.

the work lagged. Formidable and many difficulties crowded around their path. Their spirits were partially crushed and enervated by vassalage. Craven and indolent hearts suggested the time is not yet come—the perpetual apology for doing nothing, for neither finding nor making the time. To arouse them from their lethargy, God threatened them with heavy judgments; to encourage them to work when roused, he gave the promise of the text.

Their *typical* import is not less apparent than their primary reference. *That by the law of types is* not mere, not accidental resemblance, but similarity designed as well as complete and unquestionable. Man was created to be the temple of God; his intellect was kindled for the study of His works; his entire life was to be the practical illustration of His glory; his heart to be the home of the Eternal. That temple is now in ruins, as if riven by the lightning, or shaken by the earthquake, or profaned by the rude touch of savage atheistic violence. True —around it play the beams of pristine splendour, lingering as if unwilling to be for ever eclipsed. Occasionally are flashes —the memorials of the past, the portents of its future dignity. There are bursts of ambition requiring but the consecration of principle to lead to the most brilliant results. There is the tenderness of heart that weeps over suffering, and makes the pain of others its own. There are twilight gropings after truth —upheavings of mind after immortality that rise with indestructible vigour through the depressing influence of time and sense. There is the hope that trembles amid the dim conceptions of the unseen, the eternal, the infinite. There is the fierce glance of indignation against injustice and oppression.

There is the withering scorn that falls on the lie of the lip—
much more on hypocrisy, the lie of the life. All these suggest
the original majesty of our being, as from the broken frieze
you judge of the skill and taste of the artist, and from the mass
of fragments the extent of the pile. But still it is in fragments;
and fragments the more impressive from their contrasts. The
weaver's hut required to abut on the temple of Luxor to complete the picture of Egypt's degradation; and the low moan
of the solitary willow-tree on the banks of the Euphrates, adds
intensity, sublimity, awe to the silence that hangs over the
mounds of Babylon.

Now, the grand end of Christianity is to restore that temple,
to clear away the rubbish that conceals its glory, to gather from
all regions of the earth imperishable elements,—all resting on
one foundation-stone, all consecrated to one holy end, all
forming one entire, unique whole, ever filled with the presence
of God, and ever sending forth the odours of its piety and the
hymns of its praise to his glory,—a temple destined to surpass
and to survive the proudest monuments of the earth, the
colossal structures of the Nile, and the more exquisite erections
of Greece.

Survey, then, the scene; realise its magnitude; dwell on the
prospect of Christian ambition—an ambition which, if unsuccessful, would be redeemed from contempt by the nobleness of
its daring. From the contemplation of existing ruin, glance at
the ideal of future restoration—its amplitude, its completeness,
its perpetuity. Ask, How can the vision be realised? Where
is the skill, where are the resources, adequate to such a stupendous work? And if, looking at the disproportion of the

agency, and the undertaking of our hand, to reconstruct the globe into the vestibule of heaven, there comes over the heart the painful impression of inadequacy, and the corresponding, the contingent apathy of despair, then listen to the spirit-stirring voice of the text: " Not by might, nor by power, but by my Spirit, saith the Lord of hosts."

1. *We are not to conclude from the language and form of the text, which appear a contrast between power on the one hand and the Spirit on the other, that weakness is at all necessarily connected with this influence.*

Such a thought is precluded by the relation of the Spirit; it is the Spirit of "the Lord of hosts." How comprehensive, how sublime the title! Within the range of his dominion all are included,—from the tiniest, most ephemeral insect—from the mysterious existences that hover on the confines of the two worlds—the animate and inanimate—linking both, specifically identified with neither—up to the archangel that dwells beneath the shadow of his throne; through all organised forms of matter, and all orders and degrees of mind; through all the varieties of the emotional world, and through all shades of moral character; over the surges of the angry sea, and over the wilder heavings of man's passions; over the sanguinary track of human ambition, and over the desperate, maddened malignity of the lost,—over all he rules, with an authority that displays its reality and extent in the quiet, the ease, the simplicity of its operations. His Spirit, therefore, must partake of his own power, and all its emanations be sufficient for the ends they are designed to achieve.

Nor is this Spirit marked merely by power, *but by power of the highest order.* Minds, indeed, accustomed to judge by the visible and material, associate the idea of energy exclusively with physical developments, and soar to no conception of glory except as connected with pomp and parade. But as mind throws aside the prejudices which time and a forced and false state of society casts around it, such power is shorn of its attractions, and is felt and acknowledged to be the lowest of all power—mere muscular energy—the influence of matter on matter. Next, and above that, is the force of mind over matter, of thought over the arrangements and movements of physical objects; while, immeasurably above all, is the subtle but real influence of mind on mind. The emaciated student that elaborates in his solitude a great moral principle, and lodges it deep in the heart of a nation or an age, may appear to the mass feeble and sickly, when compared with the man of giant stature, or bedizened with earthly gew-gaw decorations. But, in truth, he is inconceivably greater. The humblest missionary, working in the most secluded departments of Christian benevolence,—we say it in all sobriety,—is, in the eye of right-judging minds, a greater man, wields a greater power, aims at a nobler conquest, and shall receive and wear a more glorious chaplet of honour than the leader whose whisper, or the stamp of whose foot, summons embattled legions to the field of fight. Fathers and brethren! deride, dispute it who may,—we utter it not in the spirit of self-inflated vanity, for the fact should humble us on account of its consequent responsibility,—the weakest of us is linked to an influence that vibrates through all time into eternity—the influence of God's Spirit, that pillars itself not in material and perishable results, but in spiritual, and therefore everlasting, creations.

THE LAWS THAT DETERMINE THE NATURE AND REGULATE THE ACTION OF THIS POWER *are few and simple. It must be cognate in kind to that on which it acts.* Were its scene or its object physical, we should expect the interposition of physical might; but if it is power to act on spiritual agencies and for spiritual ends, it too must be spiritual. Now, no external might can coerce thought—no dungeon-walls can confine it. The light of heaven they may exclude. Within their dreary precincts no balmy breath of spring may play on the wan cheek of the martyr—no groan from his racked and tortured frame may escape through their frowning masses. But mind is free: emotions, thoughts—all escape from the prison-cell of the body, and rise to His throne, whom the captive honours not less now by heroic patience than before he did by active labours. Whatever, accordingly, shall tell on such spiritual existence, must itself be spiritual.

Again, *mind is responsible; and to be so must be free.* Anything therefore that moves it, if rational in its impulses, must not interfere with its liberty of choice—its freedom of judgment; otherwise, it is a mere physiological machine, and no longer a moral agent. *How* this term of its moral being can be maintained untouched, consistently with the co-action of spiritual omnipotence, we cannot, nor are we required to say. But the common sense, the instinctive, the stereotyped logic of the mass, stronger than the metaphysical subtleties of the few, tells us that so it is; that the Spirit of God when working on man's heart does no violence to his emotions, and when modifying his judgment forces not its conclusions by brute, unreasoning compulsion.

And, finally, *mind is infinitely, constitutionally diversified.* Its idiosyncrasies are endless; and, under the influence of a spiritual power, we have reason to expect full tolerance of such varieties, and that no attempt will be made to reduce all into dull uniformity. Errors and imperfections, indeed, we may expect to be corrected. To the undecided and vacillating, it will impart, to a certain degree, firmness of purpose; and dogged obstinacy it will partially melt and subdue. Yet generally *the characteristic feature of the man will impart form and direction to the energies of the saint.* The melancholy man will go to heaven sowing in tears; the man of mercurial temper, of lively habits, will be the active, cheerful Christian; the intellectual man will be the thinking, reasoning disciple; while the imaginative mind will dwell in regions of religious sentimentalism, and drink in with rapture the poetry of redemption. But under all such varieties shall exist, and be traceable, the family features; and the antagonist, repelling influences of such diversities will be counteracted by the family relationship, and the hallowing thought that they who bear these varied aspects, after all form only *one home of hearts.*

2. *Nor are we to interpret the text as if teaching that the Spirit is to act independently of, and unconnected with, human agency.*

The power of coercion, indeed, our Gospel leaves to error or secularised systems. Romanism may employ it, and with restless, remorseless ambition, cast over Polynesia the cloud of its protection, from whose dark bosom comes not the shower of blessing, but the baptism of blood—converting, as that system does, the herald-sign of our faith from the dove into the vulture. Such means our religion disclaims—repudiates. It spurns the bribe; it sheathes the sword; it presents not the Cross gleaming amid the martyr-fire, nor forges chains of gold, as heavy, as vassal-like, as oppressively binding as if forged of iron.

The philosophy of the Cross, nevertheless, continually associates Divine power and human agency. In its moral canons and apparatus, the energy of God does not supersede the activity of man; nor is the activity of man efficient without the energy of God. "Work," not because you have all to do—"work," not because you have none to second your efforts—but "work,"—oh, beautiful logic!—oh, inspiring motive!—"work," for God works in you. Such is the analogy of creation and providence. Is light produced—are stars clustered in groups—or do beams of intense splendour flow from the quenchless orb of day? The voice of God wakes the echoes of the universe with the sublimely simple command, "Let there be light." Do the waters of the sea of Edom part to their foundation, and stand firm as "crystal walls?" The rod of Moses must be stretched over the deep. Are the bulwarks of Jericho to totter and fall? The blast of the ram's horn must sound around the doomed city. Is Paul caught and endangered in one of the sharp storms of the Ægéan? Though the promise of the Eternal had guaranteed his safety, no sooner did he see the mariners who worked the ship fleeing in unseamanlike cowardice and treachery, and leaving the landsmen to their fate, than he exclaimed, "Except these abide in the ship,

ye cannot be saved." And *wise* no less than universal is the
connection: the devolution of duty on man, the demand for
exertion, calls forth his powers, otherwise dormant—the promised presence of Jehovah secures success, otherwise hopeless.

These remarks lead us to the proposition of the text, namely,
that no human, no created instrumentality—however extensive
or adapted its resources are—which acts independently and
alone, is adequate to the restoration of the fallen temple; but
that the SPIRIT OF THE LORD OF HOSTS PROVIDES THE SOLE
EFFICIENT ENERGY FOR THE CONVERSION OF THE WORLD.

I am aware of, and most cheerfully recognise, the adaptation
of truth—Scriptural truth—to the nature and necessities of
man. That adaptation is universal. To the quenchless desires
of immortality it imparts the clearness and firmness of assurance. The philosopher it presents with the sublimest topics
of speculation; while to the ignorant, who have almost lost
the power by never-forming the habit of thinking, it holds out
the weightiest topics in the simplest form. It rolls over the
insensible and daring the thunders of Sinai; while it takes the
trembling penitent by the hand, and guides him to the Cross.
It has something for everybody, and for each just what he
needs. In the force of its evidence clear enough to convince,
yet not of such an order as allows of no inquiry by a rational
being; in the rules of duty it prescribes not tediously, bewilder-
ingly minute, but rather great germinating principles; in the
degree of its discoveries sufficient to guide the most fallible,
and yet so elementary as to make us pant for that world where ·
the encyclopædia of the earthly shall be the alphabet of the
heavenly student; in the proportion and blending of distinct,

practical, and comprehensive doctrines and overwhelming mysteries—in all, biblical truth is entirely accommodated to our condition and character.

Nor am I unaware of the encomiums lavished on truth, of the frequent assertion of its irresistible fascination, and the willing homage that must be paid to it when once seen. Array it, however, in what beauty you may, still the nature and the bearings of the truth will determine, if acting alone, its acceptance or rejection. If grappling with the corruptions of the heart, it tries to master them; or if presented as a mere intellectual abstraction, seeking no influence over the moral man, its reception will be very different. Give one an interest, real or fancied, in receiving a statement as true, and he will greedily believe, or try to believe, the fictions of alchemy and the dreams of astrology; give him an interest in rejecting a doctrine as false, and the finest elaborations of chemistry, or the most poetical and yet most scientific demonstrations of astronomy, will be˙disputed or treated as practically valueless. It will not surely be said that the Romish propagandist has superior resources to the Protestant missionary on the platform of Christian doctrine. Yet how often do we hear of the triumphs of the one and the failures of the other? By what is the seeming discrepancy to be accounted for? On one ground at least sufficiently palpable, that while the evangelical crusade has been maintained with the weapon of pure, uncorrupted truth, Rome has diluted even its own views of doctrine, has interwoven the dogmas of Papal Christianity with the superstitions of Paganism, frittered away the stern self-denying morality of the Bible, and, thus diminishing the difference between heathenism and Christianity, bridging over the chasm between the Church and the mosque or pagoda, made its own version of truth palatable to corrupt man by the tolerance of his sins and the licensed retention of his delusions.

Is it then said, Let truth be admitted to the heart and it must conquer? Undoubtedly it must. But a prior question exists, How is it to obtain admission there? The avenues are blocked up by sin. The first approach of truth arrays a fearful host of prejudices and passions against it. Satan, trembling for his ascendency, pours over the soul his most deadly incantations. Beautiful indeed is the flower on the hill-side, and clearly shines the star in its own serene light in the sky; and love them you must, if you behold them. But all are shrouded in heavy, impenetrable mist. Let the wind arise and disperse them, and the lovely tints of that flower and the soft brilliancy of that star refresh the eye; but, without that wind, in vain for you does the flower bloom in its mountain solitude, or the star twinkle in the far-distant firmament. So let your heart be enveloped in the cold thick mists of sin, and in vain does the Rose of Sharon blossom, in vain does the Star of Bethlehem shine, until that spiritual gust has come that will carry all noxious vapours away, and admit you to the full perception and glowing admiration of their inimitable beauty.

I.

Now it is fair to reason for the truth of a principle from the necessary inconsistencies of its opposite, to urge anomalies irreconcilable except on the supposition of the accuracy of the assertion before us.

Consider, then, these anomalies.

It will be generally granted that in similar circumstances uniformity of cause will be accompanied with uniformity of result. If, accordingly, in the evangelical plan, no power beyond the human is at work, similar external energy will issue in similar effects. Yet such is not our experience. The same doctrine has gone home to his heart at one period with a piercing force he never felt before, although preached with equal impassioned zeal. True, it may be urged he was then in an anxious frame of mind, and therefore more prepared to receive impression. As a fact this is not universally correct: on multitudes the truth has come suddenly, caught them by surprise, and their conversion has been matter of greater wonder to none more than to themselves. But even were the assertion universally accurate, a question still remains,—Whence came that peculiar anxiety of heart—that special preparedness of mind? If, then—and this principle runs through the argument—the effects of truth are not uniform, if there be a disconformity between its application and results, another power must be invoked. Who but upon this principle can account for unexpected changes in the sinner's life by the very same doctrines often heard from the same lips, nay, heard in vain from much more eloquent and seraphic tongues?

For if dependent on human power, the Gospel will be most successful when preached by the most eloquent men. The skill of an advocate often compensates for the hollowness of a cause. By subtlety he can conceal its weak points; by persevering zeal, can evolve and give prominence to its strong ones; and by his genius throw over all a warm, living tint, amid whose beauty the judgment is bewildered into dreamy powerlessness. How much more commanding and effective must eloquence be when it catches its inspiration from truth, and imagination yields its most delighted tribute, not to error, not to vice,—pours forth its stores, not to gloze over iniquity, but to emblazon righteousness and purity! We seem thus entitled to anticipate that the most logical preacher will be the most efficient with the most logical hearers, and the most fervid, with the warmest disposition; and generally the most oratorical preachers would be the most successful. In the lowest sense of the word success, they are so. They gather around them the largest, most heterogeneous masses. But if the measure of real ministerial success be the conversion of souls unto God—if the grand aim of the ministry be to multiply his image—the most logical and the most eloquent preachers of the Gospel are not the most successful. Enter that building, liker a hovel than a house of God—listen to that preacher, unrhetorical, incoherent, ungrammatical— look around, and there you see the tear stealing from the suffused and melting eye—listen, and you hear the half-stifled groans of the touched and broken heart—follow him and his audience to the judgment, and you find multitudes saved by that teaching where taste could see nothing to admire but everything to repel, and where the understanding could trace no fine process of argument before whose majesty it was constrained to bow. Another scene opens—a magnificent pile, and a dignified minister. The logic is clear and convincing; there are the finest flowers of oratory, perhaps even fragrant with spirituality: yet that scene is, after all, a richly-decorated sepulchre of souls—of souls entombed amid the most gorgeous rites and pomp. Whence is the difference? In the one scene is present the Spirit of the Lord of hosts—in the other he is not; and his absence is spiritual death.

Again, the Bible contains a system of pure ethics—of morals resting on no equivocal foundation—dictated in no trembling voice, but firm in tone, and solid in their basis. We might hence expect the most cordial reception of this system from the purest moralists of the age and scenes when and where it is ever propounded. All history attests the reverse. The mightiest conquests of the Gospel were achieved over the most unlikely elements—not among the Pharisees, the ascetic Pusey-ites of the synagogue, but among harlots and publicans ; not in Athens, with its finished manners and exquisite genius, but in Corinth, with its proverbial degradation ; not in Greece, with its groves and academies and high-toned civilisation, but on the shores of the Caspian Sea, with its rude and rugged barbarism ; not in the saloons of the self-righteous moralist ; not in the halls of the *soi-disant* philosopher, but in the hovels of wretchedness, the scenes of crime, the hearts so putrescent in corruption that the purist would shrink from their presence as from a living contagion, a moral pestilence.

Consider then, for a moment, the condition of the earth at the time of the manifestation of the Cross. In the Gentile world religion was a name, or, if its forms were maintained, it was merely the creature of the State, the instrument of politicians to keep the multitude in bondage. The Pantheon was the shrine of every impersonation of the fantastic, the voluptuous, the gross. The schools of philosophy were the scenes of vain, subtle speculation—of mental gladiatorship. Judaism was become the relic of a bygone system, to which men clung with the ignorant pride of lineage, instead of affection to a living truth. Refinement and barbarism, science and ignorance, atheism and mythology, heathenism and Judaism, the sophistry of Athens, the iron grasp of Rome, the self-interested idolatry of Ephesus, the gigantic licentiousness of Corinth— all formed one serried phalanx against Christianity; *and yet all it conquered.* How? Not by the genius of its defenders—not by their social influence—not by its patronage of existing vices—not by the physical might that could subdue the legions of Italy. By what, then? By the power of the Spirit of the Lord of hosts. Remove that influence, and the triumphant progress of a system that owed nothing to the empire, and sought nothing from it, is an anomaly unintelligible, incredible. Connect that with the movements of the apostolic Church, and the enigma is solved, and you have at once a cause adequate to the effect.

II.

Another train of illustration unfolds itself in ANALOGY.

The emblems of conversion are not more numerous and varied than they are *one in indirectly but really tracing all the results of the Gospel to the power of the Spirit of God.* Is the sinner spiritually blind? Without the interposition of God he cannot see. Conduct, then, the blind man through the most picturesque scenery; descant to him of the grandeur of that towering peak or frowning crag, of the beauty of that sunny glade or shining stream, and all your language is to him hiero-

T

glyphic, unintelligible. With colour, with form, born blind, he has no sympathy. The glow of the sun he may feel; its glorious stream of light he does not perceive. The exquisite fragrance of that flower he may inhale ; its delicate pencilled beauty does not ravish him: and without a miracle, without the hand of God, this cannot be. Guide yonder heathen pilgrim through the richest spiritual scenes, where you have drunk in the holiest inspiration ; bid him fix his viewless eye-balls on the Sun of Righteousness, and to him all is dark ; and nothing short of omnipotence can impart that visual power by which he can truly say, " Once I was blind, now I see."

Ascend the mountain belt that encompasses yonder valley, and survey its contents. Myriads of bones—dry, disjointed, bleached—lie before you. Do you ask, Can they live ? *No,* if man's power alone is to act. *Yes,* if omnipotence is to develop and apply its energies. Speak in that region of death—command its tenants to awake in human voice—and the silence that meets the sound throws mockery on your attempt. Speak with the voice of God, and at its vivifying tones they spring into life. Now, sin is spiritual, moral death. Ascend, then, the Himalayas. Sweep your eye over Hindo-stan, and one hundred and thirty millions of human beings meet its glance, prostrate in superstition, demonised or brutified in passion, spiritually dead. The missionary's arm would drop paralysed by his side, his spirit sink into despair, his voice startle at its own echo, if required to preach in his own power and might ; and he would feel his work as Utopian, as fanatical, as if commanding the dust of the necropolis to live.

Worldly, sceptical men may carp at our doctrine, and taunt

us with inconsistency. They sneeringly tell us, The sinner is lifeless, and yet you command him to turn. What egregious incoherence!—what an unphilosophical appeal! So no doubt it would be, did we speak in our own name, and to the sinner's heart alone. But we vindicate the justice and propriety of our appeal on the simple ground that He who dictates the command makes it instinct with life, opens a pathway for it, and sends it home with invincible power. What, then, we need for the Church—its revival for the world, its conversion—is not a body of men urging, establishing their apostolic lineage and authority through the heraldry of Rome or Oxford—not men possessing a species of ecclesiastical galvanism to produce on the faces of the dead the horrid contortions and mockery of the living, only making death the more appalling from the momentary mimicry of animation; but what we want is a ministry thrilled into life by God's Spirit, and thrilling men into vigorous, healthy, sustained life, by the same Spirit, superinduced by faith and prayer.

III.

Coincident with this conclusion is THE EXPERIENCE OF THE CHURCH, not only in its more ordinary and routine movements, but in its epochs that stand out in bold relief. It is true that there was a beautiful adaptation of agency,—and in this point no society has been more favoured and blessed than our own,—so that, if the languages of the East had to be mastered, or spoken languages to be reduced to writing and adjusted into form, or the rights of the aborigines to be protected, or schemes of romantic adventure to be undertaken, or the misery of squalid barbaric habits to be endured, or the subtlety of the Brahmin to be encountered, or the intellect of the Malay almost to be created—you had the men made, ready for the special end. Yet such adaptation does not supersede or exclude Divine agency; for, even were that adaptation the grand source of success, which it is not, itself is of Divine production.

Consider, then, the history of the modern revived Church. Behold the Churches of Christ at home, quivering into life under the heart-inspired and heart-touching preaching of Whitfield ; and the Churches of America, experiencing " times of refreshing under the ministerial labour of Edwards, displaying in his writings the most wondrous elasticity of mind— power sufficient to develop the subtleties of metaphysics, and yet able to stoop down to the infirmities of the most uninformed. Go back to the days of the Reformation, when the cardinal doctrine of justification by faith was exhumed from the mass of rubbish that for ages overlaid it. Amid the dim shadows of that period move giants in thought and purpose —giants the more colossal when side by side with the pigmy, heartless assailants of their fame in modern times. There is *Luther*, with his leonine courage and childlike simplicity; *Calvin*, by legal studies fitted to break through the cobwebs of error, and by classic taste prepared to group and illustrate truth in its loveliest forms ; *Knox*, noble in the manhood of Christian principle, firm in that moral intrepidity that did not quail before the fury of the multitude, nor was moved by the glance of beauty or the tears of a queen ; and *Melancthon*, full of tenderness of soul, finely contrasting with, and not only so, but powerfully modifying, the stern vigour of his great coadjutor. Go back still farther, overleap the pet specimen, the model era of Anglo-catholicism, the mediæval Church, and, fixing your gaze on the apostolic age, you find the same great fact, variety of agency, and, through that variety, adaptation of power: in *Peter*, with his burning zeal; and *John*, with his seraphic love; in *Paul*, whose imagination and intellect were so exquisitely proportioned, that you may say of him, as has been said of a great modern orator, that his logic was his rhetoric, and his rhetoric his logic; and in *James*, overflowing with practical, every-day, homely philosophy. Here, then, is vast variety of mind, of constitutional temperament, of education, of habit, of attainment. But is it not refreshing to find all ONE in *one* grand point—all delight to be lost in the blaze of Messiah's glory—all rush from human applause with instinctive veneration, to hide themselves behind the shadows of the Cross? Rich as might be the garlands they wove, lovely as might be their hues, exquisite their odours, gathered in the classic retreats of Greece, or to the Christian in the still holier and more classic soil of Esdraelon and Carmel, all with the heart of one man place first, foremost, and loveliest of all— the Rose of Sharon; and amid the variety of dialect, and illustration, and eloquence—amid the moving appeals of one, and the severe dialectics of another—amid the simple oratory of the first, and the finished periods of the second—amid the triumphs that crowned their labours—you hear the murmur of grateful hearts, the confession of self-annihilated souls: not by might, not by power, but by Thy Spirit, oh Lord of hosts! Who among us, fathers and brethren, cannot join in that heart-sprung confession that comes down to us from the remoteness of antiquity, and swells in volume by every day's experience? Who among us cannot say that those sermons have been most practically and powerfully useful, which have been most studied under the teaching of God's Spirit, and delivered with the greatest dependence on, and most fervent prayer for, his influence? Academical students of the Divine oracles, and their future ministers, catch as you may classicism of taste, cull from Parnassus its fairest flowers, acquire firmness and tone to your understanding by the most bracing scientific gymnastics, store up the largest masses of patristic lore, analyse with the most critical skill, and the most perfect apparatus, the Word of God—but oh! lodge it deeply in your heart as a great, practical, eternal truth, the recorded experience of a man of gigantic powers and inspired mind, that "Paul planted, and Apollos watered, but God gave the increase."

No illustration of these principles can be demanded more striking than that of *the relative success of the preaching of our Lord and his apostles.* Never was one more qualified to win souls than he was. That eye so clear in honesty and so melting in love; that countenance so eloquently benignant, and yet so divinely commanding; that voice, so fitted to pierce the soul by its mingled firmness and sweetness; his knowledge of all truth, intuitive and complete; the logic of miracles, the credentials of his embassage, his untiring patience,—all were fitted to attract and impress. Willingly did the people hear him; they hung with silent rapture on his lips. Never did one speak unto them like him. Yet how few were converted by his ministry! Charmed they were by the liquid melody of his tones, the condescension of his conduct, the lustre of his deeds; but under the best ministry the earth ever received, their souls remained petrified in sin. Mark the contrast! Peter appears and preaches a sermon full of the Gospel, yet distinguished by no peculiar features of eloquence, no magic to captivate men's hearts, and three thousand are added to the Church. Whence proceeds the difference? The ministry of Christ was the ministry of sacrifice, the ministry of the apostolate was the ministry of the Spirit; and no sooner was that sacrifice complete, than the descent of the Holy Ghost proved its acceptance, rewarded Him that offered it, and filled its teachers and their exhibition of it with living power from on high.

IV.

It remains for me to close this argument (if I may presume to call by such a name a simple statement of facts) by a reference to that which will compensate for all its imperfections, viz., AN APPEAL TO SCRIPTURAL ASSERTION. Nowhere do we find in the sacred volume its writers arrogate to themselves any part in the work of conversion, *except its merely external instrumentality*. Is the soul of man stirred from its slumbers into the sensibilities of life? are its wild and warring passions hushed into repose? does it possess the calmness of a well-grounded Christian hope? does it revel in the bliss of Christian joy? is it strengthened with might for the discharge of Christian duty? does it bear the sign of its glorious destination?—then all are the fruits of that Spirit that quickeneth the soul, that helpeth our infirmities, and sealeth unto the day of redemption. With equal consistency are all the transforma-

tions of the Gospel *on a large scale* traced to His operations.
Isaiah steeped in evangelical spirit; Ezekiel, whose eloquence
had the scathing power of condensed lightning-gleams, alike
associate the world's conversion with this mighty agency. "The
palaces shall be forsaken : the multitude of the city shall be
left; the ports and towers shall be for dens for ever; a joy
of wild asses, a pasture of flocks ;"—how long? "Until the
Spirit be poured upon us from on high, and the wilderness be
a fruitful field, and the fruitful field be counted for a forest."
And again : "I will pour water upon him that is thirsty, and
floods upon the dry ground; I will pour my Spirit upon thy
seed and my blessing upon thine offspring :" and, survey the
changes—"they shall spring up as among the grass, as willows
by the water-courses." Nor less distinctly does Ezekiel, in the
vision of the valley of dry bones, teach the essential, indestructible connection of the Spirit's action with the vivifying, the
saving exhibition of evangelical truth. And while the minstrel
monarch of Israel proclaims "that the people should be made
willing in the day of His power," David's Lord and David's
antitype, with clear and firm-toned authority, declares "that
no one can come unto Him, except the Father draw him."
Polished, then, as may be our armour, tried as it may have been
in many an encounter, ethereal as it is in its temper, bearing as
it may, and does bear, the stamp of Heaven's approbation,
never for a moment let us forget, in the heat of the conflict, or
preparation for the encounter, that "the weapons of our warfare
are MIGHTY THROUGH GOD."

Such, then, is the nature of that influence, and such its necessity, without whose promise and presence the Missionary enter-

prise were fanaticism. Our object is the conversion of the world to Christ, the overthrow of every idol shrine, and the erection upon its ruin of the temple of God. How quixotic the attempt if all the resources are merely human! How certain is success, if, moving in the line of prediction, we move in the track of omnipotence! Who, then, that gazes on the masses of beings prostrate in spiritual death, and turns from the survey discomfited and downcast, lifts not up his heart to Heaven and say, "Come from the four winds, O breath, and breathe upon these slain, that they may live!" And who that looks on the Church, the garden of the Lord, and sees this tree unproductive, and that flower wither and droop and scentless, does not pray, "Awake, O north wind; and come, thou south, and blow upon his garden, that the spices thereof may flow out!"

This appears the appropriate place for a reference to the manner and CIRCUMSTANCES in which this spiritual power will be imparted, and the CORRELATIVE DUTIES that devolve upon us in seeking to obtain it. These are apostolical, derived from apostolical example, and sanctioned by the Divine blessing. These I almost only name; I cannot pretend nor presume now to illustrate them. But imperfect as is the discourse, it would be unspeakably more so were no allusion made to this department of the subject. The apostolic Church had a *deep impression of the greatness of the blessing* they were to receive. I admit they did not know its nature; but as the child interprets the unexplained promise by the experience of a father's former love and conduct, so they made the past the prophet of the future, and expected large things from Him who had done large

things. Have we attempted to realise the idea of souls the
temple of the Holy Ghost?—of a Church, of the world—the
home of God—all replenished with his glory—all consecrated
to his praise?

Nor less *firm was their faith* than their expectations were
large: never had one promise of God failed: and they felt
that not one would fail now. Hence their calm, unmurmuring
waiting, through daily, frequent disappointment, in the full
confidence that, though deferred, the blessing would be imparted. Brethren, have we such faith in the coming of the
Spirit? or rather, does not the belief of the world, being filled
with his influence, not of the few drops, but of the full shower,
appear too often the dream of heated, fanatical minds?

They *continued instant in prayer.* How earnestly does the
sailor tread the deck of his becalmed ship, looking above for
the cloud, and on the surface of the deep, to see if there be the
slight curling of its waters that indicates the coming gale, and
invoking God to send it! And with what zeal and persever-
ance ought we to beseech the Seven Spirits before the throne
to breathe forth His power, to waft to her destination that
vessel laden with food for millions of perishing souls!

And, finally, *they were one,*—and to the united Church the
Spirit will come. Its influence is direct and reflex; the more
union we have, the more we shall obtain of the Spirit; and the
more of the Spirit we obtain, we shall have the more union.
For as the breezes, blow from whatever quarter they may, bring
the vessels, start from whatever part of the globe they may,
the nearer to each other, the nearer they bring them to their
common harbour—so that Spirit, the nearer to our haven it

brings the Church, the closer, the nearer will it bring its individual elements.

Such, then, is the power with which the Church is to be armed, and such are the phenomena that, so far as we are concerned, determine its bestowment; and if ever there was a time in which it was most necessary to fall back on such principles, to be ¨nerved with such energy, *that time is now*. To a mind uninspired with great faith, appearances loom on the horizon, both ecclesiastical and political, sufficiently ominous and gloomy to make the soul quiver with dread, or to prostrate it into the impotence and inaction of despair. At home, we have the development of principles,—self-aggrandizing, anti-spiritual, despotic,—principles destined, if ever they are to prevail, to prevail not through the argumentation of their abettors, the brilliant eloquence, the paraded learning, the ascetic piety of their hierophants; but through their congruity with the desires of corrupt man, investing as they do the clergy with a dim, shadowy sanctity, and basing the safety of the laity on sacramental efficacy, and rigid, exclusive ritualism, while demanding from neither personal, self-denying, thorough-paced godliness. At home, we have the great anti-Christian mystery no longer affecting the liberal, wearing the mask of an altered policy, or seeking safety in inoffensive, quiet, sequestered action, but displaying itself in the unchangeableness, the boasted unchangeableness, of its character and principles; no longer branded with the stamp of legislative and national indignation, but flattered, petted, fed by statesmen, until with tiger-craft it has acquired strength and opportunity for a tiger-spring; and worse, unspeakably worse than all that,—for here

we might meet in perfect security the onset of Popery,—it sends
forth its emissaries to India, China, and Polynesia, seemingly
endorsed by the British Government, and, to the ignorant conceptions of the natives, with the imprint and sanction of the
British Legislature. Everywhere the hosts are mustering for
the conflict—a conflict that involves no less a question than
this, Shall the dial-finger of time be put back, and the nineteenth century rolled into the lap of the twelfth? True,
the conflict is to be waged in the most favourable circumstances, with the energy of freedom, with mind unchained,
with knowledge diffused, and, above all, with the Bible cheap.
But let us not imagine that even with such advantages we can
conquer without the Spirit of God. With that Spirit we must
triumph. Changed indeed is the aspect of our work ; multiplied are the enemies with whom we have to struggle. Once
we had in heathen lands to meet heathenism alone ; now we
have to meet heathenism and · Popery too ; for the latter,
though bearing a Christian name, we never can recognise as
an ally. Thus it is in the Southern Pacific, on the plains of
Hindostan, and by the banks of the Yellow River. But,
fathers and brethren, let us not dread the issue ! The Lord of
hosts is on our side ; of whom shall we be afraid? Let us
only, then, be faithful to him, and he will be faithful to us and
to himself. Secure in her own strength sat Babylon, the banner
of the earth. Calmly reposed her shadow on the Euphrates.
Softly fell her minstrelsy on its waters. Her defences seemed
impregnable, her resources exhaustless. What is she now?
Vitrified mounds and stagnant pools—desolation so terrible
that the Arab flees from the spot—silence so deep that the cry

of the bittern breaks it: these mark the place once occupied by a "walled province," traversed by star-gazers, and the seat of a proud and powerful dynasty. The shout of liberty rang over the grave of the tyrant. Had Babylon perished in defence of her rights, or before the unprovoked assault of some new rival power, her fall had been witnessed with regret. But Babylon fell the prey of her own crimes, and because beneath the dark shade of her stupendous bulwarks, freedom, virtue, piety, withered and drooped. Better far Babylon in heaps, the sepulchre of her own vices—the tomb of the despot— than Babylon in uneclipsed splendour and untouched might, dishonouring God by her sin, and oppressing men by her despotism! Yes, and let the mystic Babylon lay deep her foundations, and extend widely her boundaries—let her rejoice in mean ambition over poor Tahiti, and aim at India as the brightest gem in her iron crown—the day is arriving,—oh Lord of hosts, in thy mercy accelerate its approach!—when over her ruins shall rise the shout caught and re-echoed from the crystal sea in Heaven by those whom she slew on earth: Babylon is fallen, is fallen, and shall rise no more! Be it ours to swell that triumphant chorus in the jubilee of the universe—the chorus of freedom over oppression—of light over darkness— of the Cross over the crucifix—of heaven over hell! Amen, and amen.

DISCOURSE II.

"THE DUKE:" A SKETCH.*

ACCORDING to the anticipation of some present, I deviate this morning from my ordinary course of exposition, to say a few things on the topic of the day—the Duke of Wellington. In the choice of this subject I have been guided partly by my own feelings, and partly by the suggestion of friends whose opinions I sincerely respect. I am well aware that almost everything has been said that can be said regarding the Duke; but every man has his own way of saying a thing, and I have mine. The views taken of the departed are strongly, almost antipodally, opposed. I am not here, however, to sneer as a cynic, or flatter as an encomiast, or trace as an historian; but to seize a few salient points, to

---

* It may be proper to state, that while the substance of the following discourse was delivered by me to my congregation on the occasion of the Duke's funeral, portions have been added which I would have thought, perhaps, not quite consistent with the character of the pulpit. I make this statement lest any of my readers should suppose that everything—whether in thought or form—was uttered as it appears in the following pages, and supposing that, condemn me.

interpret them in the light of morals and religion, and to deduce those lessons which speak most emphatically from the tomb. In the line of my remarks there are necessarily some points I would willingly have avoided—points on which there may be differences of opinion, the propriety of which you may question, the truth of which you may repudiate. I shall endeavour in their assertion to combine honesty and charity, and while respecting the sentiments of others, not disguise my own; and crave that each will give to myself the candid and liberal interpretation which I grant to all.

I select as my text the words from

Jeremiah xlviii. 17,—

"How is the strong staff broken!"

In the course of last week, it was the privilege of thousands to witness the obsequies (and those that witnessed can never describe, never forget them)—and it was the lot of hundreds of thousands to witness the funeral procession—of the foremost man of the age and of the civilised world. Every country, indeed, has its foremost man, its hero, and who, if heathen, would be its demigod; and when you wander amidst the scenes of their triumph, and hear their praises expressed in the most enthusiastic terms, one may rudely be inclined to laugh at the greatness assigned to the little dignified, or pleased to give to the praise of one hardly ever known or heard of before, the smile of approbation—the cheap tribute of good-nature to national vanity. But the fame of the Duke was not local, not insular, not Continental, not European—it was the fame of the times, of the world; and wherever our tongue is spoken, in the old or in the new regions of the globe, his name has become a

household word ; and let foreigners from any part of the globe
visit our shores, the Duke was a sight as truly and really as
Westminster Abbey or Windsor Castle, and ofttimes visited
before either, and in preference to both.

His most familiar name was—at least in my estimation—his
noblest. His titles were many ; they were enough to satisfy
the most morbid and almost insatiate ambition. He had titles
from the throne, titles from the seats of learning, titles from
the courts of Europe—and these, too, the most dazzling they
could confer ; but there is one, to my taste, unspeakably more
glorious, perhaps more enduring, than all. Chancellor of
Oxford he was made by learned men ; Marshal of different
empires and kingdoms, by their heads and rulers ; Knight of
the Garter, by the Sovereign Authority of our own land ; and
by the Regent created, in consequence of his victories, Duke
of Wellington. Garter-King-at-Arms proclaimed all these titles
over his corpse. But the people ennobled the Duke in their
own way. They shortened his title ; and by shortening they
added new splendour to it. As Duke of Wellington, he was
one of many ; as *The* Duke he stood alone ; he was a Peerage,
an Order, in himself, begun in himself and with himself extinct.
Nobody ever could mistake—so universal was the interpretation of the single, distinct epithet, " The Duke "—who was
meant, when the terms were used. You met a stranger gazing
at Apsley House (a spot now classic by the memory of its
occupant), or you saw a foreigner loitering beneath the shadow
of the towers of Westminster Abbey, and you hear the question,
" Is the Duke come out ?" or " Has the Duke gone in ?" You
might hear a number of little boys, following a person passing

quietly and thoughtfully by upon horseback, and shouting, in their boyish glee, " Why, there's the Duke !" You would never stay to ask, "What Duke?" There were other Dukes in England, some distinguished by their magnificent revenues and splendid domains, some by their large-souled liberality and boundless kindness, some by their exquisite taste, and some by their highly-polished manners; but you never thought of them when the words " *The* Duke" were uttered in your ears : to you, for the moment, there was but one Duke in England— the Duke of Wellington. How prodigious must have been the exploits of the man ! what a reality, what force must have been in his character ! how earnest, and how energetic, the man who could thus tower out in almost solitary splendour before his entire country, and by the fame of his self-created grandeur, dwarf, nay, almost annihilate, the first branch of the peerage of Great Britain ! The strippling ensign of 1787 becoming, before he was fifty years of age, the soul, the star, the life, the pre-server of the aristocracy !

But he is gone, with all his popularity, and fame, and reve-rence. Not more effectively was the rod of office broken and deposited in fragments upon his coffin in St Paul's, the other day, than the once living staff has been broken by death and buried by a nation. Look from Assaye, from Flanders, to St Paul's, and who is not constrained to exclaim, " How is the strong staff broken !"

I have referred to his obsequies. Their character, their taste, their management, I will not stop to discuss ; I may just say, in passing, it is fortunate for some that he cannot speak of them himself. Certainly they were not in keeping with the simplicity

U

of his character—they were no companion picture to the simple English funeral of his great friend, Sir Robert Peel; and I question if his successor, Lord Hardinge, was so much touched amid the grandeur of St Paul's, as when stanching with his sash the wounds and burying in the shades of night, by the lone shore of Corunna, the body of his illustrious compatriot and companion, the gallant Moore. But this is not the place, nor am I the man, to criticise such things. I must just repeat— he is gone! again—"the strong staff is broken."

The figure of my text is a very striking one. Is it applicable to the Duke? My reply to this question is necessarily limited. I will not speak now of the staff broken, so far as foreign nations are concerned—sometimes chastening, sometimes sustaining them. I will not intrude into the sacred privacy of her who loved him with a daughter's love, and in his sagacity had her best counsel, and in the kind smile of the kind old man her richest joy. Her staff, too, is broken, and that smile shall rest on her no more. I will look at home. For a moment consider *his influence among, for, ourselves*—I mean by that among, for *the middle, the trade, and working classes of the land*, to which you and I in common belong—those who live by the sweat of their brow or by the sweat of their brain—the trade, the working, the great masses of the land—the strength and backbone of society. Now, what a strong staff was he to us! I refer to measures for freeing industry, for cheapening food— measures in which his predeceased friend occupied the most prominent place, and whose very pre-eminence obscured to some degree the influence and action of the Duke. Mistake me not, as if I meant in my remarks to teach that any great

measure is in the upshot dependent upon any great man. I
cannot doubt that everything which is morally wrong, that everything which violates the sound principles of social economics,
must come to an end. The thing is a question only of time and
of means. The struggle may be protracted and fierce; ignorance
and passion may be evoked—the most determined selfishness
may assume the guise of patriotism; hypocrisy, to use a familiar
modern phrase, may become "organised," and domestic despotism may try to repress the influence of independent thought;
but *in the long run sound principle is sure to right itself.* Dr
Chalmers might die without having seen that great measure
which he predicted would sweeten the breath of society; Sir
Robert Peel may have died without being able to boast that the
time would come when his name would be mentioned with
respect in the cottages of England, as having sweetened the poor
man's bread; yet everything that counteracts the laws of God
or the ordinances and true interests of nations must terminate!

But mark, now, the strength of the staff—the power of the
Duke! A crisis came. A whisper, a doubt, much more a
direct negative, from his lips, would have procrastinated the
settlement and issue of a great controversy—a controversy
great in itself, as involving the food of millions; and, greater
still, as menacing a war—the most terrible of all wars—a
war of classes—a war of the rich against the poor—a war
of peerage against democracy. The Duke, at the risk of
every kind of misrepresentation, with the bitterest invectives
directed against himself and others, and, with danger to the
well-earned and well-worn laurels upon his brow, steps forward
to guide to its termination this great and mighty question. At

half-past three in the morning he rises, the decision then trembling in the balance. He addresses the senate in a few simple, sententious, and terse words:—"The bill comes before you with the sanction of the Commons, and it comes, too, with the recommendation of the Crown; and, my Lords, without the Crown and the Commons you are helpless. Beware how you reject this bill!" Spoken with feelings of deep, earnest truth, these words settled the question—a question which he alone at that time could have settled—which he alone could now reverse and unsettle, and which even he, young men, could not reverse and unsettle unless backed by the majesty and strength of public opinion, to which the hero himself was constrained to bend, and by which he made the senate, on that memorable occasion, a second, a senatorial Waterloo.

Again, think not only of the power which he exercised in regard to the middle classes, but also of the strength and *influence he had in regard to his own order.* His preservative influence on the peerage of England perhaps they did not feel—perhaps they do not feel universally now. There are some of them, as there are in every class of society, headstrong, impetuous men, who may possess more of the blood than the brains of their ancestry, and they accused the Duke of cowardice,—charged him with weakness and dotage! Dotage I can see none, in that old man, and certainly nothing whatever of the mulish obstinacy generally connected with age. The Duke went with the times, feeling their progressive necessities, and growingly prepared to meet them. While others lagged behind towards the middle of the nineteenth century—living, thinking, acting as if it were only about to open—dreaming that, because

they stood still the whole world around them was not moving,—
he advanced, ever a scholar (which I would have every one
of you, and myself, always to be), ·continually learning, and
perhaps gaining more knowledge—practical, philosophic, and
profound—in the last five-and-twenty years of his life, than in
the freshest and longest part of his career. A new state of
things arose; and the keen eye which could scan the man-
œuvres of a battle-field, and adjust the movements of his
army to the exigency of the moment, saw that it was necessary to carry into the political battle-field the lessons he
had there acquired. Taking time and events by the forelock,
he saved once and again the aristocracy of the country from
the angry surges which sometimes they despised, and, what
was more, saved them from themselves. That staff, their
staff, is broken; and amid the great, the good, the gentle of
their number—for there are many such amongst them—there
is not one that I can see at this moment, who by his personal
influence can control, and by controlling uphold them. Their
moral character, their intelligent forethought, their harmony
with the Crown, and, above all, their sympathy with the
people, will form in all future times their strongest and most
indestructible staff.

But whether they or we feel and acknowledge that a strong
staff is broken, there is one to whom I refer who must feel it
acutely. I need hardly say that I refer to our beloved Sovereign. In the Duke the Queen had, what few monarchs
enjoy, a friend; not a courtier, not a butterfly of fashion, not
a parasite of power, but a man — a stalwart, sincere, and
genuine friend. Relative to her, what in other cases was a

duty, part of discipline, was a pleasure—acquired almost the warmth of passion. Gallantry in old times was chivalry; devotion to the Queen was the chivalry of the Duke. The noble, true-hearted old man felt, and wished her to feel too, that beneath the shade of that arm that shivered the embattled veterans of France upon the plains of Flanders, she might rest in unbroken and undisturbed security from intestine faction and from external aggression. He was ever ready, by counsel and by action, at the sacrifice of his own repose, to uphold the integrity of the throne, and induce others to rally around it. Her strong staff, too, is broken. But great as to her is the loss of the Duke, it is not irreparable. In the hearts of her people, true and trustworthy—in the constitutional principles of Government—in the domestic virtues which at once embellish her throne and bless her life—above all, in the presence of the Eternal, the throned Monarch of the universe, the King of kings, she will find (would that the princes of the earth would seek them there!) her best defence in danger, her richest enjoyment, and her most infallible counsel amid the embarrassments of her reign.

Never perhaps, then, did so many lean upon a human staff; never was such power, so ramified or real, concentrated in the hand of one subject; and if any suggest to me that such concentration was a most dangerous and undesirable thing, at once I grant it, and pray it may never occur again. Nothing can be more dangerous to the liberties of nations than the possession, the monopoly, of enormous power in one single individual; and if ever it should occur again in the history of our country, my only hope is, that it may be committed to one who, like the Duke, will be guided by principle to regulate its use, not for the aggrandisement of himself or his family, not for the ends of human ambition, but for the great purposes of enlightened civic patriotism, the elevation and prosperity of his Fatherland !

Now, it is natural to ask, What was there in the history, in the character, of the man, to give him this prodigious influence ? To answer this, his conduct and character have been brought before the public in two different lines of action—the warrior and statesman. Now, sketching, as I wish to do, simply the man, in my own judgment I think it is impossible and unnecessary to divaricate between these two things entirely and continuously : there are so many features in common—the same directness of purpose, the same simplicity of aim, the same promptitude of action, the same firmness and strength of will. The hand that guided the movements at Waterloo upheld the Act of Emancipation to our Roman Catholic brethren in Ireland ; and possibly without the first we should not have had the second by the same instrumentality. What a sublime transition ! He who gathered laurels upon the field of slaughter should live to scatter the seeds of blessing, of plenty, and liberty on the fields of peace ! —that the same arm that sought to re-establish the thrones of monarchs should extend the freedom of the people ! Nor was this unnatural. The Duke had lived to see a large amount of his labours wasted and perverted by the folly of sovereigns he had restored, and lived to feel that the sword is not, never has been, and never can be, the arbiter of nations ; that power may force back upon a people a deposed monarch, but that principle and wisdom alone can keep him on the throne to

which he has been restored; that right alone is might; that
principle alone is power; and that while an army of bayonets
may reinstate the despot on his throne, they cannot prop the
throne up for ever. The blood that tyranny sheds has only
nourished and fertilised the vine of freedom, around whose
roots it has been poured. Besides, the Duke's own mind had
no taste for war—its barbaric splendour, its orgies of crime,
its blood-stained triumphs or defeats; and therefore, in the
Duke's second lifetime, the lifetime of the councillor and the
statesman, he profited by the lessons, and gained power by
the conquests, of the first. I shall not attempt, therefore, now
to separate the two great epochs of his life, but rather single
out a few salient features in the general character of the
man. I cannot pass, however, without one remark, and that
upon the first point to which I have alluded—his character as
a soldier. It is not because I have any taste for the exploits
of a warrior, or any knowledge of the strategy of the camp,
that I allude to the subject, but because it comes naturally in
my way. It was the habit, for some time, to call in question
the military capacity of the Duke, and for lips that should have
been sealed by gratitude, to designate him "the Stunted
Corporal "—an epithet just as witless as its sarcasm was
false. But since and before his death some of the French
have called in question his soldier-like power. Most singular
and inconsistent conduct! The last people to condemn him
are the French. The more I condemn my antagonist for want
of merit and ability, the more I depreciate myself, whether I
be successful in conflict with him or whether I should be
foiled. The more they seek to degrade the Duke, the more

they humble their mightiest soldier—the idol-star of their worship—who in his turn paled before the ascendant of England. Lower the military fame of Wellington, and you crush the laurels on the brow of Napoleon. Such, however, is generally the action of monomaniac vanity—it degrades its possessor when it seeks to humble his rival.

But it has been insinuated that he had no genius, or that if he possessed genius his deeds would have been sublime. I speak not—this is not the place to speak—of the plagiarism of that sneer. It had been well if the speaker's lips had been silent, and if he had contrived to forget all he had stolen from others, and remembered that he had a rich treasury in himself to which at all times he might appeal. To answer the charge, however, it may be fairly asked, What is genius? What do we understand by the term? Nothing is more undetermined, while certain definitions of it are most exclusive and partial. The flashy orator, the dashing novelist, the poet of the intense school, according to the modern phrase, will limit genius to his own idiosyncrasy, and perhaps even limit the idiosyncrasy to a very few—forgetful of this, that genius may be one in reality, but in action diverse; that, in point of fact, the architect of St Paul's or the author of the Crystal Palace is as truly a genius, a poet, a creator, as the orator in the House of Commons, or the novelist in his study.

But the question returns: Had the Duke genius—genius equal to his great rival, Napoleon? No; if genius consists in glitter and parade. No; if it consists in startling paradoxes, rolling sentences, and rhetorical embellishments. But if to possess an eagle-eyed mind, which could detect all the weak points in a foe—more (for these are far more difficult to be discerned), if to possess a mind which could detect all the weak points in itself, and all with whom it comes into contact —if to create from confusion serried bodies of human beings, to handle them with the greatest effect, and the least expense of life—if to move so as to convert weakness into strength, to defeat the greatest military genius of his time—if that be not genius, it is next door to it, certainly something very like it. Deny, however, genius to the Duke, and yet you find strong, masculine thought. And, after all, a prosaic life, young men, is better and more lasting than the poetic. Its light burns longer, if it produces a less dazzling flame. Seek, then, my young friends, the culture and the development of the reflective rather than the imaginative part of your nature—the practical, rather than the intense—the working and the workable, rather than the dreamy and the speculative; assured of this, that it is more essential to success to possess a steady, vigorous judgment, clear, distinct forethought, than the vivid play of fancy, uncertain though brilliant in its coruscations.

I now approach one or two points to which I feel it proper to refer in honesty and truth, before examining the general elements of the Duke's character—points on which the views of ministers and moralists should be firmly but kindly expressed. We can see—we have seen—the Duke in the camp, in the senate, in the saloon; but the thought has always crossed my own mind, and cast a shade of melancholy while reflecting on it—What was the Duke at home? Had he one? I mean by that, a scene of conjugal love and intercourse, of tender family feeling, the blessed charm of one's own fireside—

after all, the richest happiness on this side of heaven. Who has not felt the witchery of home feeling in the life of Luther? Who has not felt its charm in the history of George Washington? Luther buying a toy for his little child in the fair at Leipsic; and George Washington, the self-denying patriot of America, still panting for his domestic ease, which he had sacrificed for patriotic duty, and showing by its sacrifice the depth of his patriotic love. These touches of nature soften the grim sternness of the warrior, and make us feel we are in contact with men, not with heroes. Often have I asked myself, Did the Duke know the feelings and happiness of home life, such as you, young men, and myself, feel to be the most real enjoyment of existence? On this subject we know nothing —I wish we had known much. I draw the curtain over his domestic history with painful reluctance.

On another topic, which I have not seen mentioned nor censured in the sermons which have been published on the Duke's death, I may express an opinion—the habit in which the Duke indulged to the last; I refer to his attendance in the fashionable world—its operas and soirees—night after night, and many in a night. Without his presence no aristocratic party seemed complete; and we can easily imagine the desire of all to secure his company. However vulgar might be the assembly —and vulgarity is not confined to the cottage of the poor or the roof of the workman—his presence would redeem it from contempt; and one can readily imagine the delight which the Duke would throw into the minds of the young; perhaps his own heart had some enjoyment in the scenes; and who would grudge the old hero one moment's enjoyment? But still, still these were hardly the appropriate haunts for an octogenarian tottering upon the verge of the grave; and sure I am that if the death-scene of Walmer Castle had been a protracted one of mental consciousness, as it was one of rapid apparent insensibility, the remembrance of that part of life so spent —the waste of time which might, which should have been consecrated to the review of the past, to preparation for the future—would have come with deep and saddening influence. I grant that in this we, in our spheres, may not be the fairest, most qualified judges. We live and move in different regions. What to the aristocracy is life, may seem to us the frivolity of thoughtlessness; what to us is life and pastime may appear to them stupidly sombre. But while from this we learn the lesson of charity, let us not forget that age should form habits in keeping with the sobriety of years. To the thoughtful, calm mind, it loses venerable grandeur when mingling amid the splendid frivolities of the gay. Let each extreme of life remember that one element of its loveliness lies in the harmony of its period with its occupations and amusements; and that, while it is sad to see youth immuring itself in the conventual cloister, or seeking its heaven in the severities of unnatural asceticism, it is not less touching to some, though laughable to others, to behold old age, instead of by sober repose meetening and mellowing for eternity, clinging to the brilliant, evanescent dissipations of time.

I willingly leave this part of my subject, which nothing but a strong conviction of ministerial faithfulness would have led me to touch. I hope I have referred to it with delicate kindness.

Among the prominent features of the Duke's character, and

perhaps the most prominent, was *the conviction of the obligation of duty*. It has been referred to in every discourse and every lecture or critique upon the Duke. The words, indeed, have been almost a synonym, "the Duke" and "duty." He has been mocked by the French, who, as you know, have represented the Duke's despatches as never containing the word "glory," but as always harping upon duty. Now I will not attempt to decide the question, which principle supplies the best motive to action—whether under the stimulus of mere glory, or whether under the stern power and force of moral duty, a man will do his work best, most strenuously, most successfully; but I may just state that the affinity of duty to glory is very close. Duty is sure, young men, in the end, to be crowned with glory; and there is no glory worth coveting, worth having, except what comes in the line of duty.

When it is so often said that duty was his leading star, it is well and may be proper to see what is the meaning and force of the expression. We are not to suppose that he deemed it necessary to do whatever he was commanded on any subject; but that whatever he was commanded to do in the line of action on which he had entered, he felt himself bound to accomplish. Committed voluntarily to a cause, he was committed heartily to it, and bound to carry it out to its full issue. Personally he might shrink from the horrors of war, as we know that he did. I can conceive, indeed, of no greater contrast, in reading the history of the Peninsular war, than that between the conduct of the French and the Duke. They revelled as in a carnival of fire and blood; he tried to mitigate the horrors which he could not avert. But he felt that he was a soldier, and therefore bound to obey. A fort is to be taken, and he takes it. He becomes a statesman, and is constrained to realise his policy and plans : a bill requires to become law, and he firmly manages it until enrolled in the Acts of Parliament. From 1799, in India, to 1850, in Britain, the principle embodied in the letter which he addressed to General Harris, in Mysore, is that which breathed, and was embodied, in after life. A movement was suggested, of which the future Duke felt doubtful (and his doubts were completely justified by the result), and he writes to his commander,—" However, you are the best judge, and I shall be ready." That was all ; he gave up his own judgment, his opinions, to his superior, and simply says, "I shall be ready;" and throughout all his life this principle reigned. It is my duty, and must be done. This principle, young men, may, no doubt, be carried to excess. Without any limitation it may be highly dangerous, and unregulated it may stoicize, may petrify your hearts ; but if combined with virtue and wisdom, and, above all, controlled by the religion of the Lord Jesus Christ, it is the certain principle of power and the sure foundation of progress.

In its practical evolution there were two accompaniments— that whatever he could do himself he left nobody else to do, and that in duty nothing is a trifle ; that is, that everything acquires importance when it becomes a matter of duty. These might be apophthegms ; but in his case they were practical realities. Amid difficulties almost overwhelming, amid demands upon his time and thought requiring almost omnipresence and omnipotence, in cases in which the least disarrangement would have been fatal, these, while multiplying responsibility, only seemed to augment his power and resources; attending to the care of the sick and the general comfort of the army as if they were his own family, he raised around him a noble band of fellow-soldiers who followed him in his victories, and the other day wept over, his grave, worthy of their chief and their country.

Here, then, young men, is the lesson—Duty, its obligations and demands; that is the great secret of success. The Duke has been described as the. chance victor of Waterloo. Some have had the hardihood to designate that battle as only a lucky hit, the mere good fortune of the day. Napoleon—the Napoleon—has been called the child of destiny, beneath the *star* of Josephine. Singular, that upon the field of fight chance and destiny should come into collision, and that the luck of the Duke should overwhelm the destiny of the Emperor! No, no, it was not so. The secret of his entire life and its success lies in the simple motto on his hatchment—" *Virtutis comes Fortuna*"—fortune, prosperity, is the companion of virtue. He looked only for success in doing his duty. Young men! trust neither in chance nor in fate: feel that duty and prosperity are inseparably associated. They may not always appear to be so linked at the moment; but discharge your duty to your employers, to your parents, to your brethren, and to your family, faithfully, and depend upon it that in the end you will be crowned with God's blessing. Above all, remember that you profess to have given yourselves to him, and that you have only one rule to guide you, his law; one principle by which to be prompted, love to him; and one end to gain, his everlasting glory.

Such is the first feature. The second I shall briefly refer to —that, connected with the felt obligation of duty, was *great concentration of action*. The value of that property it is impossible to exaggerate, but I have not time now to expatiate upon it. I may just say, that without it the highest genius is comparatively valueless ; it may be developed in fits and starts, now and then, but it is an aimless and powerless thing, only weakening itself by spasmodic efforts. He, on the contrary, who has concentration of mind, can bring his powers to bear at all times on any particular subject, and by that very concentration multiplies and strengthens them. Now, it is scarcely necessary to say that this formed a bold point in the Duke's character. Whenever he felt a thing to be right, a matter of duty, he made directly for it—he brought the powers of his nature and influence upon it, as if he had nothing else to do in the world. Young men, aim after that self-control. You may spend years in reaching it ; but if you gain it at length, you will have done more for the acquisition of knowledge, for the culture of your minds, and for your influence in society, than if you had stored up in your memory masses of information ; for you will obtain the power to employ them to advantage. Above all, carry out this great principle in religious matters. In all your conduct, as professed believers of the Gospel of Jesus Christ, aim at one great end, and concentrate all your powers upon the acquirement of it, using everything for one purpose, and doing it as if you had nothing else to do.

I might here allude to another obvious feature of the Duke, and one which I think is not the least instructive in its character—*his perfect reality and transparency*. Transparency I define in a single sentence as truth in life, truth in action. In this you are assured that you have not before you the actor, but the man. The Duke may have resolved wrong; from his opinions you may have utterly dissented, as many dissent now; he may have argued wrong, and the breath of your lips might have scattered all his words and arguments; but you always knew what the Duke meant. His logic might not be clear, but it never sank into sophistry; his rhetoric might not be very elaborate, but still it was always connected with the honest manifestation of truth; you feel that he might have deceived himself, but he never meant to deceive you. There was the secret of the Duke's eloquence! He never professed to be an orator, though Lord Brougham tried to make him one; but he proceeded upon the principle which I would impress upon every one here, that the best logic is to be found in a clear head, and the best rhetoric in a warm heart; and if you have these two things combined, ignorant of the scholastic rules of rhetoric or of logic, you will become successful speakers. The Duke's words were not meant, according to Talleyrand's plagiarism, to conceal thought—not a loophole, which so many tricky politicians make speech, through which, by double interpretation and oracular ambiguity, to escape in the future from the pledges of the present. He spoke in terse, nervous, Saxon English— plain, distinct, simple thoughts, so that they who heard could not mistake his meaning. Everything about him was clear as the day, though it might seem a day of mid-winter, icy, icy cold.

Here, then, is a warning to you against appearances, against hypocrisy, or, to use a Carlyleism, a warning against shams.

x

The Duke was none. He could not tolerate one. An earnest, real, transparent, living man himself, he liked to come into contact with such, and with such to have to do. And what man would not? Who that knows, possesses the manhood of human nature, does not like to associate or to come in collision with men of intellectual sinew and strength, and moral transparency? Give me a rough touch of nature rather than the *finesse* and finish of artificial life. There is something in that to charm you, and make you feel yourself secure, safe, and at home; but shams and hypocrisy are untrusted lies. Seek, then, young friends, always to be what you appear to be, and always appear to be what you are; work in the day, broad-breasted and open before the light of heaven, transparent in the purity of your motives, and distinguished by the truthful energy which ever marks the noblest children of God. Need I say, that in acting thus in religion you resemble your Master? Transparent, living, real, was the Son of God and man. The little child rested in His arms, and, as it looked up to the brow beneath which the thunders of Omnipotence slept, it saw the sweet smile, the sunny light, of that blue eye, and felt itself at home. The Pharisee looked upon Him, and the lightning of His eye flashed conviction and terror into his soul. The child breathed and felt sweetly there, as on its mother's lap; the Pharisee quailed in terror before Him. The loving, real child knew the transparency of His nature, and the Pharisaic hypocrite felt and trembled before it. Study His character, make Him your ideal, and copy His example.

Another element in the Duke's character which strikes me, was its *perfect truthfulness*. It has been graphically said, his

life was a battle against falsehood. Amid political changes in
which the most violent attacks were made on the honour of his
compeers, the most reckless political assassin scarcely ever
dared to aim one stab at the fair fame and truthful character
of the Duke. His plans were condemned, his judgment im-
peached, and himself represented as the tool of crafty and
treacherous men; but his own personal honour was almost
never assailed and never suspected. He stood firm, because
sincere; respected by those who politically differed from him
most diametrically.

Nor is this feature less obvious in the history of the soldier.
What a contrast he presented to his antagonists! Look at the
bulletins of the marshals of France, often composed of poetic
fiction, in contrast with his truthful prose. Even when a little
colouring in his narrative would have been acceptable, and
would have cheered the people of England, he resisted the
temptation. His own nature was true as the steel of his own
sword. He knew that truth is always the most honourable
in itself, and the most safe in its consequences, and therefore in his despatches never departs from it. By that he,
too, baffled all the diplomacy of the age—diplomacy which
may be defined to be the art and mystery of international
overreaching. When he came into contact with diplomatists
who had undergone a course of thirty or forty years' training in the art, his simple, downright, English truthfulness
baffled them all. Young men, carry this with you—one grain
of truth is better than a bushel of policy. Through the whole
of his life the Duke acted on this principle in all departments of service, in the senate and in the camp. As has

been well and beautifully said by the Poet Laureate, Alfred
Tennyson,—

> " He never sold the truth to serve the hour,
> Nor paltered with Eternal God for power.
> His eighty winters freeze with one rebuke
> All great self-seekers trampling on the right.
> Truth-teller was our England's Alfred named,
> Truth lover was our English Duke ;
> Whatever record leap to light,
> He never shall be shamed."

Now, mark the influence of truth on his success in life !
Never yielding to temptation to exaggerate victory or ex-
tenuate defeat, his representations of either were verified in
the result, while broken squadrons of men and the flying
marshals falsified the boasting of his rivals. Truth with him
was power ; and the converse is just as correct, that falsehood is weakness. While the Duke was lying dead, a great
American orator died. Daniel Webster aimed at the highest
object of Transatlantic ambition, the Presidential chair, and
might have reached it ; but the splendour of his talents was
obscured by the versatility of his conduct. Betraying the
North to the fancied interests of the South, he was not trusted
by the South because he had sacrificed the North ; having,
as has been sarcastically said, broken as many pledges as
would have qualified him for being an Emperor of the French.
The contrast is startling, and its lesson prodigiously important.
Firm to his purpose, true to his word, the Duke had energy,
success, in his fidelity. Truth to him, I repeat, was power.
Nor was this all : truth begets truth, as surely as falsehood
propagates itself. Napoleon had a strong inventive memory,
and he was surrounded by men with whom an oath had no

sanctity, and who could, on the faith of one, receive an army from the Bourbon only to transfer it to the escaped prisoner of Elba. Around the Duke's coffin stood an array of officers of the highest rank and of the greatest achievements—his companions in arms—trained under his eye; and it was a proud thing to think of their uniform, unsullied honour, and how his character, as a true man, was perpetuated in them. Young men, carry this thought with you; and remember that, if you become employers, you will be best served by true servants through being true yourselves. Lodge it in your heart—*truth is power*. It is power in the merchant, for it conducts him from poverty to riches—from obscurity to fame. Truth is power in the politician: the right, plain-hearted Speaker in the House of Commons, upon whose word its members can distinctly rely, has, after all, more influence than the most ingenious but sophistical and uncertain advocate. Truth is power in God; without it the universe were a blank, and eternity were a dark and terrible thing. Truth is power in God, for it keeps the universe revolving round *his* throne in peace—the universe of mind dependent upon *his* word for joy, or trembling in *his* condemnation with terror. Many of you are starting in life; rest then assured, that this will be the best basis of a substantial character and of an enduring prosperity.

One single sentence may be uttered regarding another characteristic of the Duke—*his great disinterestedness.* I mean by that, his freedom from self-seeking, from seeking honours for himself or family. Here is a lesson which we should not forget. He rose to great power. Every wish he could frame would be at once responded to. There was nothing too great for him to ask—nay, the struggle would be to gratify his wish—ay, to anticipate it. Now, look at his conduct. He never used his influence for his own honour, or the aggrandisement of his family. What a contrast to many!—I don't speak as a politician, but as a patriot,—what a contrast to many on both sides of politics, in whose cases to bear the family name of the Prime Minister is enough. The genius of the Premier would seem to run on indefinitely to the most remote relative, would appear to fit them for any employment —to tread the quarter-deck, to adorn the mitre, or to rule the Colonies, the future Britain of our globe. There is a sort of political popery, a kind of politico-apostolic succession, where commonness of descent and relation to the Minister, without which a person would be nothing, is galvanized with power, qualified for anything, and desirous of everything. Mark the Duke's conduct! He left office with clean hands, and gave to the Ministers of England, in all future times, an exhibition of a noble-hearted and true Minister, that did not take place to enrich himself, and would not prostitute station to elevate his friends.

Such was the Duke; but he is gone—*whither*, I profess not to tell. I have spoken in regard to his domestic life; I should like to know more than I do of his inner being before I should speak of his doom. There may have been workings within, of which we have never heard (I judge none)—the unseen workings of the Spirit of God—upon his mind, while the dark shadows of death approached. At least one thing we believe, and that is all I would say—that he is in the hands of a kind and merciful Judge. I would not have the rashness to send him or any to heaven on the knowledge of the habit to which reference has often been made—his mere attendance on the daily service at St James'; but God forbid that I should be guilty of the uncharitableness of asserting that he is lost, because I may be ignorant of the inner workings of his spirit before God!

Again : he is gone. None in our country before him ever equalled him. Marlborough, notorious for meanness and untruthfulness, degraded the warrior by the man. Nelson, magnificent upon the quarter-deck, was a babe on shore, and held in the leading-strings of a designing woman. Wellington, in the camp, in the senate, in all the different departments of life to which we have referred, was a man, a noble and magnificent man. Nor can we expect to look upon his like again, as we have never seen it before ; but if, in the changes of nations, the collisions and struggles of the empires of the earth, another European war should burst out, my prayer to Almighty God is that—hate war as intensely as I do—Britain may never want an arm like the Duke's to grasp the sword in the hour of her danger, and a mind like his, which, by its prudence and counsels in the senate, shall extend and defend its liberty, its order, and its peace !

I cannot close without alluding to the illustration furnished, in the history of the Duke, of *the temporary fickleness and the ultimate stability of popular opinion.* We have seen last week thousands pouring into London from all corners of the land, many, no doubt, coming as to a show, and many touched with sincere respect for the memory of the mighty dead—nay, from all European States from which he had received honours while

living, special military representatives to honour him when
dead, with an exception which, after all, need cause little
regret in a free-breathing soul. The absence of a delegate from
a court which cannot discriminate between Haynau and Wellington is a matter of no great concern to us, whatever it might
be to them, and appears in humiliating 'contrast with the
conduct of the nation whose capital the Duke entered in
triumph, and nobly saved from spoliation and ruin. Now, go
back little more than twenty years. I remember placards in
this neighbourhood, " To stop the Duke, run for gold." I
heard him hooted in Lincoln's Inn Fields, saw persons try
to unhorse him, and accompanied him as one of a bodyguard
to protect him. Thus it is, has been, and will be : the martyr
of the day is the hero of the morrow, and the voice that makes
him either, seems uncertain as the wind. But feel that however uncertain popular opinion may be at the time, let a man
be right in himself, and the people are sure to be right with
him! Personal justice is, like social equity, a question of
time—the upshot is sure to be right. Some, indeed, may
perceive the claims of the suspected or injured sooner than
others ; they may have clearer heads, or warmer, more trusting
hearts, and anticipate the general verdict ; but ultimately all
will correct itself. History will vindicate character mistakenly
regarded—nay, if a man lives long, he may, like the Duke, get
his due. But certainly, if not in this life, amid the unchanging
realities of eternity will character here maligned, and principles
now misrepresented, stand forth for ever and fully vindicated,
eternally unassailable !

DISCOURSE III.

THE WAR: A FEW THOUGHTS ON IT.*

"The shields of the earth belong unto God; he is greatly exalted."
PSALM xlvii. 9.

THE general peace which crowned one of the severest European struggles, which has lasted nearly forty years, and whose duration was such that we hoped it would never be interrupted, is now ended. It is impossible to measure the progress of improvement made under its sway. During the time, commerce has extended almost indefinitely, not only in enterprise but in its principles. The means of intercourse have been prodigiously increased. Steam has diminished distance both by sea and land, and, by facilitating and cheapening travel, has multiplied the travellers. The

---

* An opinion having been expressed, by friends on whose judgment I rely, that the publication of the following thoughts might be profitable in the present crisis, I commit them to print. The sentiments and language are as nearly as possible those uttered on the Sunday evening of the 9th of April, from my own pulpit—very imperfect in thought and style, I acknowledge; but very honest and sincere in intention, I know.

lightning, which when we were children was a terror or a toy, has been pressed into the service of man, and surpassed steam, which diminishes space by annihilating it. Science has made great and rapid strides, and perhaps its most important, not in reaching the loftiest heights, but in journeying among the masses; and thus realising one of the sublimest truths of one of our sublimest thinkers (Sir James Mackintosh)," Diffused knowledge immortalises itself." National intercourse has been diminishing national prejudices, has fostered mutual respect, and been binding commonwealths by the consciousness of relative necessities and resources. This feeling of national sympathy so advanced that the Crystal Palace of Hyde Park seemed the Temple of Concord of the world. Alas! the green grass waves not more entirely over its site, obliterating every trace of its existence, than the hopes of peace—undisturbed, blessed, advancing peace—seem to have perished now. Forty years' tranquillity close amid the mutterings of war. How long, how loud, shall be their sound—how fiercely it shall swell—how soon it shall subside—who can tell? Amid the uncertainties of human motives, and the clouds that encompass all human action, let us refresh ourselves and brace our hearts by the language of the text, "The shields of the earth belong unto God; he is greatly exalted."

I depart this evening from the usual and appropriate order of pulpit ministration. I sympathise with the saintly Leighton on that point—the man who added to the gentleness of the Christian the heroism of the martyr and the wisdom of the sage, and who, living in days of eventful and stirring moment, when all with quaint, heartfelt, heart-reaching eloquence preached to the times, claimed the prerogative of preaching to eternity. Yet there are occasions when we may deviate from the routine course, and the present is one. We have entered on a war whose duration and issues we cannot predict. We are sure of many things connected with it—of the anguish it will inflict, the death it will deal, the crime it will create, and, last and lowest, the expense it will entail. But, begun, let it be examined in clear Christian light, and waged with the principle which rises above the cowardice that trembles and the rashness that scorns, and whose result is weakness and danger.

It is not my purpose here to discuss the lawfulness of war in the abstract. On that question minds are divided—minds strong in force and clear in honesty, and from whose antagonism we can conclude the difficulty of the subject, and should learn the lesson of moderation on either side. I have no sympathy with the tide of ridicule with which the peace principle is met, although I do not recognise it. I am alive to the obvious absurdity and inconsistency of men hating with a birthright hatred all tyranny, yet trusting the tyrant; loving simplicity of manners and style, yet fascinated with the palatial grandeur raised from the coerced labour of serf. But surely principles are occasionally to be regarded beyond the men, as men are occasionally above the principle; and in war, whose horrors none can exaggerate, there is enough to palliate the ultraisms, the eccentricities, of peace advocates, and even to sanctify their efforts.

Nor shall I pause to discriminate between the comparative lawfulness of defensive and offensive war. The line of demarcation between them has always seemed to me very faint; and the longer I regard it, it fades and melts away. The most daring offensive warfare is often the securest defence. It is no stretch of fancy, that British freedom would be best pro- moted by an invasion of its assailant, and London saved most practically by an occupation of the capital of its enemy. In Chatham's time, and since, the battles of England have been fought in Flanders ; and even now the battles of the Seine and the Thames may be waged on the Danube, and Western liberty vindicated by hurling back from the Baltic and Black Seas the barbarous hordes of Russia.

Nor shall I introduce to my present subject the symbols of apocalyptic vision. Of these I at once confess my utter ignor- ance, and in their interpretation my thorough want of faith. This may be my misfortune or my fault ; but such is the fact, and my conscientious judgment. Nothing, indeed, is easier, and with many classes nothing is more popular, than to deal with the mystical, and to decipher the hieroglyphics of the future. Prophetic interpretations, piercing into the distant, forecasting into the remote, have always had their votaries, their professors, and their students, whether in Egypt or in the glens of Scotland, or in our city, the Metropolis of the world. For my own part, believing that prophecy was never given to reveal the future, but only to confirm the Word,—not to super- sede the law of God, but to corroborate its claims—not to be its own interpreter, but to be interpreted by the fact,—I appeal in the following remarks to the past—the most prosaic, but the most certain guide of present conduct, the surest interpreter of coming circumstances.

In the preceding remarks the lawfulness of war has been

assumed; but it must be obvious that certain laws and circumstances can justify it—and what are they? My reply shall not be from the jurists, the dry expositors of international law; nor from the suggestions of traffickers who might be supposed, however unjustly, to measure principle by the purse. I will quote the writings of one distinguished not more by his Christianity than by the elegance of his mind and the beauty of his productions—I mean Dr Alison, the author of the "Essay on Taste." In a sermon delivered by him, the reverend preacher thus speaks, in 1801 :—

"If the war we pursue be one which is neither founded in justice nor necessity; if it be a war undertaken to overturn the independence or abridge the prosperity of any other people; if it be to add to our wealth by the spoils of the world, or to seek our glory by the tears of innocent or the blood of unoffending nations; if these be our secret objects in the war, let us not think, nor hope, nor pray for success. Victory may follow victory; achievement may succeed achievement; the pulse of national vanity may beat high; but 'the counsel of the Almighty' is against our devices. The secret vice which silently pursues its end is undermining the fabric of all our prosperity; and the Destroying Angel, who comes from the throne of God to 'justify his ways to man,' rejoices in the triumphs which his hand is so soon to wither, and in that attitude of presumptuous elevation which must so soon be humbled in the dust.

"But, my brethren, on the other hand, if it be a war of a different description that our hearts tell us we are pursuing; if it be a war necessary in its nature and just in its end; if it be to maintain the rights, the freedom, and the independence of our country; if it be to protect that constitution which is the fountain of all our best enjoyments here, and that religion which is the source of all our hopes hereafter; if it be to continue to our children that freedom to which they were born, and that faith in which they were baptised,—if these be our sole objects in the war in which we are engaged, then, in the name of the living God, let us fear not. Defeat may for a time succeed defeat, misfortune may follow misfortune, and the hearts of the weak and the timid may turn cold, but the counsels of God are with us."

But, *à fortiori*, if war be lawful when undertaken for ourselves, for our independence, how much more is it just when undertaken for the preservation of the weak in the brotherhood of nations against the unprincipled aggression of the strong! how much nobler, if one grand ulterior end of war be the promotion of thought, virtue, liberty! Here, what seemed to be the resistance of power for self-preservation, and might therefore be chargeable with selfishness, rises into generosity, and becomes dignified with the unselfishness of philanthropic humanity.

Now here rises the question, Are these principles applicable to the present juncture? Are our hands clean in this crisis? Do we as a nation war without an unjust motive, and having exhausted every means to avoid an appeal to arms? Perhaps —nay, certainly—a higher question may remain: Are the objects contemplated prospective rather than present—are we about to struggle for a great principle, for civilisation and progress?

To reply to these questions, let me suggest a few reflections.

I.

IN THE WAR LET US MARSHAL THE FORCES.

And here a combination of powers meets our view, almost unexampled and incredible—three great States, with nothing seemingly in common, moving under the guidance of one standard. Four centuries ago, and two of these kingdoms were arrayed against the third. The spears of France and England bristled against the shields and scimitars of Turkey. The voice of the Hermit of Picardy had appealed to the chivalry, the Christianity, of Europe; and, keen for adventure, its martial spirits rush against the Saracen—and for what? and how? For the rescue of the imagined sepulchre of our Redeemer from the Moslem grasp, and degrading his tomb by the most monstrous violations of his living law. Forty years ago, and these powers, one under Godfrey, were two under Napoleon and the Duke—pouring out the best blood of both lands like water in a fierce struggle, *for what?* Can we say now?

Who, looking from the former *time-point*, the elevation of four centuries, or even from the nearness of forty years, could imagine that the *three should be one*, moving in one mighty line of united action, and forming one common buttress for the civilisation, the freedom, of the earth? Who, looking down on human movements from either of these points of view, could suppose that the stoic fatalism of the Mussulman, the lively, burning zeal of the Gaul, and the sturdy, indomitable energy of the Saxon—that the Crescent, the Crucifix, the Cross—should all be combined in one serried mass? All seems dream-like! But it is the dream of fact; and, like all such fancies, more poetic and startling than those of imagination.

Extraordinary, however, as is this grouping, it is not less suggestive and cheering. Its existence shows that old antipathies are disappearing, and that a purer and nobler principle is seizing men than that of conquest. Let me say, that especially this is hopeful for the Truth—the Cross of our Saviour. The prejudiced, the armed isolation of nations, has been and must be a barrier to the progress of the Gospel. Let men come more into contact, and they will see each other more clearly. Antagonisms will abate; grudges, wounds, will be healed; and the inquiry will be forced—Whence the imagined or real inferiority of my foe once, my friend now? In such a juxtaposition of men and nations, mind will be taught, not from the lessons of books, but the conduct of the living. Mahomedanism will find that Christianity is kinder, more tolerant, than it was once believed to be; and the Romanism of France, rising from the embers of its unbelief, be constrained to ask—What has made Britain what it is? why its bulwark, strength to all parts of the earth? its shield to the weak, its defiance of the strong? To what can all this be ascribed—its level with us? To what but the purity of its creed, the manhood of its thought, and the personal and home virtues they germinate and mature. Singular! but why should it not be the fact, that the present struggle in behalf of Turkey should not eventuate in the exaltation of the Cross?

On the other side are ranged, *at present*, the vast military resources of Russia. These are but the body of the Czar—its thews and sinews, moved by one fierce and indomitable will. Souls, thought, they have none. They were born slaves, are kept slaves, and impelled, whether by the knout or by the priest, to do the behest of their imperial god ; and his command is the voice of Heaven. It is vain to disguise the formidable nature of this fact. They are serfs ; but they have muscle, though no thought; and they have purpose, though no light. A summons from Neva, and millions move at its bidding. The display of a consecrated banner, and millions more advance to a religious crusade, impelled by a sentiment the most easy to raise, the most fierce to act, and the most difficult to guide and to allay--religious fanaticism.

I have said that on the opposite side, *at present*, is Russia. The words "at present" I have purposely used—for who can tell what may be? War spreads as well as diplomacy. Self-interest in States begins to have a real or imaginary stake. The pusillanimity of one kingdom, the ties of gratitude by which a second throne is or fancies itself to be linked with Russia, may cast either or both into the arms of the wolf-like grasp of Moscow. Many dread this possibility,—first, as complicating the position, and second, as deferring indefinitely the decision, of the war. No doubt can exist, indeed, that from such a combination we might have reason to anticipate, and with horror, a greater flow of blood. Others might lament the departure of Austria from professed neutrality; but, expressing my own opinion, the open hostility of such a power were safer than a professed neutrality, during which Vienna waits the opportunity to betray the weaker and join the stronger and victorious side. Again: instead of complicating the circumstances, it would

Y

really simplify them. The Ottoman dispute alone settled, leaves multitudes still to embroil Europe. The spirit of freedom will still struggle; and better its demands be settled at once. Let Vienna remain in hypocritical neutrality, and the struggle is not ended—it is only deferred. Let Austria embrace Russia, and the fact leaves Western Europe free and unentangled, and spreads the torchlight of independence over the plains of Lombardy and the fastnesses of Hungary!

Such, then, are the forces now mustering to the conflict; and it were vain, worse than vain, to disguise that their meeting is awfully portentous. It is easy—but is it not idle?—to speak of the matters at issue being settled in one short, sharp campaign. The number of the foes assembled, assembling—the momentousness of the points at stake—the iron firmness of purpose of the parties—these imply that the present is a death-struggle. All may and should hope and pray—who does not? —that the conflict may be brief and glorious. But it may be protracted, severe, and clouded; and our only solid hope for its speedy and lasting termination is not in the prowess of our men, the science of our leaders, the stimulating rivalship of companions in arms (long foes, may they be still longer friends!), but in the truth that "THE SHIELDS OF THE EARTH BELONG UNTO GOD," and that, over the intrigues of cabinets, the passions of the people, the strategy of the camp, the valour of the tented field, he will, he must be exalted!

II.

LET US NOW ASCERTAIN THE CAUSES AND THE CIRCUMSTANCES
OF THE WAR.

Remembering the principles before announced, two points naturally present themselves: Have all means short of the sword been exhausted? and is the cause for which the sword is drawn, just—adequate?

The former of these questions has been answered by public sentiment and language. Negotiation had almost, if not entirely, exhausted patience. Diplomacy, on one side, indeed, played a cunning, unprincipled game, and realised a definition I ventured to give in a sermon on "The Duke"—that "diplomacy is the art and mystery of international overreaching." Certainly, Carthaginian faith has found its modern match in Russian honesty. English and French honour have shunned, have spurned the snare, as French and English force will crush the tempter. In the progress, however, of diplomatic plans, a strong impatience of their continuance was manifested in some organs of the press and from some platforms. "Why all this delay? War is the only means of arresting the Czar!" Now, nothing is easier than to utter such sounds, by those who have no risk in the encounter—no responsibility for its results. War is the last appeal of nations, and is fitted by its solemnity to make the rashest pause. But who, thinking of its ravages, of the homes it desolates, of its burdens, nay, even of the danger it gathers around our national existence, will not pity, excuse, honour, the apparently timid delays of those who conduct the counsels and affairs of an empire—the throbbing heart of the world? In a crisis of this order, how tremulous, how awfully anxious, must be the thoughts of the Minister! What difficulties must arise of which we know nothing! what opinions have to be united on most delicate matters! what plans have to be invented for future action! what preparations have to be made for their successful execution! And should not the consideration of such difficulties make a people compassionate of their rulers, and induce a large allowance for seemingly unnecessary and impolitic procrastination?

That in this war everything has been done to avert it, we cannot doubt. It is forced upon us, forced by boundless ambition and unblushing hypocrisy; and not till all expedients which skill and principle could suggest have been employed, has Britain accepted the gauntlet thrown down in contemptuous bravado, in defiance of Ottoman independence, European equality, and British honour.

I am aware that it may be and has been said, Why should we interfere at all? Why not leave nations to settle their own differences; or, if they will fight, fight their own battles? My answer is, that such a course would be unmanly, as it is unwise and unsafe. Leave Turkey in the grasp of Russia, and you would lay Europe at its feet. You would thus augment an empire already colossal, inordinately ambitious, and utterly unscrupulous, and so increase it as to destroy the balance of power. The term, I know, is derided as unintelligible and illusory. What is the balance of power for which you are going to war? It is a phantasy, a mere dream! So might appear to some our balance of power—the checks of our Government. They are our boast, and a reality. Our Constitution is a system of checks, and their relation and working strengthen and advance our liberty. By it we are saved from the autocracy of Petersburg, from the oligarchy of Venice, and from the throes of democracy in the first Revolution of Paris. And so with the safety of nations. In the balance of their powers there is the protection of the weak against the strong. In its feebleness, the victim-land can appeal against the oppressor. Different commonwealths, of corresponding resources, can restrain any one of their number; and, above all, by mutual confederation, can prevent the feeble from being overridden by the otherwise resistless might of one. To save Europe, Russia must be kept checked by the Eastern and Western world.

We pass now to the second question—Is the cause good? Are we now to be engaged in a war which contemplates a right end? I am aware of the difficulty arising from the pictures drawn of one of the mustered forces. Descriptions of Turkey have been widely circulated, of the most sombre cast; and such descriptions can be easily got up. A little reading and much prejudice are all the necessaries, and with them you may be able to say that the war is for a worthless ally. But from all such statements I appeal to men whose testimony is as firm as their position is worthy and dignified. The first of these is one of the most accomplished statesmen of our times, and whose official life has afforded larger opportunities than most men have enjoyed of knowing the condition of nations. The second to whom I appeal is one who, with the energy of Saxon blood, has dived into the retreats of the past, and mingled with the thoughts and homes of the living—throwing

light at once on the palaces of Nineveh and the mind of
Turkey. My last appeal is to one whose coronet is his least
distinction, and who by his conduct and character ennobles
the peerage. And on the testimony of Lord Palmerston, Mr
Layard, and Lord Shaftesbury, I have enough to fortify my
argument that the cause is good. Far indeed be it from me
to deny—much farther to palliate, to vindicate—the oppres-
sions, the cruelties of Moslemism. These are too palpable to
be gainsayed. Mussulman rule has been almost the synonym
of degradation. But that is not the question. We war not
for the Koran—we adopt not the licentious and cruel of the
system. We war, not for Turkish crime, but against Russian
hypocrisy and crime and barbarism and perfidy. The battle
now to be waged is not for the Crescent, although beneath
its light liberty, religious freedom, has more scope than within
the scope of its foe. True it is that Turkey is a barbarous
land; but is Russia a type of civilisation? True, Turkey
along the Danube is oppressive, or said to be so; but is there
no serfdom on the Volga? True, Russia once allowed the
Bible, under the patronage of Alexander, who admitted the
book and unlived its doctrines and precepts; but is it not now
a sealed, a tabooed book? True, once Turkey oppressed
Christians: but is not the difference this—that while Russia
has been going back, Turkey has been advancing; and that,
while the former has chained the Bible, in the latter, from
Ararat to the Bosphorus, from the Dardanelles to the Mediterranean, the Word of God, its missionary, is free! The cry has
been heard, from the shadow of St Sophia, for help, for help to
souls; for light, for light to heaven. And who does not believe

and feel that, Turkey once prostrate to Russia, the Mussul-
mans would be reduced to as thorough physical, mental, and
religious bondage, as its own slaves? It may suit the policy
of some to mystify the question, and others may overlook the
facts of the case; but, so far as I can see, the war is not
designed to add splendour to the Crescent, nor forge chains to
the Christian. It is a struggle of freedom against despotism,
of justice against iniquity, of right against might, of growing
civilisation against wide-spread and down-trampling barbarism;
and who can doubt that, in such a conflict, however long and
terrible it may be, He to whom the shields of the earth belong
will and must exalt His own throne on the ruins of tyranny
and crime!

III.

WE MIGHT NOW ADVERT TO THE PROSPECTS OF THE WAR.

The difficulties on this part of my subject are so great, that
I envy not the man who can speak on it without hesitation
and diffidence. In any great and general war the contingencies
are numerous and varied—dramatically, startlingly so. There
is almost no certainty in them. An event may hang on a
life—nay, on the frame, the momentary frame, of one man's
mind. Our views, beside, of any great line of action are
coloured by our own complexion. If we are of a gloomy and
morbid temperament, we indulge in the vision of long-pro-
tracted years of woe. We see in its course trade paralysed,
the resources of the country exhausted, the progress of the
arts arrested, class armed against class, and manners demo-
ralised. If, on the contrary, our minds are more sanguine,
we anticipate a few great exploits, and then peace. Amid the

uncertainties on which we enter, it were rashness, it were madness almost, to prophesy. Our only great work is, rising over the vista, to anticipate, to pray for the end; and if my text is true, of that there can be no question. Our God, the God of Liberty, never can, never will, touch, anoint the shields of despotism. Our God, the God of Truth, never can, never will, touch and anoint the shields of untruth and knavery. Our God, the God of the Weak, never can, never will, touch and anoint the shields of the strong and oppressor. Our God, the God of the Cross, never can, never will, touch and anoint the shields of superstition, against his Word or evangelical cause. Let us therefore hopefully look to him, and humbly implore his presence and help, for on him alone we depend.

As a nation, let us bear manfully what we must endure in this struggle for the independence of another land; and let us rest convinced, that if, in the course of time, we as a country should be imperilled from the incursion of tyranny—which catastrophe may our Father avert!—the God of nations will reward our efforts now for the maintenance of truth and equity, by our protection then.

Let us, as Christians, mourn over the terrors, the crimes, of war, and seek to mitigate its evil results.

Let us, as sinners, deplore the awful power of one unsanctified heart to produce such havoc in our earth—to involve his own subjects, and those of other nations, in such calamities; and pray for the Spirit of God, that can correct such unholy passions.

Let us pray for them who have gone or are to go forth to

fight the battles of freedom, that, if spared, they may return to forget the art of war in the pursuits of peace; and that, if they should fall, they may die in the arms of victory, and forgiven through the blood of Christ.

Let us pray for our Queen and her advisers, that all wisdom may be imparted unto them—all firm attachment to the nation's honour and weal; and that, in our present crisis, our throne may rest on its most solid earthly basis—the hearts of the people.

Let us pray that they whose fathers fought under the banners of Godfrey to rescue the tomb from the infidel, and who now unite side by side in a struggle for a living reality— lands, once thought to be necessarily enemies, eternally foes— may be rivetted together in the chains of common interest and common principle, no more to meet on the field of blood, but to prosecute the noble rivalry of science, civilisation, and virtue.

Above all, let us pray and hope for the jubilee of peace, and truth, and love—when all nations shall repose in well-ordered, Heaven-defended independence, and shall learn the art of war no more.

And now, O God, to whom belong the shields of the earth, crown our cause with thy blessing! and oh, accelerate the period, when from all regions of the earth—when from the Danube and the Neva, the Thames and the Tiber, the Bosphorus and the Seine—shall rise the gladsome song of liberty and peace—the arm of despotism shall be broken—and mind, body, MAN, *shall be free*—and THINE! Amen.

DISCOURSE IV.

PHILOSOPHY OF THE ATONEMENT.*

OULD I entertain the unfeigned belief that the topic of this evening was realised in all its solemn moment- ousness by my audience, I could calculate at once on the most breathless attention. The relations of the atone- ment are so vast, so enduring, and so incomprehensible, as almost to prostrate with awe the mind that ventures to treat it. Its influences touch even the moral character of the throne of the Eternal, and thus affect its stability; while its relations to us stretch into the undefined, ineffable realities of eternity. The results of the atonement are such as no imagination has ever been able to describe, not even to grasp. I will not stop for a single moment to divert the attention of my hearers from my subject, by any reference to the speculations which are now afloat as to its influence on other planets than our own; nor occupy your attention by discussing the question whether those planets are inhabited by intelligent and moral and responsible agents like ourselves, or whether the light of "the Sun of

* Delivered as a Lecture in Exeter Hall in 1854.

Righteousness," that shone over Calvary, has ever cast a solitary beam into those remote parts of the universe. These speculations of the present may become the certainties of the future, and in heaven shall undoubtedly be solved. It is enough for us now to fall back upon the great ascertained and practical facts, which are sufficient to swell the soul with admiration of the atonement, and the Book that reveals it. I am aware that my theme is old, and possesses none of the crispness and freshness of novelty. Nor am I to appeal to any of the passing events which thrill men's hearts, and almost monopolise their thoughts. I will endeavour to keep close to my subject; and if I draw more upon your patience than perhaps you are inclined to give, I trust you will find a recompense for it in the result of our present examination. May I express my hope, that the object of what I shall now state may be realised, and that this night some young man, who has never embraced the atonement of Christ, may be led to accept it, and that all who have embraced it hitherto may be induced the more firmly and determinedly to cling to it.

I have referred to the grandeur of the topic before us. No more striking proof of that could be furnished than by the attempts to undermine and to destroy it. The value and the strength of a citadel are proved by the fierceness and number of the attacks made upon it, by the blood shed in assailing it, and by the resources of skill and sagacity and money applied to achieve a perfect and lasting triumph over it. Let us take this test, and apply it to the subject of present reflections, and ascertain in what way the subject of the argument this evening has been assailed, and how especially it is assailed now. I admit, in the remarks which I have to meet, and in the manner in which I meet them, there is nothing whatever new. The character of heresy is old and unchanging ; and the modes of defence against it are just as old in form as those of assault. We admit, nay, rejoice in the antiquity of our doctrine. Hoary and venerable in years, it has all the vigour of youth. Its antagonists affect novelty in their onslaught, yet, after all, only repair and refurbish weapons which have been broken against the shield of truth, ages before the present combatants were born. It is well, however, to glance at the modes in which the doctrine of atonement is attacked.

First and foremost, of course, is direct assault. Its form is that of open, avowed Socinianism. Its denials are absolute and dogmatical. It ridicules the idea of an atonement; it scorns the fact. No one acquainted with the literature of that system for the last fifty years, but must be familiar with instances of that to which I now refer. On the one hand, we have had coarse invective; on the other, more modest and refined language ; but in both cases the point of attack has been the same—the authority and ascendency of the Cross of the Redeemer. It is in modern times described as it was years ago. It is ranged among the " tricks of fancy ; " it is an "ancient superstition ;" it is a " superstitious mystery, into which Jesus was forced contrary to his intentions, to uphold his sinking cause." Why, one's blood boils with abhorrence at the thought suggested by these words of Strauss. The thought of our blessed Redeemer conducting a falling cause is contrary to all fact; but there is something abhorrent to the manhood of Christianity in the charge that our Lord had recourse to subterfuge and untruth to prop up his system! Abhorrence, however, is mitigated by another feeling; and when we read and quote such words, we must remember that these are the words of the Strausses and the Mackays of the nineteenth century: men characterised by intellectual and moral dwarfishness, compared with the Pauls and the Johns of the first—giants in mental stature, and angels in hearts of love.

Another mode is far more dangerous, because far more insidious, and which has many advocates—may I be allowed to say, sir?—in certain quarters of your own Church. Some, indeed, of the parties to whom I allude have left the Church of England; and perhaps I may be allowed to hint—and brethren and friends in this meeting belonging to the Church of England may perhaps agree with me in the hint—that it would be no great loss if those they have left behind would follow their predecessors in their pilgrimage to Rome. Their doctrine is what is called the doctrine of reserve. They love the atonement so much that they like to keep it to themselves! It is something so peculiar, so commanding, that no neophyte is to be introduced to the knowledge of it. It is not to be openly and indiscriminately broached. Its very grandeur is the reason for its concealment. It is not fit for the uninitiated. It is to be the possession of the serious and the practised alone. "The prevailing notions of bringing forward the atonement explicitly and prominently on all occasions, is evidently quite opposed to what we consider the teaching of Scripture; nor do we find any sanction for it in the gospels. *If* the Epistles of Paul appear in favour of it, it is only at first sight." Hence the senses are to be regaled. The eye, the ear, are to be appealed to. The homage of faith in the Cross is cast into the shade. Religion becomes histrionic; consisting in ceremonies and genuflections. The priest is exalted; the Church is everything. They reverse, if I understand it aright, the ecclesiasticism of the New Testament. Its policy was this—"The road to the Church is the Cross." Their principle is this—"The road to the Cross is the Church." The way in which a sinner is to enter the Church of Christ, according to the evangelical principles of the Anglican Church, is the atonement of the Saviour of the world. Their principle is this, that through the door and the pathway of the Church sinners are to approach the atonement. Who could fail to anticipate the results of this principle? or be astonished that from the one starting-point the roads should diverge in opposite directions—the one leading to the bogs and swamps of Rome, the other to the mists of Germany —and somewhat farther?

Again, another and third form of attack is equally indirect and perilous. Books are written possessing a degree of sparkling, attractive beauty. Their authors belong to a school which I may be allowed to say, without feeling anything like cynical contempt or professional jealousy, is perhaps the most pedantic and canting of all schools of modern times—the intense school of writing. Something striking is presented to the imaginations and feelings of the readers. Certain compliments are kindly paid to Christ. The writers speak of the benevolence of the man; they describe his wisdom as being something very extraordinary; they admire, whether really or

not I cannot say, the character of Christ. But the God, the
Cross, the atonement, all are lost behind. Let me repeat: this
policy is insidious and perilous in the highest degree. Downright atheism is bad, but it revolts; it keeps the soul wakefully
on its guard. Pantheism is more dangerous. It makes everything God, and therefore God nothing. It deifies nature—
it undeifies the Creator; and, by apparent reverence to nature,
steals over the lulled, unthinking soul. It is exactly so here;
for mark how the writers to whom I allude speak: "Jesus
Christ is the greatest person of the ages;" "he belongs to
the true race of prophets"—of which, I suppose, Theodore
Parker reckons himself one; "he is the proudest achievement
of the human race." Not one word of sacrifice—not a word
of atonement—not a word of bloodshed—of sacrificial martyrdom. It is on the mere externalities, the mere humanities of
the Son of God, that the mind is fixed, and by which it is
diverted from the interior and sublimer truths. The rock they
feel they cannot blast; it has stood too many tempests and
assaults for that. But they veil it; they throw over it a mist-
cloud, fringed with the golden beauty of genius and poetry.
The mind of the young man is fascinated; the moral chloro-
form is administered and acts. He awakes in broken sleep
from his cloud-land, and awakes on the confines of eternity,
only to exclaim, in the anguish of despair: "Ye have taken
away my gods, and what have I more?"

I solicit your thoughts now to another form in which the
atonement is attacked, and whose exposition has been recently
published. To this development of the atonement I feel the
more bound to refer, from the character of the author and the

relation of his book to you. The author is Mr Maurice; his work is on the doctrine of the atonement, and it opens with a dedicatory letter to the members of the Young Men's Christian Association. The volume is a reply to one by Dr Candlish, connected with a lecture delivered by him last year. Let no one think that I am trying to take Dr Candlish's place—that I am taking the shield or the quiver for him : he does not need it. And I know this, that while I stand here to advocate some of those points that Mr Maurice calls Scotch theology, and while Dr Candlish would rejoice in finding a brother Scotchman, of another denomination, upholding the theology of his own heart, he might say, "Stand aside; let me fight for my own hand, and let me fight with my own hand." I am not, therefore, to undertake the defence of Dr Candlish's argument—to anticipate Dr Candlish's logic; I leave that to himself: but I cannot in my argument omit a reference to a volume which, from the position and character of its author, may work for good or evil on the public mind. Mr Maurice, as I have said, in the opening epistle, dedicates that book to the young men of the Young Men's Christian Association; and he speaks of you with great affection, and in terms which indicate that he has a kind and good-feeling heart to young men;—you are his friends. But still he objects to the jury and the judges before whom he is summoned. He speaks of you as the jury impanelled, and before whom he was tried in this hall by Dr Candlish, a Scotch divine, sent forth from Edinburgh to maintain certain opinions—opinions in reply to Mr Maurice's teaching. I believe I may say, in vindication of this Association, that such was not the purpose, Dr Candlish having selected, as other lecturers do, his subject for himself. That by-the-bye, and in passing. However, Mr Maurice says, that in that lecture Dr Candlish "appealed to your passions and your ignorance, and to the passions and ignorance of the clergymen and Dissenting ministers who were countenancing him on the platform of Exeter Hall. You were impanelled as a jury to try his treasons against a higher authority than that of our sovereign lady the Queen." Mr Maurice does not consider you his judges, though Dr Candlish does. He leaves "his own cause and his own character ' to that day.' " Now, may I be allowed to say, that you were not then, and you are not now, judging Mr Maurice. We say nothing personally whatever of Mr Maurice. We do not condemn him in regard to his motives or principles of conduct; for I demand for him— at least, allow me to say for myself—I demand for him the same liberty of judgment, and the same freedom of conscientious speaking and acting that I, as an honest man, claim for myself. We would not touch one single hair of Mr Maurice's head. We do not condemn Mr Maurice for any secret opinion which he entertains, or for the entertainment of any opinion which he avows openly. Nay, more; I can admire the independence of his thinking, although I agree not with the results to which that thinking brings him. I can admire the zeal with which Mr Maurice, with many others, is trying to bridge over the chasm of the gulf between the rich and the poor, the capitalist and the labourer, the learned and the ignorant. All this I can admire. But then, I sit not in judgment upon the man, but upon his doctrine; and in judgment upon that doctrine in a simple way: Is it Divine? Is it to be found in the Word of

God? Mr Maurice says he might have challenged his judges. Now, I cannot see exactly upon what ground. Had this been a question of law, and this cause come before a jury, he might have urged, " You have nothing whatever to do with that ; it is a matter for lawyers." But this is not a case of law, but of fact. Did this depend upon the meaning of a Greek preposition, or the turning of a Greek or Hebrew sentence, or some point of pure metaphysics, I would leave those questions to scholars and metaphysicians. But I must remember that the Book whose doctrines we appeal to, is not a book written for the learned, not prepared for metaphysicians, but *a Book for the world,* for men of plain common sense, for them to judge of and judge from, and to fetch out those doctrines by which they hope and trust they shall be everlastingly saved. I therefore say that you, as jurors in this case, are just the persons to whom I should like to come for determination on any of those points where common sense and practical honesty, and not scholarship and metaphysics, are to be the standard and the criteria of judgment.

I have pointed to the different ways in which the doctrine of the atonement is assailed. Now, Mr Maurice maintains sacrifice. Mind that. Mr Maurice does not deny sacrifice; he grants the existence of sacrifice ; he asserts and assumes the existence of the sacrifice of Christ. But mark in what way. " The Gospel shows him, who is one with God and one with man, perfectly giving up that self-will, which had been the cause of all men's crimes and all their misery." Sacrifice, according to Mr Maurice, " manifests the mind of God, accomplishes the purpose of God, in the redemption and reconciliation of the creatures—enables these creatures to become like their Father in heaven by offering up themselves." With this he contrasts those sacrifices which men have often "dreamed of, in one country or another, as means of changing the purposes of God, of converting him to their mind, of procuring deliverance from the punishment of evil whilst the evil still exists." Let me just say, in passing, that we never have entertained the dream of any sacrifice, of any atonement, changing the purposes of God; that anything has been done by Christ to change the plans of God. Our belief has always been that the atonement of Christ is part of the development of that system of means by which the purposes of God are carried out; that atonement was no change of plan, but part of the plan itself. Far be it from us to entertain the supposition of mutability in the Divine mind. We should shrink from such an idea as much as Mr Maurice, or any one of his school. Consider now his words; the idea they convey is this: that sacrifice, atonement, is the renunciation of self-will—that sacrifice in Christ and sacrifice in man is one and the same thing in this respect—the abnegation of our own self-control to follow our own devices. But the abandonment of my own will implies the assumption of some other; that is a simple axiomatic truth. If I abandon my own will, I must adopt something else in its place. Now, where is the will adopted by Christ and the believers in common? I grant that both make a common sacrifice. The sacrifice which I make as a Christian, is the abnegation of my will and the assumption of the will of God. But what does he require of me? It is to live for him, and to do his work in living for him. But what does he demand of

Christ? To live for him? Yes! but more, immensely more. What end did Christ contemplate in his life? Obedience? Yes; but unto what? and for what? The end—if the Bible be true—was death, and salvation by it! Sacrifice on the part of Christ, therefore, did not consist exclusively, nor principally, in self-abnegation, but in the fact to which self-abnegation led; in other words, the atonement of the Cross. In one sense, then, his life and that of the Christian are a sacrifice, namely, abandonment of self-will, the adoption of the Divine. But the sacrifice of Christ transcended this; for he not only lived to God, but he died for others.

Hitherto I have proceeded upon the assumption that we know what atonement is.; and perhaps, in some measure, the last sentences I have uttered may present some of the ideas we attach to it. Let me now, however, in a sentence, state what I understand by an atonement. I speak not of the Biblical atonement alone, but of the idea of propitiation generally. *An atonement, then, is a scheme, an expedient of Divine wisdom, to harmonise the outgoings, the practical developments of Divine mercy, with the demands of Divine equity and law.* This definition includes the existence of both—of Divine goodness and of Divine equity. It does not demand them—it does not by any means create them. It assumes the fact. And here I may be allowed to say, that these things existed and exist anteriorly and independently of any atonement whatever. If no atonement had been made, God would have been holy; if no atonement had been made, God would still have been just; his equity and goodness are completely independent of the atonement. Away, then, with the assumption, with the misrepresentation, that in the atonement we contemplate something which is to make God good and merciful! Away with the aspersion which Socinian and Pantheistic writers alike have uttered against our views of Jehovah—as severe and stern, requiring the death of his Son to render him gracious. I go back to the Gospel of our Lord, as recorded by his disciple John, and adopt the simple statement: "God so loved the world," *because* he gave "his only begotten Son?" No, but "*God so loved the world,* THAT *he gave his only begotten Son, that whosoever believeth in him might not perish, but have everlasting life.*"* Atonement, then, is not the root, but one of the fruits of mercy; it is the effect, not the cause, of Divine goodness.

Now, to understand the force of this idea of sacrifice and its necessity, it is requisite to consider two matters of consciousness—one relative to ourselves, the other to the Almighty; first, that we are sinners; second, that he is just. If either of these terms fail, the atonement is superfluous, or may become so. If I am not a sinner I need no atonement; and if God is not just he may not require or demand one. Redemption and slavery are correlative terms; the antithesis of reconciliation is alienation; and if I speak of atonement for a human being, it involves the fact that he has done something which demanded the existence of sacrifice. Here, then, comes the argument as to our natural condition. On this point much diversity of opinion is expressed. The moral condition of the race has been a moot point in many ages. The most opposite pictures are drawn of the normal state of the race. One

* John iii. 16.

speaks of the thorough defilement of human nature ; represents
the man up from the child, in all his stages, as alien from God,
in a state of moral recoil against the commands and authority
of the Eternal. Another dilates on the charms of childhood.
Poetry has sketched its prattling innocence, its physical
beauty, its unsuspecting, trusting heart; while the aberrations
of the man have been traced by others, not to the original
nature of the child, but to temptation and its force, forgetful
to show how temptation could act on perfectly pure minds !
Not only, however, have poets, who sometimes mistake the
ideal for the real, thus spoken, but others, from whom something more sober might be expected, have asserted the same
fact,—the original purity of our nature. One of the most
accomplished statesmen of the day has recently said : " You
will find that all children are born good ; it is bad education
and bad associations in early life that corrupt the minds of men.
Be assured—be assured, that the mind and heart of men are
naturally good." Now, is this off-hand dictum, pronounced
with categorical authority, in a quiet nook of Hampshire—
carried by the press over the country, and greedily embraced
by many—is it true ? Is it true that all children are born
good ? " Be assured that the mind and heart are naturally
good." My Lord Palmerston, ask the mothers of Romsey—
carry your views and your questions a little further ; ask the
mothers of England—if the children whom they have born into
the world will meet the description which your lordship has
given of them. But they are not poetical, they are not
philosophical ! True, but they are practical observers, and
come continually in contact with the tempers, the intellectual

character, and the moral feelings of the individuals to whom
they have given birth. Do you tell me that there are sometimes exceptions to this rule, and that their corruption is the
result of education and association? I demur to that statement. I hold that the wicked influence of that association
and that temptation with which they are encompassed, has all
its power in the innate and natural corruption of the heart.
Why, if they were in this state of purity, would not the beautiful thought of St Clare, in regard to Eva, be universally
exhibited; and just as he fancied that Eva was so pure that
a drop of rain would not run more rapidly off a cabbage-leaf
than temptation would from her heart, so all the children of
England would be so pure that the shower-drops of temptation
would just roll away from them, and leave them unstained,
unspotted as they came from the hand of God?

But perhaps it is said that those are the opinions of only
practical people like myself. I appeal, then, to the Articles of
that Church with which the propounder of that statement is
connected; and I ask your judgment on the meaning of these
words :—"Original sin standeth not in the following of Adam
(as the Pelagians do vainly talk); but it is the fault and corruption of the nature of every man that naturally is engendered
of the offspring of Adam; whereby man is very far gone from
original righteousness, and is of his own nature inclined to
evil." Or if human experience and the doctrines of the
Church of England will not satisfy, then let us go to the words
of the oracles of eternal truth, and hear the statements of
David reiterated and re-impressed by Paul in clear, distinct
harmony with each other :—"The Lord looked down from

heaven upon the children of men, to see if there were any that did understand and seek God. They are all gone aside; they are altogether become filthy; there is none that doeth good; no, not one."* Now here we have the record of the Divine inquisition into the conduct and character of the human family. The moral world appeared before the all-searching God, and, wherever his eye fell, it rested on scenes of ungodliness and guilt. Varieties, no doubt, there were in thought, in emotions, in actions; but still all rose before him, a fallen temple, a temple in ruins, a temple where, to use John Howe's idea, lay here and there the fragment of a column, the wreck of a statue, indicating the skill of the Architect and the glory of the design—but still in ruins, and ruins the more melancholy by the very grandeur of the remains. Such is man;—guilty, prostrate, lost! Here, then, I may assume the existence of that first term, the necessity of such an atonement. A few words now upon my second.

I have said that the second term is this, on the part of God, that he must be just. If he is not just, there may be an atonement required, or there may not; we cannot speculate on that point; but certainly, if he is not a just being, no atonement need of necessity be demanded. Who would then deny this simple statement—that he is just, that he is king, that he is head of creation, that he rules by law, that that moral law has been revealed, and that that moral law is yet dear to him? A world without a governor forms part of few people's creed. That the moral world should be subject to law is perfectly obvious. That God rules by law is distinctly

* Psalm xiv. 2, 3; Romans iii. 10, 11.

clear; and if that law has been broken, he must, so far as we know, be just to punish it, or require an atonement for it. On this the opponents of the atonement are not agreed with us. Now here, my dear young friends,—for it is with you I deal more emphatically this night,—here let me again urge a word of caution. The danger in the literature of modern times, so far as theology is concerned, is not in direct assault, but in subtle undermining; and often much more—not in assaulting any truth of the Word of God, but in ignoring it. An illustration here occurs. Nature is described as beautiful. God is represented as a kind, beneficent, universally loving Father; but his existence as governor and king, though not dogmatically denied, is practically ignored. The primal law of government is not contradicted, but the law itself is not mentioned. Divine equity is dethroned by human silence. God is portrayed as a Father—we are pictured as his family; but nothing is said of a Father's rights, nothing of the children's duties, and nothing of the children's rebellion. All is radiant with love. The voices of creation are the echo of his own; the beauties, the grandeur of nature are the footprints of his majestic throne. Well, I trust I too can hear him in every zephyr sound, in every forest song, and in every ocean melody. All about me bespeaks of a God of pure and perfect love, in the survey of whose works I am lost, and where with the poet I am led to exclaim,

"Come, then, expressive silence, muse his praise !"

But is this all? Is the goodness of God the only feature of his character with which, as members of his family, we have to do? Is he nothing more? Has he no rights to maintain?

Is there no other feature of his character with which, as rebellious children, we have to do? Is he not the God of law as well as the God of love? We have not out-lived, my dear young friends, the belief of Scripture—nor drowned the utterances within—nor forgotten the records of nations—nor shut our eyes to the approaching period when around our Father's throne the voices of unnumbered myriads shall proclaim, on the sea of glass mingled with fire, "Just and true are thy ways, thou King of saints. Who would not fear thee?"

But I forget. These views are antiquated; they are quite obsolete; they are the dreams of old superstition, not fit to engage our thoughts or disturb our peace. What have we to do with such views in relation to atonement now—to judgment hereafter? "They practically give to Christianity a character, which, though it may have an ill sound, it would be vain as well as dishonest to dissemble—that of a religion of Moloch." Their religion, according to one of their hierophants, which calls God Father, and not King, is the religion of beauty, the religion of truth; it is spiritualism: but our system "makes God a King, and not a Father." To this my reply is very simple. The charge is not true. We own the Eternal in both relations; they recognise him—if they recognise him at all—in one. We can divaricate between king and father, and the relative work of each. So can they. But while both define the varieties—they dissociate, we unite. They strip the Father of the equity and authoritative power of the king; we surround the throne with love. While they resolve Deity into paternal affection, and say we array God with Draconic severity, we repudiate the charge, and fearlessly assert ˙that our system denies neither of his characteristic relations: it admits both, and owns him at once Father-king and royal Father.

This point introduces the necessity of some mode of harmonising these ascertained facts in the Divine and human character—that is, of some atonement. As sinners we need one. God, as just, has a right to demand one. Has one, therefore, been made? Our reply is Biblical. The Scriptures assert that atonement has been offered—and offered by Christ. Their language continually implies this sacrificial character—his atoning death. Of this let me give a few specimens :—

" For the life of the flesh is in the blood: and I have given it to you upon the altar to make an atonement for your souls : for it is the blood that maketh an atonement for the soul." " But he was wounded for our transgressions, he was bruised for our iniquities: the chastisement of our peace was upon him ; and with his stripes we are healed. All we like sheep have gone astray ; we have turned every one to his own way; and the Lord hath laid on him the iniquity of us all. He was oppressed, and he was afflicted, yet he opened not his mouth; he is brought as a lamb to the slaughter, and as a sheep before her shearers is dumb, so he openeth not his mouth." " The next day John seeth Jesus coming unto him, and saith, Behold the Lamb of God, which taketh away the sin of the world." " For when we were yet without strength, in due time Christ died for the ungodly. For scarcely for a righteous man will one die : yet peradventure for a good man some would even dare to die. But God commendeth his love toward us, in that, while we were yet sinners, Christ died for us." " For Christ also hath once suffered for sins, the just for the unjust, that he might bring us to God, being put to death in the flesh, but quickened by the Spirit." " Unto him that loved us, and washed us from our sins in his own blood, and hath made us kings and priests unto God and his Father ; to him be ˙glory and dominion for ever and ever. Amen."— Lev. xvii. 11 ; Isaiah liii. 5, 6, 7 ; John i. 29 ; Romans v. 6, 7, 8 ; 1 Peter iii. 18 ; Revelations i. 5, 6.

These sentences I have grouped in this particular order, because it is the order of Biblical manifestation ; and I have chosen one sentence from the different writers, for each sentence or paragraph is the writing of one or other teacher of the Old or New Testament. I have done so for the purpose of showing the complete identity, the homogeneousness of Biblical teaching on the death of Christ. It is delightful to feel that, go where you will in the sacred volume, you find this. Ascend Mount Horeb, and a vast valley, a great trough of a petrified sea lies below you, crowded with Israelites ! Descend, and enter a tent approaching in size the palace of a Bedouin chief, and you are surrounded with the symbolism of atonement ! Ascend Calvary, and, standing amid a sea of heads, you gaze upon the wondrous development of the fact, the reality of atonement ! Pass on to the Ægean, and as you gaze from Patmos, you hear, wafted over the waters from the home of the redeemed, the songs and praises of its wonders, ever swelling in volume with each admission of its new trophies into heaven !

This perfect unity of teaching in the sacred volume is to

me one of the most clear and delightful proofs of the reality of the atonement of my Saviour. It sparkles not in Scripture as one solitary star gemming the night, but as a cluster of stars, each rivalling in brilliancy its sister star, and all throwing their combined radiance on the hill of Calvary, on the work of the Redeemer. In short, whether there be an atonement or not, whether Christ made one or not, this at least is clear, that atonement by him is a doctrine of Scripture, *the* doctrine of Scripture—" the pillar and the ground of truth." To deny this requires a new Bible. But as we cling to the old, the Bible of our fathers, the standard of their opinions, the fountain of their joys,—and so, God helping us, we shall cling amid all the pretensions of literature and philosophy so called, that now spurn it because they fear it!—let us still hold by its central truth, " Christ crucified," and crucified for us. Here let us not seek the wisdom, or rather the affectation of wisdom, of too many modern oracles : let not our aim be to be wise with the Priestleys and Belshams, the Martineaus and Emersons. We—at least I do ; do not you ?—prefer being fools with Isaiah, and Paul, and John ; with Wycliffe, and Latimer, and Ridley ; with Luther, and Melancthon, and Calvin ; with Wesley and Whitfield ; with Edwards and Martyn ; with Hall and Chalmers ;—in a word, not with the men of this time or that, but the men of all time, and now of the spiritual aristocracy in eternity !

You will remember that, in the idea which I threw out of the nature and character of atonement, I stated that it was the expedient, the creation of Divine wisdom, to harmonise the outgoings of Divine goodness or mercy with the demands or claims of Divine law and equity. The principle embodied in the first part of that sentence is essential. If we have sinned, the atonement, in its nature and degree, rests with the party against whom we have offended. He alone has a right to say whether we shall be saved at all, and if so, by what agency. If, therefore, means have been revealed by Him at all, they must be right, for he is infallible. There may, however, be many difficulties about the scheme which we cannot master, positions we cannot reconcile. But if they are facts—if they be revealed in his Word, they must be true. If the discovery is made by God of such an atonement, whatever be its difficulties, as his atonement it must be certain. Here philosophy comes to our aid—not the philosophy of Faneuil Hall, in Boston, or some of the schools of Germany; not the philosophy of mere speculators, or of Pantheistic dreamers; but the strong, massive philosophy of England—the philosophy of Bacon and Newton, of Locke and Boyle; the experimental, the inductive logic, whose great practical principle is that we have not to treat the question, *How* does a thing exist? but, *Does it exist?* I need hardly say that the introduction of this principle has revolutionised the worlds of science, of astronomy, chemistry, and geology. This principle, applied to physics and metaphysics, was employed by one whose name should and will never be heard without admiration,—I mean Dr Chalmers,— with great force in regard to revealed facts, where we have only to ascertain the truth, and reverently embrace it. The Book is to be our oracle, and when it speaks we are to be dumb. The great point, then, to which I come is—Is the Book authentic and true which contains the discovery of an atonement? If so, whatever clouds may envelop the Cross, or whatever splendour may embellish the speculations of its foes, then you and I are bound to rise above both; and knowing that this doctrine is in Scripture, we take as our motto, " To the law and to the testimony ; if they speak not according thereto, it is because there is no truth in them."

It may be well, however, to look at a few principles which reason might suggest as essential to an atonement, and ask if they are found in the atonement of the Bible? Do they meet in the Cross? I am quite well aware that what I now urge is familiar to the student of theology, however superficial almost his knowledge, and limited his reading is. The principles, however, are important, and as heresiology is one repetition of itself, and yet may have power, so truth often repeated is sure to suffer no loss from its repetition. A few salient principles, then, and only a few, I will present of the fundamental requisites of atonement.

Purity, then, is the first element essential to the existence and the character of an atonement. The man himself in debt cannot liquidate the obligations of another; the rebel, himself amenable to the laws which he has violated, cannot expiate the crime of a brother rebel—he has his own to atone for; and he that would be the atonement for a guilty world must himself be free from the guilt which is chargeable upon it. Otherwise to imagine were to suppose that the person so atoning was free from responsibility, and that in his case the great sentence had been rolled back—" The soul that sinneth it shall die." It is obvious, therefore, that the first element of this atonement must be the purity of its victim. *Christ*

was perfectly pure. He could challenge all his foes and
boldly say, "Which of you convinceth me of sin?" Their
silence was his defence; and glancing to the malignant attack
of the bitterest foe of himself and the whole human family, he
could say, "The prince of this world cometh, and hath nothing
in me." His character was perfectly immaculate; and in the
whole history of his life (although some have now and then
attempted to throw insinuations and slurs over it), we behold
a purity and an innocence unchallenged and unchallengeable.

Next in the statement of the terms and mode of an atonement, I observe that *it must be dependent on the will of the
offended party.* The offender can dictate nothing, can prescribe
or may suggest nothing—his life is forfeited; and if that shall
be saved, it is in consequence of the will of him whom he has
opposed, and at whose hands he deserves nothing but utter
condemnation. All that the offender has to do in the case
of an atonement is to accept or reject the offered terms: no
more has he to do, and no more can he. In the present case
all is in consistency with the Father's plan; every act and
word of our Saviour is coincident with the Father's will.
Oh! how absorbed was the mind of Christ in that! and how
frequently did he refer to the harmony of himself and Father
in all the movements of redemption and redeeming love! "I
came not to do mine own will, but the will of him that sent
me;" "My meat and my drink is to do the will of my Father;"
expressions but the fulfilment of ancient writ, when the royal
prophet of Israel said, "It is written of me, I delight to do
thy will." I quote the principle for this reason, that it completely supersedes an objection often urged by Socinians and

Deists against our representations of the atonement. " Do you say that an atonement of such a character would be required, and that such an atonement was presented for the sake of propitiating the Father's wrath, and of making him merciful? that the Father could be moved into tenderness and compassion by the effusion of his Son's blood? In how gloomy and repulsive an aspect do you thus present the eternal Godhead! Is this your view of God? We should shudder to entertain it." And so should we, but we never held it. We say, *the Father gave the Son,* not *that the Father should be* merciful, but *because* the Father *was* merciful; and that the Son was given by the Father, not for the purpose of awakening the Father's love, but because that love was brightly burning. The whole arrangement of the atonement was of the Father's appointing, and when the Son came to die as an atonement, he came in consistency with the Father's will.

Again, *an atonement,* from its nature, *must not be often repeated.* It is an extraordinary remedy. In human affairs it is a great experiment, and oftentimes a dangerous one. Frequently employed, an atonement would cease to be that which it is,—the exception to the operations of law,—and become the law itself. It would lose, therefore, its peculiarity, and be stripped of its impressiveness. *There is but one atonement for the world.* " Then must he often have suffered since the foundation of the world; but now, once in the end of the world hath he appeared to put away sin by the sacrifice of himself. And as it is appointed unto men once to die, but after this the judgment, so Christ was once offered to bear the

2 A

sins of many, and unto them that look for him shall he appear the second time without sin unto salvation."[*]

Another great fact, it is obvious, must characterise an atonement: *it must be such as not to destroy the force of law and the claims of equity.* It is easy to conceive of a case of a person substituting himself for another, and destroying the very law under which he suffered. He may complain of its severity; the law itself may not be completely vindicated in his own individual conduct; he may not allow its justice while he bears its stroke; and therefore, instead of honouring the law by being subject to its condemnation, he himself in truth degrades and weakens it; and the effects of this it is not difficult to imagine. How different the case of Christ! Through the whole of his course, from the cradle to the grave, from the first step of his mediatorial course to its final consummation, no murmur, no whisper against the integrity of God, or the authority of the law of God, ever escaped his lips. Never was victim so patient, so enduring, so heroic, so sublime in submission. Never did one tread a path at all approaching his with such resignation to the authority of the law, and such reverence to the authority of the Lawgiver. It cannot be said, therefore, that the law was degraded by the language of Christ, or that its morality is impaired, or that its demands are limited, or that its motives are enfeebled, by the example of Christ. All rather swell into strength and clearness the more they are contemplated in the light of the life and cross of the Son of God.

It is but an expansion of this truth to affirm that *an atone-*

* Heb. ix. 26, 27, 28.

ment is most successful which, while it gains its primary end (that is, the pardon of the guilty), *adds force to the obedience of the pardoned.* Atonement is ruinous if it weaken law by narrowing its claims or diminishing its obligations. Atonement is adequate if, while it yields to law, it maintains its sanctions. But atonement is glorious if, while it maintains law, it adds. new authority to it. Now, the atonement of Christ illustrates the law as it had never been seen before, and brings before us its claims with a force and an ardour to which hitherto they were strangers. The command of God is binding, and the immediate benefits of obedience, justly considered, recommend that command, while the awful terrors with which it is encompassed and upheld persuade men into subjection. But every Christian heart has felt a holier, gentler, and yet more potent impulse to obedience in the contemplation and acceptance of the Propitiation.

This last point is one of the most practically important in examining and determining the philosophy of an atonement, its moralising influence. Here, accordingly, have the strongest charges of its enemies centred. It is represented as subversive of pure ethical distinctions and of practice. I may just quote the words of a recent antagonist of atonement, which he describes as "equally unsatisfactory as a scheme, and immoral as an example." Now, it is very natural to ask of the author and his coadjutors—What have you done in the presentation of moral examples, or of satisfactory schemes? You boast of your new schemes, your new philosophy. The Cross is an effete thing. The world, which world is yourselves, wants something new. Well, what have your new plans, satisfactory

as schemes and moral as examples, done? What has Secu-
larism done? What is it doing? What has Socinianism done?
What is it doing? What has Pantheism, or, as it prefers
calling itself, Spiritualism, done? What is it doing? What
have they all done, what are they all doing, for the advancement of morals, for the elevation of man? What barbarism
have they civilised? What darkness have they illumined?

It is cheering to turn and reflect on the achievements of the
Cross, the atonement of Christ. Where, I repeat, have its foes,
ranging between the extremes of materialism and spiritualism,
done anything? WHERE HAS ATONEMENT NOT TRIUMPHED?
Its preachers, never aping the philosopher, but preaching the
Cross, *which is philosophy*, have penetrated scenes of heathen
darkness and degradation. Where, indeed, have they not
been, from the kraal of the Hottentot to the temple of the
Hindoo; from the rude superstition of the Caffre to the
Pantheism of Brahma, or the Buddhism of the Cingalese?
In the cold regions of Greenland, under the shadow of the
Andes, on the coralline reefs of the Pacific, this doctrine, the
atonement, has been preached, and never failed. Under its
shadow the cannibal savage has emerged in the civilised man.
And all this has been effected, not by literature or philosophy,
but by faith—the humanising, the sanctifying power of THE
CROSS!

In these facts another great law of atonement is evolved,
viz., its *adaptability*. *Atonement must be applicable to the race
for which it is made.* Now, other systems may do for one class,
though even that is problematical. *This is for all*, and *certain*
in its results where applied. The Rose of Sharon is universally

transplantable. It blooms with equal beauty amid the snows of Labrador, the sands of Africa, or on the sides of the Himalayas. It is fed by the blood of "the Man," and all men can be saved, nurtured by it!

I have thus addressed you on a subject of greatest moment in a very sketchy way; may I trust, a suggestive one? After all imperfection, however, in my argument, who cannot adopt the language of Young?—

> " Oh ! what a scale of miracles is here !
> Pardon for infinite offence, and pardon
> Through means that speak its value infinite !
> A pardon bought with blood ! with blood divine !
> With blood divine of Him I made my foe !"

In these remarks I have appealed to you as judges and jurors at once, not of Mr Maurice, nor of Dr Candlish, nor of myself. But I have appealed to you upon PRINCIPLES, not *persons*. The latter may die, the former live—live for ever. My address has been on a topic of universal as well as imperishable interest, and not to be determined by metaphysics or scholarship, but the facts of our consciousness and the discoveries of Scripture. My address has therefore assumed the form, not of a *concio ad clerum*, but *concio ad populum*. I have addressed your common sense, and not tried to turn Exeter Hall into a gymnasium of metaphysicians. How far I have succeeded it is not for me to say. If I have failed in the vindication of the principles announced, ascribe that failure to the feebleness of the advocate, not to the unsoundness of the cause. Above all, let me implore you, my dear young friends, to re-

member óne thing—THIS:—I may sit as a judge, and clearly
expound law; or as a juror, and pronounce a just verdict on
fact, and personally have no interest in either. It is not so
here; *you are judging for yourselves.* This is no question of
theory. If the atonement is anything, it should be real, home-
going, heart-reaching truth, characterising our habits in time,
determining our destinies in eternity. I may now speak to
some who have never felt its magnitude—never trusted in its
application to them. Think, my friends, what you are—what
you must be without it. You are now in the flush of youth—
its freshness and buoyancy. You may, by the play of your wit
or the sparkle of your genius, be the very soul of the circle in
which you move. But what is all that? The prospect of com-
mercial success may be before you, and you may rejoice in its
reality and brilliancy. But is that all? Does not your ambition
soar beyond? Have you no consciousness of alienation from
God—of disobedience to his law—of recoil from his society?
Have you no inward struggle between right and wrong? no
temporary forebodings of a world and judgment hereafter? If
you have—close, I implore you, that struggle at the Cross,
where only it can safely terminate.

I address others—many, I hope—who have embraced this
atonement, who have bowed to its philosophy, and felt the joy
it inspires. Keep firm on that rock of your faith and hope!
It stands firm as ever. Ages have swept over it, but not
crumbled it. The artillery of hell has played against it; but
not one angle of it has been destroyed. The sophistry of earth
has tried to undermine and blast it; but the mine has not
sprung. Here it stands, colossal in its own strength—pouring

defiance on its assailants, while casting a refreshing shadow on all who walk confidingly and lovingly by its sides. Let no storms, my dear young friends, drive you from its shelter—let no wiles of false philosophy lure you from its elevation. Feel that here is power to sustain and brace you in the moral battle of life. You may in this struggle sometimes be prostrated; but remember Antæus, who, when wrestling and falling to the ground, no sooner touched the soil from which he sprang, than he rose refreshed. The fiction of Greece may be more than realised in you. Touch, in your grapplings with sin and in your occasional falls, the soil of Calvary, and, saturated as that is with the blood of atonement, you will start from it with new spiritual muscle—with renovated hopes—with holier ambition! Time, my dear friends, is passing along, and carrying you, me, all, on its bosom. Oh! never forget that, as it flows on, sometimes amid hidden reefs, sometimes amid bolder crags, sometimes treacherous eddies—the thing, the only thing, that can support, amid all its surges and dangers, amid the breakers and maël-strom, alike securely, is the Cross of Christ! Embrace it, then,—grasp it—cling to it thus with the earnestness of a drowning man, until you touch the shore of Eternity, and feel yourselves everlastingly safe beyond the approach of danger—temptation—death!

Schenck & M'Farlane, Printers, Edinburgh.

ERRATA.

Page 57, line 19, *for* Mary Ray, *read* Mary Gray.
,, 73, ,, 3, ,, her, ,, his.
,, 101, ,, 28, ,, concerns, ,, conversion.
,, 105, ,, 27, ,, Media, ,, India.
,, 108, ,, 9 & 20, ,, 1841, ,, 1840.
,, 120, ,, 22, ,, Oratorio, ,, Oratoire.
,, 182, ,, 26, ,, not, ,, wet.
,, 245, ,, 13, ,, bereaved, ,, beloved.

WORKS

BY

REV. JOHN MACFARLANE, LL.D.

In handsome Crown 8vo, Price 7s. 6d. Third Edition.

The Life and Times of George Lawson, D.D., Selkirk, Professor of Theology to the Associate Synod. With Glimpses of Scottish Character, from 1720 to 1820.

"This is the most spirited of all the author's productions. He has fairly risen to the height of his subject. His memorial (Dr Lawson's) is like fragrance on the breeze; and this volume, like a golden casket, has collected within it much of the perfume which will be there retained to regale generations to come."—*United Presbyterian Magazine.*

"The volume is rich to an unusual degree, abounding in anecdote, and flashing with wit. It will command a host of admirers."—*Baptist Magazine.*

"Seldom have we taken up a book so full of anecdote. Fresh and racy."—*Eclectic Review.*

Price 3s. 6d. Fifth Edition.

The Mountains of the Bible: Their Scenes and their Lessons.

"It is no mean praise to certify that Dr Macfarlane has produced the best series of discourses on the subject which as yet has been published. The production alike of an accomplished and devout mind."—*Eclectic Review.*

Price 2s. 6d. Third Thousand.

Why Weepest Thou? A Manual for Bereaved Parents.

"This is a delightful volume. Yes; delightful, though its theme be sorrow. It is more than worthy of the author of the 'Night Lamp.'"—GEORGE GILFILLAN.

"It is told with the touching tenderness, the beauty, and artistic skill for which the author is distinguished."—DR KITTO.

Price 5s. · Ninth Thousand.

The Night Lamp: A Narrative of the Means by which Spiritual Darkness was dispelled from the Deathbed of AGNES MAX-WELL MACFARLANE.

"It will ever remain green and fragrant while the world lasts, and while youthful piety continues to be an object to the Church of God."—*Evangelical Magazine.*

"We do not wonder at its popularity. It is a story of thrilling interest."—*Journal of Sacred Literature.*

Price 5s. Third Thousand.

The Hiding-Place; or, the Sinner found in Christ.

"Dr Macfarlane's work reminds us greatly of the works of Flavel and of Baxter; and well will it be for the Church of Christ when such efforts are duly appreciated, and such works extensively read."—*Eclectic Review.*

The Life and Correspondence of Henry Belfrage, D.D. (conjointly with Rev. Dr M'KERROW).

"A work highly honourable to Dr Belfrage, creditable to the compilers, and profitable to the Church."—*United Secession Magazine.*

12mo. Price 2s. 6d. Pp. 264.

Memoir of the Rev. John Campbell.

"Mr Campbell deserves to be held in grateful remembrance by the Church."—*D. Dewar, D.D., LL.D., Principal of Marischal College, Aberdeen.*

An Aged Christian: A Sermon preached on the Occasion of the Death of the Rev. Dr KIDSTON.

The Spiritual Life Developed: A Sermon preached on the Occasion of the Death of the Rev. Dr BAIRD.

Good Will to Israel: A Sermon preached before the Glasgow
Society on behalf of the Jews.

Memoir of Rev. Dr Mackelvie (with Remains).
"It is worthy of its author and of its subject."—*United Presbyterian Magazine.*

Price 1s. Second Thousand.
The Martyrs of our Manse: A Sketch.

Apostolic Preaching: A Sermon preached on the Occasion
of the Rev. Dr Beattie's Jubilee.

The Power of Christ and the Power of Preaching: A Sermon
preached at the Opening of the United Presbyterian
Church, Bristol.

Price 1s. Fourth Thousand.
Altar-Gold: A Sermon preached before the London Missionary
Society.
"Few discourses are superior to this for point, profundity, force, and
pathos."—*British Banner.*
"The working out of the idea in this most noble sermon has never been
surpassed."—*Christian Witness.*

Price 1s. Second Thousand.
Altar-Light: the Funeral Sermon of the late ALEXANDER
FLETCHER, D.D.
"We are thankful to say that we heard this masterly discourse delivered.
The clear, solemn thinking, the imposing imagery, the venerable appear-
ance, the full, rich voice—all gave immense effect to this admirable dis-
course."—*The Homilist.*
"Dr Macfarlane has employed the purest English in the embodiment of
remarkable thoughts."—*The Bulletin.*
"It surpasses all his previous publications in force and vigour of style,
originality of thought, and aptness of illustration."—*Stirling Observer.*

Price 1s.   Second Thousand.

Altar-Zeal; or, Paul in the Pulpit.

"It is characterised by the same sparkling and popular qualities which have often been referred to in this Magazine as those of Dr Macfarlane's writings."—*United Presbyterian Magazine.*

By the same Author.

Preparing for Immediate Publication, Crown 8vo, Price 5s.,

PULPIT ECHOES:

OR,

PASSAGES FROM DISCOURSES AND EXPOSITIONS

DELIVERED IN KINCARDINE-ON-FORTH, ERSKINE CHURCH, GLASGOW, AND CLAPHAM, LONDON.

LONDON:

JAMES NISBET & CO., 21 BERNERS STREET.

CPSIA information can be obtained at www.ICGtesting.com
Printed in the USA
BVOW05s0016070815

412297BV00012B/59/P